The International Library of Sociology

THE SCHOOL INSPECTOR

Founded by KARL MANNHEIM

The International Library of Sociology

THE SOCIOLOGY OF EDUCATION
In 28 Volumes

I	Adolescent Girls in Approved Schools	*Richardson*
II	Adult Education	*Peers*
III	Down Stream	*Dale et al*
IV	Education after School	*Stimson*
V	Education and Society	*Ottaway*
VI	Education and Society in Modern France	*Fraser*
VII	Education and Society in Modern Germany	*Samuel et al*
VIII	Education and the Handicapped 1760 - 1960	*Pritchard*
IX	Education in Israel	*Bentwich*
X	Education in Transition	*Dent*
XI	The Education of the Countryman	*Burton*
XII	The Educational Thought and Influence of Matthew Arnold	*Connell*
XIII	English Primary Education - Part One	*Blyth*
XIV	English Primary Education - Part Two	*Blyth*
XV	From School to University	*Dale*
XVI	Helvetius	*Cumming*
XVII	Mission of the University	*Ortega y Gasset*
XVIII	Parity and Prestige in English Secondary Education	*Banks*
XIX	Problems in Education	*Holmes*
XX	The School Inspector	*Edmonds*
XXI	Sixth Form and College Entrance	*Morris*
XXII	Social Class and the Comprehensive School	*Ford*
XXIII	The Social Psychology of Education	*Fleming*
XXIV	The Social Purposes of Education	*Collier*
XXV	Social Relations in a Secondary School	*Hargreaves*
XXVI	Total Education	*Jacks*
XXVII	Values and Involvement in a Grammar School	*King*
XXVIII	Who shall be Educated?	*Warner et al*

THE SCHOOL INSPECTOR

by

E. L. EDMONDS

Routledge
Taylor & Francis Group

LONDON AND NEW YORK

First published in 1962 by
Routledge

Reprinted in 1998 by
Routledge
2 Park Square, Milton Park, Abingdon, Oxon, OX14 4RN

Simultaneously published in the USA and Canada by Routledge

711 Third Avenue, New York, NY 10017

Transferred to Digital Printing 2007

Routledge is an imprint of the Taylor & Francis Group, an informa business

First issued in paperback 2013

British Library Cataloguing in Publication Data
A CIP catalogue record for this book
is available from the British Library

The School Inspector

ISBN 978-0-415-17770-2 (hbk)
ISBN 978-0-415-86863-1 (pbk)

CONTENTS

	FOREWORD BY SIR WILLIAM ALEXANDER	*page* vii
	PREFACE	ix
I.	THE EARLIEST INSPECTORS	1
II.	NATIONAL SOCIETY AND BRITISH SOCIETY INSPECTORS	15
III.	THE FIRST GOVERNMENT INSPECTORS	25
IV.	INSPECTORS IN THE EARLY 1840's	30
V.	KAY-SHUTTLEWORTH	46
VI.	MID-CENTURY DEVELOPMENT	51
VII.	THE 1860's	68
VIII.	SCHOOL BOARD INSPECTION	86
IX.	BOARD INSPECTORS AND ORGANISERS	97
X.	HER MAJESTY'S INSPECTOR AND OTHER INSPECTORS	114
XI.	THE EARLY TWENTIETH CENTURY	137
XII.	SINCE 1944	148
XIII.	WOMEN AS INSPECTORS AND ORGANISERS	154
XIV.	SOME PROBLEMS OF INSPECTORS	173
	SELECT BIBLIOGRAPHY	186
	INDEX	191

FOREWORD
by Sir William Alexander

THIS book by Dr. Edmonds is an important contribution to educational literature. So far as I know, there is nothing available which sets out the part of inspection in the organisation of the educational system. Dr. Edmonds traces the history of inspection in the organisation of schools from its beginnings, which is in itself important for we are apt to forget that inspection is an essential part of the organisation. More important, however, in the later chapters of the book he examines the position of inspectors and the work of inspection in modern days. There are many interesting questions in this field. It is essential to recognise the difference between the functions of Her Majesty's Inspectors and those of the inspectors to a local education authority. The general functions of what I like to call the advisory service to a local education authority, that is, the work of inspectors and organisers, have come in recent years to be increasingly recognised as of major importance. The establishment of the Soulbury Committee to negotiate salary scales some fifteen years ago was in itself a recognition that this was an important arm of the education service.

It is therefore a pleasure to write this foreword to a book which puts on record so admirably the history of the development of this section of the education service. It is to be hoped that it is widely read by those responsible for the administration of the schools and by members of the teaching profession.

W.A.

PREFACE

No more emotive term exists in our language than 'inspector', whether in the professions or industry and commerce. Indeed, freedom from outside inspection is the supreme status-symbol of today, properly epitomised in our universities. To press home the idea of subjection to supervision, particularly if by the Government, would be anathema to clergy, lawyers and doctors alike; and as the teaching profession (which is no less a public service) reaches out towards its own 'education for responsibility', the precise nature of school-inspection may well be subject to scrutiny. This book seeks to portray the growth of inspection in England, in a framework of its relations with teaching on the one hand, with administration on the other.

In a work of this kind, it is impossible to thank by name all who have contributed by precept, practice and advice. The number of Heads alone would run into hundreds. I should however like to mention the following:

(a) Professor W. H. G. Armytage and Professor W. Walsh, in whose Departments the two theses were compiled which form a basis for this book; also Dr. M. Cruickshank, Dr. S. J. Curtis, and Mr. W. E. Tate.

(b) The Secretaries of the British and Foreign School Society, the Catholic Education Council, the Congregational Union, the National Society, the Methodist Education Committee, the S.P.C.K., the N.U.T., and the N.A.I.E.O.

(c) The Chief Registrar and the Librarian, Ministry of Education, Her Majesty's Superintending Inspector of Factories, the Trustees of the British Museum.

(d) The Clerk or his representative and the City Librarians of Birmingham, Bradford, Brighton, Bristol, Hull, Leeds, Liverpool, London, Manchester, Newcastle, Norwich, Nottingham, Oldham, Sheffield.

(*e*) The Archivists of the East and the North Ridings of Yorkshire, Lancashire, Newcastle, the L.C.C.; also the Director of the Borthwick Institute of Historical Research.

(*f*) Sir William Alexander, Mr. J. E. H. Blackie, Mr. C. B. Freeman, Mr. E. W. Fryer, Dr. A. G. Hughes, Dr. J. G. Kellett, Mr. C. Borlase Parker, Mr. E. C. Wright, Mr. V. Clark.

Also my personal thanks are due to Professor W. J. H. Sprott, Dr. M. Pickett, Dr. O. P. Edmonds and my wife.

E.L.E.

'Cuimhnich air na daoine bho'n d' thanaig thu.'
(Remember the men you came from.)

Chapter One

THE EARLIEST INSPECTORS

(a) The Ecclesiastical Matrix

'INSPECTION', said the Rev. Edward Feild in 1840, 'strengthens the links binding the various parts of the ecclesiastical system.'[1] In so saying he reflected something of the long visitatorial tradition of the Church. Initially, as demonstrated by St. Paul himself, it was a cohesive force: visitation was spontaneously undertaken, likely to be very infrequent, and entirely hortatory. In this country, a similar 'primal sympathy' linked visitor and visited who were all of one family. The occasion was one of great dignity, but it was also domestic, as Archbishop Thomas Musgrave of York was happy to claim even as late as 1849. Early forms of visitation were closely associated with the general missionary impulse of the Church, opposing to the 'vain superstitious folly' of the pagan Anglo-Saxon 'the right rule of life' of the Christian.[2] It sought to persuade rather than threaten, to encourage rather than dismay, to endorse the good whilst eradicating the bad. Above all, it was no sinecure for the Visitor himself, who needed to combine physical toughness with his saintliness and scholarship, if he were to survive the long, even perilous, journeys.

With the establishing of more permanent administrative patterns in the Church, the visitatorial hierarchy also became clearer. Monasteries, for example, might receive several types of visitor, external (as in the case of the Pope's own legate) as well as more internal (e.g. local Order Visitors). The parish

[1] National Society *Annual Report 1840*, Appendix VI.
[2] Bede *Historia ecclesiastica gentis anglorum* Book V. C.VIII and Book IV C.II (translations after C. D. Douglas(ed.) English Historical Documents I.S. 151).

priest and his congregation might expect a series of visitations. There was that of the bishop, in whom was vested the ancient canonical right of visitation—and the duty to maintain schools. At more local level, there was the visitation of the rural dean, who

> was appointed by the bishop to have the inspection of clergy and people within the district in which he was incumbent under him.

Furthermore, 'this office of inspecting and reporting the manners of the clergy and people rendered the rural deans necessary attendants in the episcopal synod or general visitation, which was held for the same end of inspecting in order to reformation'.[1] Archi-diaconal visitation also sought to ensure 'good moral instruction' but included inspection of a good many administrative matters too, such as care of the ornaments and fabric of the church.[2] But at all levels, questions of inspectorial training and administrative loyalties were hardly likely to be raised as they came to be later; nor were inspectors to be plagued by the dichotomy of religious and secular education as they were after 1870 in this country. The whole of life could be viewed *sub specie æternitatis*.

The results of the Church's being the keeper of the public conscience can be seen in other ways than a routine insistence on conformity, and underlined the need for regular visitation. Irregularities in the schoolmaster's private life were as much a cause for reproof and correction as professional incompetence. Indeed, that particular form of inefficiency arising from lack of class-control can hardly have troubled the schoolmaster when he had the whole spiritual and moral power of the Church behind him; John Everard, for instance, did not hesitate to excommunicate Richard Hall for assaulting his usher.[3] Again, the Church, as supreme *fons et origo* of learning, could and did both prescribe and proscribe certain class text books. Secular inspectorates have since toyed with this idea

---

[1] R. Burn, *Ecclesiastical Law* (Fifth edition). Vol. II p. 114, 117: this may give too precise a picture of ruri-decanal visitation. If it ever was so sedulously practised, it lapsed with the growing power of the archdeacon in the fourteenth century.

[2] J. V. Bullard and H. Chalmers Bell (ed.), Lyndwood's *Provinciale Book I*; Titulus 10 cc. I–IV *cf.* also Book III; Titulus 22, cc. I–VII.

[3] A. F. Leach, *Educational Charters*, p. 253.

at certain phases of their development, but in this country at least, have not adopted it.

It was only natural, therefore, that the Church should, as Patron of this whole business of temporal living, hold a watching brief over all the professions, and should most zealously guard its monopoly of the right to license

> all rectors, vicars, curates, parish clerks, schoolmasters, physicians, chirurgeons and midwives . . .

who must, at the time of visitation by bishop and archdeacon:

> exhibit, or cause to be exhibited . . . their respective letters of Orders, certificates of subscriptions, institutions, admissions, faculties, dispensations and licences, upon pain of Law.

Unlicensed rivals were sternly dealt with, and the threat of the ultimate 'executive' act of excommunication was a potent one.

In the thirteenth century, the so-called golden age of visitation, men like Thomas de la Mere most nearly recalled the early visitors like St. Theodore from whom 'rivers of wholesome knowledge daily flowed to water the hearts of the hearers'. When morale is high in those inspected, this approach serves admirably, public persuasion of the many bringing the few up to the same high standards. Bishop Grosseteste's visitations indicated he had not this initial advantage; but he had all the true administrator's art of knowing how to find out the facts, interpret them shrewdly, base a decision on them and see it carried through. Thus, a dozen monastic superiors were deposed after his first visitation. Perhaps his tact hardly matched his zeal;[1] nevertheless, it was his persistence that kept the doors of the secular cathedrals open to diocesan visitation. In this connection, in one of his letters, he made that most important of all distinctions between inspectors, namely 'visor' the one who comes from within (in this case the Dean) and 'visitator', the one who comes from without (in this case the Bishop): not surprisingly, in Grosseteste's view, the latter only was the true visitor. Certainly, as a form of inspection, it is more easily impressed on the mind, though mention might be made of a development which seems to partake of the nature of both as well as providing an early if regrettably obscure example of how function is delegated. The first schools were primarily for

---

[1] Matthew Paris, *Historia anglorum V*, p. 419.

the training of priests, were attached to the cathedrals, and in them the bishop could act as prototype headmaster and inspector. Gradually, over the years through pressure of other diocesan duties, both offices were delegated (though the bishop still retained ultimate supervisory responsibility), and, in addition, the one school became sub-divided into schools of song, writing, grammar, logic and theology. In the smaller collegiate churches all the specialised schools might come under a single master—usually a senior priest, termed 'magister scolarum' or 'scholasticus'; but by the eleventh century the schools attached to the larger collegiate churches like Warwick, or the secular cathedrals like York and Salisbury, had become very important and, in consequence, more elaborately organised. By 1215 the fourth Lateran Council made obligatory the foundation of a school of grammar in every cathedral church, with a Master of Arts to teach therein, and a theological college in every archi-episcopal church. Such schools inevitably required someone in high authority in the cathedral to supervise them: the erstwhile 'magister scolarum' became 'cancellarius' and his duties expanded likewise. Besides being in charge of the schools of theology and chief lecturer there, he was also expected to keep the cathedral library (if it had one), act as chapter secretary, arrange the lectionary and act as senior preacher. Over and above all this he had to choose the teacher(s) in the school(s) of grammar, and license all teachers: any of the inevitable attempts by unlicensed teachers to set up schools in rivalry to the cathedral school could be and were combatted by the Church's weapon of excommunication. Any question of discipline within the schools was always referred to the chancellor, and he had to keep a watchful eye over his teachers—sometimes over the teachers of the whole diocese—so that, if anything was going amiss in the schools, he might make the necessary corrections.

In this way he gradually developed as a kind of diocesan, and also local authority, inspector, whilst, at the same time, he was ultimately responsible to Rome itself. Incidentally, the first specialist subject-organiser emerged from the same source: the precentor in the cathedral was not only responsible for the singing in church but for the organisation of the song school (duties which in turn could be delegated to the succentor). The precentor had authority over schools of song and no less than

4

the chancellor could cause adulterine schools to be dealt with sternly.

Judging from what records of visitation are extant, its tremendous potential was but uncertainly realised. It could reveal grave abuse and ensure stringent reform on occasion; it could also be so infrequent as to nullify its best efforts. Worst of all, it inevitably became caught up in the winds of religious change in the sixteenth century, when its powers of visitation became vested in the Crown. In Archbishop Grindal's visitation in 1571, deviationist dogma was as much in quest as pastoral ineptitude.[1] Again, a tradition of diocesan visitation was hard to sustain when as many as 25 sees might be vacant at one time. The family in fact had broken up, though some of the old familiar patterns were retained. The Church still kept a hold on education in that all grammar school masters had to be licensed by their diocesan or by the diocesan chancellor or his deputies.[2] Individual clergy too continued to show their enthusiasm for education by founding, or helping persuade lay folk to found schools of various types. In the way of things, such clergy retained their interest in these foundations and often acted as visitor-inspectors of them: often they were the only educated persons in the area capable of dealing continuously with inspectorial problems.

(b) Eighteenth Century Anglican Charity Schools

The breakdown of ecclesiastical organisation following on the Reformation in this country had dire effects on education at all levels, and the inspecting power of the Church of England was practically non-existent, apart from the power it retained to license the masters of grammar schools. It was not until the eighteenth century that any nation-wide effort to offer some kind of schooling to the illiterate poor came into being in the form of the charity school movement, such schools being instituted by individuals or by the Society for the Propagation of

---

[1] For his "Injunctions", *v*. E. Cardwell, *Documentary Annals of the Reformed Church of England*, Vol. I, p. 369.

[2] *cf. Constitutions and Canons Ecclesiastical 1603*, LXXVII. *cf.* further "The ecclesiastical licensing of teachers in the past." (*Gentlemen's Magazine*, Dec. 1902) and "The episcopal licensing of schoolmasters in England." (*Church Quarterly Review*, Oct.–Dec. 1956).

B

Christian Knowledge and kindred societies. Such a voluntary movement, dependent largely on spasmodic charity, inevitably had many twists and turns of fortune, but whilst it lasted it frequently received noble support from many country parsons who acted as unpaid teachers, organisers, examiners and inspectors in their local charity schools.

The S.P.C.K. itself grew out of the religious societies founded in London and Westminster from 1678 onward and out of the societies for the reformation of manners, about 1691. The latter were more latitudinarian than the former both in make-up and outlook, and even nonconformists readily supported some charity schools in the early years. From the first meeting of the Society on 8th March, 1699, when, among other aims, one was announced 'to further and promote that good design of erecting catechetical schools in each parish in and about London', the growth of charity schools was rapid. By May, 1705, there were 36 in a ten-mile radius of London, and by 1718 an estimated 1,378 in the whole country, educating 28,610 children. The quota of a large county like Yorkshire was 48 in 1724 and 61 by 1732, the peak period of expansion. There was a subsequent falling off in this rate of increase, though the over-all figures for the country in 1758 were 2,044 schools with 51,161 children on roll; and by 1792 the estimable Mrs. Trimmer still reckoned some 40,000 children to be receiving charity school education. By far the greater majority of the schools were in England and Wales. The Irish charity schools never met adequately the greater (if to them more dangerous) appeal of the Roman Catholic 'hedge-schools'. In Scotland, the schools of the S.S.P.C.K. were very thinly scattered. The inspection of their schools was always controlled fairly tightly from the central parent Society; e.g. in 1787 Dr. Kemp, the then Secretary, undertook the arduous tour of inspection of the charity schools in the Highlands and islands. Thus, perhaps, is already forecast the pattern of development of later inspectorates of schools in Scotland.

Insofar as the first appointment of an inspector of charity schools is concerned, London, as so often later, led the way. But the name of the Rev. Mr. Coghan, appointed inspector of London's charity schools at £20 a year under a Minute of 13th June, 1701, does not appear in Newcourt's 'Repertorium' (1708-10); and as the agents paid his salary quarterly he may

6

well have worked under them. From the start, the Church of England clergy were inspectors in that all Anglican charity school teachers had to be approved by them on appointment. In conception, the agents of the S.P.C.K. were merely men who would 'begin an endeavour of setting up schools'; and the first three appointed, 'willing to undertake the care of taking subscriptions to set up schools', could have had little idea of how important they were ultimately to become to the Society. Their multifarious activities cover so many agenda-items of a modern education committee.

Their first duty was to nurse sedulously new subscription lists for schools in different localities and then keep a watchful eye on collections (of money) made for the same purpose. When the school was built, they were responsible for finding, interviewing and appointing a schoolmaster (or mistress), paying him through funds allotted to them from the parent Society. Only rarely did this Society recommend candidates to its agents for consideration—though this was tantamount to appointment. The agents also paid for the school books that were ordered, and, like a present-day Local Authority Treasurer's Department, kept a watch on all school outgoings—duly noted in their (at first) weekly reports on the school(s). They were the Society's interpreters of policy, e.g. they advised how legacies could be left to the Society and kept lists of benefactors to each charity school in the vestry of the local parish church.

It is not surprising that other duties began to devolve upon them, for not even the most visionary of the early members of the S.P.C.K. could have foreseen such a rapid expansion of schools. The agents became the only men who could advise them on how many schools they had, where they were and how many children were on roll; what monies were subscribed for their upkeep; who the staff were; which were the brighter children (with 'pregnancy of their parts'); to whom the leavers were apprenticed and in what numbers; how many boarders there were and how many were clothed and fed free. Again, it was the agent's responsibility to see that the children were brought to church at least four times a year 'in order to be publicly examined by their respective Ministers'.[1] Inevitably, therefore, the agent became something of an attendance officer, and always on the look-out for irregularities such as the

[1] S.P.C.K. *Minutes*, 30th Dec. 1700.

7

acceptance by schoolmasters of fee-paying pupils alongside the poor, non-paying children for whom the benefits of charity school education were really intended.

By 1703, the agents had acquired enough experience to be conducting in London a 'general visitation of the charity schools', and their report on the whole was favourable; 'hitherto, all things relating to them (being) in very exact order, saving that in one school some of the trustees do cause their own children to be taught with the poor children; and that in some other schools one master will undertake to teach more than fifty children'. Needless to add, the parent body 'resolved . . . to endeavour to obviate these two mischiefs by a proper application to the trustees'.[1] Far more serious (to the S.P.C.K.) was their agent's report on the Clerkenwell charity schoolmaster Mr. Honeycott who publicly performed with his children *Timon of Athens*: it warranted at very least a severe reprimand by the Bishop of London.

It was, perhaps, some recognition of their importance to the Society that the agents were allowed expenses for messengers and bill-posting. This latter concession illuminates an activity of the agents as 'tractators', for time and time again the Society used them to distribute the pamphlets it printed. In 1701 these same agents were asked if they would 'lay before the Society a scheme or method for the management of the Trust of charity schools in general', and, two years later, they were asked to submit 'proposals about the training up of masters for the country schools', this being one of the earliest hints that training of teachers for rural schools might be a problem separate from that of general teacher-training. Regretfully, therefore, one reads of the Society's decision, on 11th November, 1708, to leave this most vital of matters to the religious societies, which:

> have hitherto furnished the charity schools in and about London with discreet masters at far less charge, and to better satisfaction, than by any other method that has been tried.[2]

To these onerous duties, the agent added others of a local character which have affinities with those of a later race of local inspector. They were called upon to investigate complaints against school teachers, and in at least one recorded

---

[1] S.P.C.K. *Minutes*, 22nd April 1703.
[2] S.P.C.K. *Minutes*, 18th Nov. 1708.

case, they settled satisfactorily the question of a teacher's debts. Fully acquainted with the needs of the localities in which they worked, the agents were of sufficient social standing to enlist, usually, the interest and support of local gentry (the mainspring of eighteenth century private philanthropy, educationally speaking) or to report to their parent committee cases where such local encouragement and support were not forthcoming. It was only natural that agents should be made corresponding members (22nd June, 1704).

In short, it is hardly surprising that the officially appointed inspector for the London district sinks out of the picture; indeed, apart from his name appearing in the Minutes as being duly appointed to the post, he has no further mention. The more powerful agent, in fact combines within himself the functions of a later Organiser, Inspector, and Chief Education Officer. In the nineteenth century the British and Foreign School Society developed further the idea of agent by making him peripatetic over a wider area.

Outside London the Society relied on 'local correspondents' for the furtherance of its plans, and the response of these correspondents varied enormously from area to area, being largely dependent on the correspondent's own enthusiasm and ability and also on the amount of co-operation he might (or might not) receive from fellow clergy. His task was a heavy one—to rouse enthusiasm and collect subscriptions for the charity school, build it, and organise the work therein, often taking a share in the instruction given. Over and above all this, he, along with others appointed by the subscribers, was required to 'have immediate care and government of the school and shall report the state and condition of the same at the said quarterly meetings of the subscribers'.[1] At its most efficient, group visitation of this kind, loosely linked with the larger lay Committee in which executive power was vested, admirably fulfilled all that was best in the vigorous tradition of local inspection of schools. But there were far too few men of the calibre of the Rev. Dr. John Ellis of Gonalston, who blended personal piety with administrative ability. Six months after accepting the position of correspondent on 11th January, 1700, he could report a school was being built; a later letter to the S.P.C.K. states in a clear firm hand, 'the subscribers meet once in six

[1] S.P.C.K. *An account of the S.P.C.K.* 1716, p. 12.

9

months to regulate their charity and appoint inspectors of schools'. Many causes contributed to the failure of the Society to develop any definite pattern of inspection or inspectorate, but a most important one was the failure of Henry Newman, Secretary of the Society from 1708 to 1743, to visit any of the 'corresponding' charity schools outside London. Such personal visits might indeed have helped bind the different parts of the educational system together.

(c) Early Sunday Schools

Generally speaking, Sunday schools were much more popular than any other type of educational establishment in that they catered for all ages, up to, and including, adults, and did not interfere with the week's work. As a result, such literacy as existed among the working class in the early nineteenth century can be traced mainly to the influence of Sunday schools.

Insofar as inspection of Sunday schools was envisaged clearly, it was influenced by charity school procedure. The Tetbury Code of Rules, for instance, provided for 'two subscribers of at least 10/6d. to visit, in rotation, and report', altogether reminiscent of the local visitors in general, and of the agents of the S.P.C.K. in particular, in their periodic reports on visits to schools. The same Code enjoined upon 'subscribers, visitors and churchwardens' the solemn duty of preventing any 'idling and playing about on the Lord's Day', suggesting they might be regarded as an early form of attendance-officer.

The early history of the two types of school is not dissimilar, particularly in the rapidity of growth. London again gave a lead to the rest of the country. The Society for the establishment and support of Sunday Schools throughout the Kingdom of Great Britain was formed in 1785; and its procedure was clearly influenced by S.P.C.K. precedent: e.g. the same qualifications were looked for in their teachers, who were also paid in a similar way. Eight years later was founded the London Society, as latitudinarian in inception and make-up as the S.P.C.K. had once been. Ironically enough, however, it is only after the loss of this tolerance in the early nineteenth century, with the consequent crystallising of attitude in the various denominational bodies, that a more definite form of denominational inspection emerges. The British and Foreign

School Society's travelling agents show the influence of a charity school agent-cum-adviser-cum-inspector. The term 'official agent' is also used as an alternative to 'inspector' in the early records of the indefatigable Wesleyan Education Committee, and their functions were obviously regarded as inter-changeable. In the case of the National Society, an inspector and an 'inspecting agent' were also to be appointed. All these inspectors of the different denominations might regard Sunday schools as coming within their purview (upon request). All had in common a fondness for the catechetical method. Nor was this surprising, stemming as it did from the Catechism itself. Familiar to Church of England clergy through its own inherited visitational procedure, it was a natural means of examination of Anglican Sunday Schools no less than of charity schools, when education meant predominantly religious education. The first of Her Majesty's Inspectors of Schools could be expected to use it too. Their denominational background was also advantageous when comment was required, as it sometimes was, on the links between teaching in week-day and Sunday schools.

At local level, it was only natural that persons selected to inspect Sunday schools should be ministers, and that the masters or mistresses, often voluntary workers as they were, should need to be approved by the Minister. The charity schools had worked under a similar system insofar as internal inspection was concerned: the master must follow the minister in 'the business of religion'. Besides this 'clerical' inspection, the Sunday School movement, being voluntary in spirit and local in application, relied on a sufficient number of interested, socially adequate local folk coming forward to give of their time and energies in service on local Sunday School Committees which were directly responsible for supervision. Such supervision was carried out regularly and thoroughly by means of a rota of 'visitors' duly appointed by the Committee. In the case of the Manchester and District Sunday Schools Association, 'the Management of the Association is vested in the Committee appointed at each General Annual Meeting: and such a Committee is bound to · meet at least once a quarter'. The visitatorial programme here was well formulated: the 'Visitor' was placed under the direction of a visiting sub-committee to which he reported. The Annual Report for 1867 affords a good example of procedure.

Article 11 of the Articles of Association of the York Incorporated (Church of England) Sunday School Committee,
instituted in 1786, stated that 'the clerical visitors, at their
discretion, (shall) open and close the respective schools,
catechise or address the scholars, preside at the meetings of the
teachers, and communicate with the Committee on any matter
relating to the schools that they may think desirable'. Article
12 goes on: 'the Committee shall, from time to time, appoint
two of their body to visit and examine the schools, and report
thereon'.

The rules for the regulation of Sunday Schools in the parish
of St. Stephen's, Norwich, stated:

> that two of the visitors visit the school by rotation on every
> Sunday, that they make their report written down in a book for
> that purpose: and that these visitors, at the recommendation, and
> with the concurrence of the Superintendent, do grant proper
> rewards to the diligent and orderly, as to them shall seem useful
> and of general advantage.

The Rev. W. Ellis, who drew up the rules and regulations
for the Stroud Sunday Schools in 1781, included one that:

> "some of the subscribers will in turn visit these schools to see
> that their design is duly pursued, and give some little reward to
> the first, second and third most deserving in the school."

In clauses like these are apparent the essential features of
Sunday School inspection. Supervision was not entrusted to
one man, as was all too painfully true in some cases fifty years
later. The protocol of patronage required that the whole body
of managers should have opportunity in turn to visit their
Sunday Schools, thus being, as it were, their own eyes and
ears. The idea was by no means a novel one, looking back, as it
did, to local inspection in early Anglican charity schools and
forward to that obtaining in 'National' schools for the children
of the poor in the second decade of the nineteenth century.
Individual visitors in themselves had no executive power,
relying rather on their powers of public persuasion. Policy
(including finance) was reserved to the whole Committee
which was not afraid to assert itself vis-à-vis the internal supervisor, the Superintendent himself. Thus, at Blackburn, the
Superintendents of the four Church of England Sunday schools

were forbidden to pay bills 'whether relating to the ordinary expenses or of repairs to the school'. It should be added that only locally-raised funds were available: the National Society refused any financial help to Sunday-schools. The spectre of debt, therefore, was never far away.

This visitatorial pattern was not exclusive to the Church of England: for example, the Wesleyan Sunday School Union in Sheffield stressed more than once 'that the system, which has long prevailed, of visiting all the schools in this union by deputation, at least once a year, is very useful, and ought to be maintained, as it promotes religious intercourse in general; but especially because it increases that Christian charity and circulates that mutual information so necessary and acceptable among Sunday school teachers'.

Such visitation-cum-inspection, when the visitors could do nothing more than advise and encourage was doomed, in the long run, to fail. Many visitors realised beyond all shadow of doubt that Sunday school teachers were, all too frequently, hopelessly inadequate and needed some sort of training before they could achieve any really worth-while results.[1] But where to find that training? The help of the National Society's training or organising masters was sometimes sought by the local diocesan societies on behalf of Sunday schools, but both H.M. Inspector, Mr. H. S. Tremenheere, and the National Society's Inspector, the Rev. E. Feild, commented in their very first reports upon schools about the need for organisation.

It was always to the visitors that Sunday Schools looked for suggestions as to improvements, occasionally with success, as in the case of the Manchester and District Sunday Schools Association. The inexhaustible John Chadwick, in his Visitor's Report for 1867–68, commented wryly: 'One of the greatest difficulties in the way of improving our schools is the want of teachers who possess some tact and skill to impart knowledge suited to the capacities of their scholars'. He referred to the need for books and pictures, for more suitable premises, for more care by teachers in the management of junior classes. Yet his technique was quite sound; holding conferences with the teachers to discuss these matters, and attending by invitation meetings of local unions. The visitors, too, were fortunate

[1] *cf. Report of the Commission on the Employment of Children.* (Trades and Manufactures) 1843, p. 142.

in being encouraged to visit each others' Sunday Schools, such visits being 'of great benefit to us, and no doubt the other visitors will find the same, as they will see what is profitable and what to avoid in their own school". Specific weaknesses commented on by visitors were the ceaseless gossip and chatter of the pupils even when singing or being read to, the lack of equipment, the unpunctuality and the general incompetence on the teachers' part. Few, if any, of these faults could be remedied, even by the most willing and enthusiastic visitors, when these latter were as ignorant of teaching techniques as were the teachers themselves.

Chapter Two

NATIONAL SOCIETY AND BRITISH SOCIETY INSPECTORS

THE Church of England, with its long traditions as inspector-general and administrator, was well fitted to undertake once again a system of education on a national scale, and nothing less than this was envisaged by the National Society, with its charter of 1811 for 'the provision of the education of the poor in the principles of the Established Church'. The earliest annual reports of the General Committee of the National Society are full of confidence that this self-imposed task could be accomplished. By 1817, according to the Annual Report for that year, 200,000 children were estimated to be receiving instruction—a truly magnificent effort. The hard lesson had yet to be learned that it was beyond the financial resources of any voluntary body or bodies to provide free universal education.

As in the case of charity schools, the emphasis was on local effort, prompted and encouraged by the parent National Society, in turn exhorted by men of the calibre of G. F. Mathinson. The aims of these up-springing local education boards were to stimulate and foster interest, obtain information, collect subscriptions, and then get the school(s) built—good eighteenth century S.P.C.K. procedure, in fact, brought up to date. The Annual Report of the National Society for 1816 included a recommendation to these diocesan and district societies that they should appoint one of their own members to visit and examine annually the schools in connection with them, 'distinguishing superior proficiency by small rewards and pointing out defects, together with the means of their correction'.

Such as it was (for it was by no means a clearly defined

ministration and varied from district to district) such inspection was akin to visitation, except that no hard and fast rules about frequency existed. It was an integral part of Dr. Andrew Bell's Madras system of education:

> 7th. Last of all comes the superintendent, or trustee, or visitor, or chaplain, or parochial minister, whose scrutinising eye must pervade the whole machine, whose active mind must give it energy, and whose unbiased judgement must inspire confidence, and maintain the general order and harmony.
> For this purpose there is kept by the ushers, teachers or others equal to the office
> 8th. a register of the task performed; and by the schoolmaster
> 9th. a register of daily offences, or black book . . .[1]

Dr. Bell himself was appointed Superintendent of 'national' schools in 1812, but the many calls on him of a more general nature, coupled, no doubt, with his own restless ambition, tended to militate against his devising any routine of inspection. The Secretary of the Society also inspected schools as and when he was able—probably the forerunner of the 'Clerical Superintendent' mentioned in the Annual Report of the Society for 1839 as being available for inspection purposes.

This attempt at schools inspection at a national level was a very real achievement of the National Society, hampered as it was by complete lack of any inspectorial traditions, not to mention a great lack of schools and an attitude towards their conception of education for the children of the poor ranging from apathy to downright hostility. It was fortunate, therefore, that the Society should possess certain initial advantages. In the first place, it had 'ties as light as air yet strong as iron' with many influential sections of public opinion, could count on the whole episcopacy for support, and even enjoyed royal patronage under H.R.H. the Prince Regent (later, from 1820, King George IV). In addition, it could, and did, learn from the mistakes of the S.P.C.K. in matters of supervision. The Rev. Dr. T. T. Walmsley, for example, Secretary of the National Society, was a tireless correspondent, and never failed to visit promptly any school which needed help. Furthermore, the National Society touched the feelings of men and women of the so-called 'leisured classes' who were sufficiently interested

---

[1] *Experiment in Education made at the Male Asylum in Madras*, 1797, Part I, ch. III.

and altruistic to be willing to carry out inspections of their local schools.

Above all, the Madras System, which was the method of education favoured by the National Society, both for economy and to ensure the fullest use of the very few teachers available, depended for its very existence on supervision of an organisational as well as inspectorial nature. Dr. Bell himself was consulted by the General Committee of the National Society on the principles of inspection and organisation, and was given very wide powers when co-opted to the same Committee on 24th January, 1812:

> (he should) be requested to act as superintendent in the formation and conduct of the Central and other schools under the direction of this Society, with power to engage such persons as masters and mistresses as shall be adequate to carry the purposes of the Society into effect, and to retain, suspend or dismiss the masters or mistresses.

These were large personal powers indeed; so large that an amendment followed five days later, when after 'superintendent' were inserted the words, 'under the direction of the Society'. A slight amendment at first sight: in fact, one of major importance. It enunciated a principle integral to local educational administration today: Dr. Bell, no less than those he might appoint, was to be the servant of the National Society, and 'Committee approval' of his actions, however nominal it might be, was essential. This was demonstrated in mid-July, 1812, in the matter of revised editions of elementary textbooks. The General Committee was, in fact, a prototype 'Finance and General Purposes Committee' so familiar in present-day local administration. To it the Schools Committee reported and sometimes had motions 'referred back'. When the Rev. W. Johnson became Dr. Bell's assistant in June, 1816, it drew up a set of regulations which left him in no doubt as to his terms of reference. Much later, in 1842, it pointed out to Mrs. Field that no bills should be paid without its prior approval; reminded Mrs. Bridges that knitting as a subject should remain on the teacher's certificate; and required any dismissal of staff to be sanctioned by its approval. It also authorised items of school expenditure which would today be classified as school requisitions or supplies, e.g. the purchase of a clock and candles in

November, 1812. It was of this Committee that even Dr. Bell was the servant: nevertheless, the Committee recognised his greatness and his potentiality of becoming the ideal school inspector, and gave him a very free hand. As he so rightly believed in personal contacts, his time was fairly evenly divided between the Central School and a series of voluntary 'circuits' in the country, planned by himself,[1] and seemingly followed by no official reports to any National Society Committees.

Besides being inspector, Bell was also organiser: he felt that he knew the way, and there *was* only one, to teach, and he set it down in his 'Instructions to Schoolmasters', which were intended to be used in every National School. His suggestions about suitable school books were also intended to become the basic book-list for the schools. Teachers were indoctrinated in the Madras system at the Central School, under his eye and guidance, given ample opportunity for school practice—he was a firm believer in the principle of 'learning by doing'— and then sent out to organise other schools on the Madras lines, their appointments being either on a temporary or permanent basis. These training teachers, both male and female, were closely watched by both officials of the National Society and by the Vicar of the area in which they worked (the latter, of course, acting in his ex-officio capacity of local inspector) and they were reprimanded or rewarded in accordance with their performance. For example, one Catherine Smedley first appeared in School Committee Minutes under a deferred appointment, 15th May, 1818, was further mentioned on 3rd July of the same year, was sent to organise a school at Staines on 25th September, and another at Sigglesthorpe on 6th November. Seven months later, the School Committee:

> received a communication from the Ladies Committee, (and) resolved, as Catherine Smedley had arranged no less than twenty schools and always given great satisfaction, that the Ladies be requested to present her with such clothing as shall appear to them proper, together with a Bible and a Prayer-book; and to inform her if she shall continue exemplary in her behaviour and that an appointment to a school should offer to which she may seem fitted, the School Committee will not forget her past good conduct.

[1] National Society *Annual Report*, 1816, pp. 20–21.

She was still peripatetic in February, 1820, but, after two more assignments the School Committee agreed that she should be permanently appointed to Chiswick, by request of the Vicar of that parish. Because of the great shortage of trained teachers sometimes mere boys and girls, after a short period in Central School, were sent to continue work begun by a more expert training master or mistress in some local schools. On all these, trained and half-trained alike, the Committee kept a watchful eye. By March, 1817, a School Committee Minute required:

> that a report of masters and mistresses sent into the country to arrange or inspect schools, or for any temporary purpose, be made by them once a fortnight, addressed to the Secretary, and regularly laid before this Committee and introduced into their list of agenda.

Despite the odd wording of the above Minute, it seems certain that such training masters and mistresses were not intended to be inspectors in the strict sense of the term. They were supervised by local managers, and depended on them for an 'ample testimonial' as to their performance, conduct and behaviour. As early as 12th January, 1812, the School Committee recommended:

> the weekly or more frequent visiting of the schools and the superintendence of the master be undertaken by one or more of the governors.

This mixture of genuine belief in local inspection and of a centrally directed advisory service may have been calculated to enlist local support: it is significant that both advice and assistance had to be asked for before being given, but there was soon an almost universal clamour for someone with both educational and administrative information. The thirst for knowledge of the National Society system had prompted 'several persons of great respectability in the higher ranks of life' to undertake the course of training at the Central School, being thus equipped to act as visitors to their local schools. Such 'experienced visitors', observed the Society's Annual Report of 1816, 'are of the very essence of the system'.

The Society even from the beginning was very much concerned about the delicacy of its inspectorial relationships with the schools in union. On the one hand, it was almost overwhelmed at times by 'representations from the clergy and others interested in the welfare of schools, setting forth the benefits which would result from occasional visitation': such visitation, it was felt, would check the natural tendency of the schools to fall into torpor or even error when the first enthusiasm which caused their foundation had waned. On the other hand, the Society was hesitant to take any step which might be construed as interference in the internal management of any particular school. This was inevitably the dilemma for any voluntary system of local supervision: in practice, most of the supervision of church schools seems to have been left to the parish clergy, whilst the lay-managers, generally, sank into apathy; such apathy in the end brought about local disasters in the shape of schools collapsing, sometimes literally, for lack of subscriptions to support them. Even nonconformist schools, where the lay element among managers was more predominant, suffered in the same way; most of the actual inspection was tacitly left to the minister.

In the face of such variable enthusiasms on the part of local groups, the best preventive remedy against decline was soon recognised as being inspection by some officially appointed and paid inspector. As early as May, 1814, the energetic Society of Secretaries was pressing for the Central School to have a visitor who could be sent out to local and diocesan district societies, whenever required; in other words, an inspector, as distinct from an organising master whose services were already available on request. It was also suggested that:

> whenever it is practicable, local visitors perfectly versed in the mechanism and discipline of the System should at stated intervals be deputed to this important function.

In 1820 a motion was passed:

> that it be recommended to the Secretaries and Superintendents of the different schools in each diocese or district to meet and appoint a visitor; to fix upon the remuneration to be given to such visitor, and to offer the benefits resulting from his visitation to any school subscribing a certain sum, to be determined by the meeting, towards defraying the necessary expense.

This conception of local visitation, paid yet non-profit making, recurs frequently during the nineteenth century.

The basic problem to be settled was, however, 'Who was

there capable of undertaking such visitation, involving, as it did, examination of the children in such things as liturgy and catechism, as well as the distribution of rewards to staff for such things as the best conducted class?' The obvious answer to this question was, 'The clerical Superintendent'. Therefore, it is not surprising that the initiative in such inspectorial visitation came from the clergy: for example:

> in the district of West Sussex, County of Norfolk, Diocese of Durham, Archdeaconry of Coventry and Archdeaconry of Bath, one or more of the clergy have kindly undertaken the office of inspecting visitor, and their services have been considered acceptable and beneficial.[1]

By 1826 the apparent wisdom of this scheme was being pressed home by the Society, particularly in view of 'a partial departure' from the National system by some country schools. The Committee stressed that:

> they consider it essential for the well conducting of the school to have only one official visitor, who would, very frequently, and at uncertain hours, inspect the schools and examine into the improvement of the children. This duty can never be so well performed as by the resident minister of the parish; but in the absence of a resident minister, it would be desirable that this duty should be undertaken by the treasurer, the secretary, or some one of the subscribers well acquainted with the system. It seems desirable that only one person should take upon himself this interesting task, with a view to secure uniformity in the instruction and discipline of the school; although the assistance of weekly or monthly visitors, especially if they would direct their attention only to the general state and discipline of the school, would be highly advantageous.

The Committee went on in similar strain:

> Other points of equal importance with the preceding are that the official visitor should especially direct the master's attention to the necessity of taking care that there should be a constant supply of teachers; that particular attention should be paid to the detailed instructions recommended by Dr. Bell on this matter, as well as to all the other leading principles laid down in his manual; and that, for this purpose, his manual should be invariably placed in the hands of every master and mistress.[2]

[1] National Society *Annual Report*, 1821, pp. 26–27.
[2] National Society *Annual Report*, 1826, pp. 16–17.

It would seem then that the visitor-inspector's duty was to ensure orthodoxy even more than efficiency: in this he had much in common with the organising master. In fact, some local Committees, notably the one at Bath, urged the appointment of 'some person thoroughly conversant with the Madras system as an inspecting master of a certain number of schools within some allotted district of each diocese', the advantages being:

> 1. constant communication between teachers in different schools, 'ever tending to an increase of zeal and attention to the duties of their respective posts';

> 2. 'constant exertion' from managers and masters to 'ensure the approbation' of the inspecting master and hold a creditable place in his occasional report on the progress of schools;

> 3. uniformity with the Central School.

It is clear, therefore, that the two functions frequently merged; nor is this surprising. Any training master who carried with him the latest information about *the* system, including details of approved textbooks and manuals, was well on his way towards being regarded as an inspector. This is epitomised in a request by the Durham Diocesan Society for the help of a training master:

> he will also be understood as engaging to superintend such instruction; to support, whenever there shall be occasion, the authority of the teacher; to promote to the utmost of his power the harmony and goodwill which ought to subsist between the teachers and the masters so to be taught; and to take upon himself the office of visitor to such school or schools when organised.[1]

It is equally clear that the idea of some combination of local inspectors with a centrally controlled inspectorial body was evolved and put into practice by the National Society; from this beginning has developed the complex system of inspection of the present day.

The British and Foreign School Society, no less than the National Society, was very much concerned with the welfare of its schools, and recognised at once a place for regular visitation. Although labouring under shortages of money even more grievously than the National Society (what voluntary Society

[1] National Society *Annual Report*, 1818, pp. 130–131.

ever had enough and to spare?), yet, in the period 1820–1830, it developed the idea of travelling 'agents'. These were men, who, like the S.P.C.K. agents, could proselytise, get local groups of interested people together, raise funds, build schools, and then go on encouraging managers and teachers with advice, inspiration, and even by direct help such as providing school reading books.

At first, these agents were somewhat limited in their work by the sheer impossibility of their being in more than one place at once, but they had considerable success in areas in which they operated for any length of time. In 1830 the Society took the really big step of appointing Lieutenant Fabian as their permanent 'travelling agent', and in the following year Henry Althans was appointed inspector for the rapidly expanding metropolitan district. In 1833 the general report of the Society gave the considered opinion of inspectors and travelling agents:

> while they lay no claim to any right of interference with the internal economy of schools which may have received assistance at their hands, but on the contrary are satisfied that the best guarantee for their being efficiently conducted is to be found in the independent management of local committees, they yet feel that many important advantages are gained by the occasional and friendly supervision of a qualified inspector.

The report added that visits of this kind, if properly conducted, were equally advantageous to the teacher and the taught. Nevertheless, the onus lay always on the local committees, in which the lay element was often more predominant than in similar National Society Committees, although frequently the minister was the power behind his committee, just as the local vicar was.

Althans was based on London, and in the course of a year he intended to visit each school at least once, and preferably twice. But already, in 1833, a pilot-investigation was being undertaken of schools outside London: the sample of Yorkshire schools, for example, was made up of three schools in York, three in Hull, two in Whitby and Scarborough, and one each in New Malton and Barton-on-Humber. These visits were accompanied by a public examination of the children at which parents were encouraged to be present, by addresses to parents, and by lectures on education at public meetings—everything, in fact, which might be expected to commend the schools and their work to the public. Althans and Fabian, therefore, combined within themselves the functions of diocesan 'visitor', central and Local inspector, and even of Chief Education Officer of twentieth century local Education Authorities. The extent of their work is indicated in the general report of the Society for 1835: Althans made 237 visits to schools and 'inspected' 21,176 children, all of whom were 'brought under the course of examination'; Fabian visited 38 schools and examined 5,708 children. In every case they were cordially received. Similar figures were presented for the next few years, but soon the inadequacy of their visitation, good as it might be, was squarely recognised:

> these occasional visits do not by any means meet the needs of the country. Nothing short of frequent, regular and systematic inspection will ever secure the general efficiency of schools.

The success of the organising-inspector of the British Society did not go un-noticed in other non-conformist circles, and much the same results were forthcoming. Thus, the Report of the Congregational Board of Education, presented to the Assembly 16 May, 1856, noted with satisfaction that:

> the Rev. John Ross has been engaged since last June in visiting various parts of the country to disseminate information relative to the principles and operations of the Board—to obtain more general pecuniary support—to visit and inspect schools—to hold meetings of the friends of voluntary education, and wherever practicable, of parents whose children are attending the schools which he has an opportunity of inspecting.

Well might the Board express satisfaction with the work of 'its valued friend' in faithfully representing its claims, and aiding local efforts to promote education. The scholarship of Ross was not wasted in such context.

Chapter Three

THE FIRST GOVERNMENT INSPECTORS

THE government of a country which was rapidly becoming industrialised was far more likely to be interested in the development of industry, and it was in the industrial field that the first government inspectors made their appearance, with the duty of considering the working conditions in factories, particularly in their impact on the young. But even in this field the government was hesitant over the nature and degree of its supervisory role. The early nineteenth century Acts dealt with the improvement of conditions of work and employment: for example, under the 1802 Act, factory walls and ceilings were to be lime-washed yearly, adequate ventilation was to be provided, apprentices were to work no more than twelve hours daily, excluding mealtimes, and compulsory night work, between 9 p.m. and 6 a.m., was forbidden. During the first four years of his indenture an apprentice in mill or factory was to receive instruction daily, during working hours, in reading, writing and arithmetic, under a 'discreet and proper person . . . in some room . . . set apart for that purpose'; and on Sundays he was to have an hour's instruction, including appropriate questioning, in Sunday school. Mill-owners were required to obey these rules, and, as a 'double-check', magistrates were required to appoint as visitors two persons, one a justice of the peace, the other a clergyman of the Church of England, neither being in any way connected with the establishment they were to visit and both of them being given 'full power and authority from time to time throughout the year to enter and inspect any such mill or factory at any time of day, or during the hours of employment as they shall think fit'. Moreover, they were required to submit to the quarter sessions periodical reports in writing on such things as the condition of the factory buildings, how the work was being done in them, and how, in general, the Act was being observed. The penalty for any obstruction offered them in the course of their duty was a fine of £5 or £10. Such local inspecting visitors had no real impact. Apart from the lack of any agreed policy upon what they should all be set to look for or how to look for it, if they found any faults they had no executive power to ensure amendment. There was no central office for the collating and summarising of their reports and no well-defined government department to supervise enforcement.

But in 1833, with a new Factory Act came a new type of inspector, a paid professional responsible for ensuring that what Parliament intended by the Act should be put into practice effectively. There were four of them, each with a salary of £1,000 (less travelling and hotel expenses); they were required to send quarterly reports (half-yearly after 1844) to a central office, and also required to meet together at least twice a year to standardise procedure and pool information. As it was quite impossible for the four to inspect more than 4,000 mills and factories, each was empowered, after due application to the Home Office, to appoint one or more superintendents, or sub-inspectors, to help him. Their powers were far more limited than those of the inspector: whereas the latter could enter any part of any factory at any time, the former could only enter 'any schoolroom, counting house, or any part of any factory or mill, excepting such part or parts as may be used for manufacturing purposes'.

These four inspectors were given practically a free hand to make any rules, regulations or orders regarded as necessary to fulfil their duties, and they had magistrates' powers and authority to impose fines, or even commit to prison any transgressors. They also had wide supervisory and executive powers, educationally speaking. Under the Act of 1833 children under 9 years were not to be employed; and attendance at some school provided by arrangement of the employer was made compulsory for factory children between the ages of 9 and 13. The school could be chosen by the parents, but in the case of their default, by the inspector, who could direct the employer to deduct one penny per shilling from the child's wages for

26

'education'. If schools were lacking, then the inspector could, if he saw fit, 'establish or procure the establishment of such schools'. Where the money was to come from was left an open question: it might even appear at first sight that the inspector was to find the money from the fines he imposed! He also wielded a certain amount of control over the teachers, and could disallow the salary of any teacher whom he adjudged to be incompetent.

Such powers as these were almost dictatorial, but in 1844 a new Factory Act codified their duties much more clearly and relieved them of the embarrassment of having first to make law and then administer it in a magisterial capacity. Under the 1844 Act both inspectors and sub-inspectors could visit any part of any factory or mill at any time, and could visit any school, whether on factory premises or not, at which factory children were educated. A central office was set up for them in London, complete with clerical staff. The inspector was responsible for fixing the salary of the school master, whose certificate of proficiency could be annulled by him from reasons of 'incapacity to teach to read and write, from his gross ignorance, or from his not having the books and materials necessary to teach them reading and writing, or because of his immoral conduct, or of his continued neglect to fill up and sign the certificate of school attendance required by the Act'. The teacher, incidentally, was given a right of appeal to the Home Secretary, and, before any such drastic action as annulment could be implemented, there must be a suitable alternative school for children within two miles of the factory. School pence up to the value of 2*d*. a week were to be deducted from each child's wage and each factory child between the ages of 8 and 13 must spend weekly either three whole days or six half-days at school; so it was that the 'half-time' system was born. It was only natural that the National Society, the largest of the voluntary societies, should require to have these factory children in its schools on a regular, not a casual, footing; the time was at hand, in fact, for much closer co-operation between the voluntary societies and the central government if the country's children were to be educated efficiently.

The new conception of Her Majesty's Inspector in the 1830's did not envisage training as a pre-requisite. None of the first four appointed Factory Inspectors had previous experience;

nor had the first appointed Mines Inspector a decade later (though all set about quickly to acquire it by judicious inquiry of 'management'). Perhaps a House of Commons Select Committee in 1835 best showed the prevailing attitude to pit inspection by recommending that 'men of known ability be encouraged to visit mines, whether in the character of distinguished scientists, chemists, mechanists or philanthropists'.

By 1850, however, the importance of some form of preparatory training was beginning to be grasped, for under the Mines Act of that year, four skilled mining engineers were appointed inspectors. As in the case of Factory Inspectors, their regulative function was very apparent, though they were expected at the same time to be 'diffusing everywhere intelligence and counsels without imposing directions'.

Insofar as the factory inspectors' relationships with the Home Office and with one another were concerned, many early tensions existed, which only time would resolve. 'Quis custodiet ipsos custodes?' was by no means an easy question to answer. The four inspectors were co-equal, no less than coeval, and continued to send in their quarterly reports to the Home Office quite independently of each other, though the need for some co-ordinating agency or influence was becoming increasingly apparent. The Home Secretary himself intervened in 1849, Sir George Grey going so far as to say that he deemed it 'very inexpedient' that the net result of their joint conferences should be to make their reports a vehicle for contentious argument 'on points wherein they differ in opinion'.[1] Any system of appointment by nomination could react against hierarchy in this way, and it speaks well for it, as then currently practised, that so large a measure of agreement should have been reached by these four very different types of men. Their sub-inspectors or superintendents were at first even more sensitive to discipline: two had to be reprimanded and two more were dismissed later. In all, some five of the first fifteen embarrassed their particular inspector and the Home Office either by minor indiscretion or more serious insubordination. Beal's carelessness, for instance, to put it no worse, sparked off Fielden's polemic in the House of Commons 17th July, 1840, that the government was using the factory inspectors as its spies, a charge levelled three years earlier by R. H. Greg in his book

[1] *Factory Inspectors' Minute Book.* 22nd Jan. 1849.

The First Government Inspectors

The Factory Question. Only gradually were the firm foundations laid upon which any inspectorate must rest: on the personal side, absolute loyalty to one's colleagues and superiors, unimpeachable integrity, constant vigilance to ensure the good name of the service; on the administrative side, uniformity of approach and procedure, and 'all of one voice' in *public* utterances. Some of these early tensions were part economic, part social in origin. The salary of the sub-inspector was only a quarter of the inspector's, out of which he had to pay all his— considerable—travelling expenses. Their job, as the early minute-books of the inspectors show, was no sinecure: journeys were long, roads bad, and they were exposed to much local obloquy. They most certainly were not the mill-warden type which may at one time have been envisaged; Horner was at pains to say so. Their usefulness depended upon their being able 'to occupy respectable positions in society'.[1] The four inspectors did succeed in getting sub-inspectors' salaries raised in 1844. Much the same pattern could be traced in the case of mines inspectors: their attitude of fierce 'lone wolf' independence persisted even into the early twentieth century. In their case too, there were to be tensions of a socio-economic kind.[2]

[1] Joint-letter from Inspectors to Home Office, 30th Nov. 1844.
[2] *cf. Transactions North of England Institute of Mining Engineers.* 1871–72, Vol. XXI, p. 21; and M. Dunn, *A Treatise on the Winning and Working of Collieries.* 1852, p. 225.

Chapter Four

INSPECTORS IN THE EARLY
EIGHTEEN-FORTIES

IN 1833, Parliament made its first grant-in-aid to the voluntary societies. It was only a matter of time, thereafter, before Parliament would begin to seek more effective control over these grants-in-aid if only to find out how they were spent; the most obvious way of getting such information was by inspection. The immediate problem was, 'To whom should these inspectors belong? To the Churches? To the State?' An effort was made to settle the problem in 1838 when 'the Lords of Her Majesty's Treasury' directed

> an inspection to be made with a view to obtaining specific and detailed information on the schools, towards the erection of which grants have been made by the public.

Both Societies were requested to supply the necessary information and a grant of £500 was made to cover expenses. The National Society (with 425 schools built) asked for more than British and Foreign School Society (with 117 schools), but the Treasury rejected the claim. In consequence, 64 National Schools remained uninspected when the report, mainly a 'fact finder', was made.

Stemming from this report came an Order in Council, dated 3rd June, 1839:

> The Committee recommend that no further grant be made, now or heareafter, for the establishment or support of normal schools, or of any other schools, unless the right of inspection is retained, in order to secure a conformity with the regulations and discipline established in the several schools, with such improvements as may from time to time be suggested by the Committee.

The immediate concern was the establishment of the principle, without giving offence to the many different gradations of religious scruples about the State's role in education; hence the general terminology. A further Minute by the Committee of Council on Education some four months later (24th September, 1839) embodied regulations governing the appropriation of grants:

> the right of inspection will be required by the Committee in all cases; inspectors, authorised by Her Majesty in Council, will be appointed from time to time to visit schools to be henceforth aided by public money: the inspectors will not interfere with religious instruction, or discipline, or management of the school, it being their object to collect facts and information and to report the results of the inspections to the Committee of the Council.

This was a very cautious approach, indicating that the State had no wish to quarrel with the various denominations. At the same time the State had been provided with an opening because of the dissatisfaction expressed, by the National Society in particular, with the £500 offered by the government to the two voluntary Societies to inspect and report on their own schools.

Meanwhile the Societies, no doubt suspecting that the Treasury's request for information might be but the prelude to further State intervention, had already begun to make similar plans for inspection on their own denominational lines. In fact, even before the 'Lords of the Treasury' had made their request in 1839, the National Society, conscious of a need for 'considerable improvement' in its supervisory powers at local level whilst, at the same time, loth to interfere too drastically with the work of local managers, had, in May, 1838, appointed a Committee of Enquiry and Correspondence. In the following month the Committee presented its recommendations, namely that every diocese should have a Board consisting of the principal clergy and laity, acting under the authority of the Bishop; the Diocesan Board should form subordinate Boards in archdeaconries, rural deaneries and towns, and should also encourage, where expedient, Committees for the care of particular schools; it should also be responsible for the collection and administration of monies for educational purposes and 'for making arrangements for the visitation and inspection of schools, to be conducted in such manner and by such persons as the Bishop shall direct'. When this elaborate scheme of Boards and Committees had been formed at diocesan level, it was the duty of each Board to work out a system of school inspection for its own area. In anticipation of the old problem of variation in standard and method, the Committee reverted to the technique of the questionnaire; this was certainly a move towards meeting the General Committee's directive of 7th July, 1838, for the establishing of

> some general system of inspection best calculated to raise the standard and increase the efficiency of church education.

In November of the same year the Committee of Enquiry announced its 'Suggestions for the guidance of local schools', two of these having particular relevance:

> 1. the clergy and laity supporting local schools be requested to place them in connection with the local board for the purpose of general information and mutual improvement.

The permissive nature of this request was likely to be a weakness, but, nevertheless, it was a wise suggestion in the light of current circumstances.

> 2. These clergy and laity likewise 'receive a visitor properly appointed', in the next breath, however, adding, 'this should on no account be pressed; the advantage of inspection will soon be apparent wherever it is tried, and its introduction must be more or less gradual. The clergyman of the parish is of course the natural and constant inspector of all schools connected with the Church, and except in the case of a legal visitor of a Trust, no visitation should be attempted without his consent or the authority of the bishop. But when this can be obtained, the Board, in order to ensure frequent and regular visits by persons aquainted with local circumstances, may appoint two Examiners, of whom their Secretary will probably be one; the headmaster of a grammar school, or some one well versed in the details of practical teaching, may be another. They should undertake to visit every school in the district once or twice in each year. As soon as the arrangements can be made for the purpose, it will be desirable that an inspector should also be appointed by the Diocesan Board to act in concert with the local visitors.

This interesting statement reveals the possiblity of variants upon local inspectorial systems, but entirely consonant with the spirit, expressed earlier, that:

> Your Committee, in mentioning inspection among the proposed terms of union, are anxious to guard themselves against being supposed to contemplate anything of an inquisitorial or invidious interference with the local managers of any schools in union; but they entertain a strong conviction that a personal inspection, by qualified and authorised examiners, when carried on with the concurrence of the clergyman and managers (without which it should never be attempted) will tend at once to raise character and quicken the zeal of the master and stimulate the energies of the scholar.

These diocesan boards multiplied quickly, by 18th February, 1839, growing greenly in Exeter, Bath and Wells, Norwich, Salisbury, Lincoln, Chester, Gloucester, Bristol and Worcester, whilst Chichester, Ely and Ripon were also 'about it'; in all cases inspection was envisaged as under the sanction and aegis of their respective bishops. Of the diocesan boards following suit, London's was significant; though the idea was not entirely original, it proceeded to appoint the Rev. F. C. Cook to a two-in-one post of paid Secretary and Inspector in March, 1841. In the latter capacity, he visited some 150 to 200 schools in connection with the Board, his 'reports upon the proficiency of the scholars and other circumstances' being sent to the managers of these schools. His visits were not 'confined to National and parochial schools, but have included commercial schools; and are extended to all those of which the managers are willing to avail themselves of the obvious advantages of inspection'.[1] As diocesan inspector (and later as Her Majesty's Inspector) Cook was well-liked by the National Society: in 1843 the London Board was quite prepared, at the request of the Society, to send him to examine and report upon the schools of the Middlesex Society. Chester Board in like manner proposed 'that a paid Secretary and inspector be appointed to visit schools in union, under the Diocesan Board'; alternatively, Bath and Wells Diocesan Board appointed the Rev. H. F. Gray to the dual posts of Principal of the training school and Inspector, paying his expenses incurred qua inspector but leaving the bishop to provide his stipend. The intention was most sound:

[1] Essex Branch Board *Summary Report*, 1841–42.

33

The Principal, having an accurate knowledge of the state of education in the diocese, would understand better how to direct the studies of those under instruction; at the same time that his journeys of inspection would bring him into acquaintance with those pupils whom it might be desirable to send to Wells.[1]

Gray included in his itineraries 'schools for the middle classes', again indicative of a widening scope for inspectorial processes beyond schools for the feckless poor. In like manner the Rev. William Reed, Principal of the York Diocesan Board's Central School, undertook a comprehensive inspectorial tour of schools in the diocese in 1840–41; the report he presented on 9th November, 1841, has all the qualities of model inspection. Yet a further development, repeated elsewhere, was that 'as the inspector has proceeded, ruri-decanal inspectors have been appointed by the bishop for the several districts'. In Chichester, a further development was the appointment by the Bishop of three clergymen from one archdeaconry to inspect a neighbouring one, and conversely three more to return the compliment. This obviated certain dangers of a too local inspection, though possibly creating others. Ely, by contrast, relied upon inspection at ruri-decanal level, two or more inspectors being appointed for each deanery. From 1840, Exeter had 18 local boards in Devon and Cornwall, with from one to four diocesan inspectors in each. There were thus some thirty or forty in all, nearly all clergy, reaching out to joint-consultation at an early date.[2]

So large and so varied a number of inspecting bodies obviously required some kind of co-ordination which would bring about approximate equation of standards of schools in the various dioceses. The use of standardised questionnaires was only a partial answer; the local correspondents showed very clearly their ability to interpret the standard questions with almost embarrassing diversity. Some centrally directed system of inspection was demanded, and in June, 1839, the Committee of Correspondence was born. Its particular task was that of handling communications with schools in union or wishing to be received into union, with diocesan and other local boards already in existence or to be formed in the future. It was also to deal with the general correspondence of the Society, excepting

[1] National Society *Annual Report*, 1842, pp. 27–28.
[2] *Monthly Paper*, Dec. 1850.

that relating to the business of the School and Finance Committees, its special duty being 'to correspond with parishes in the country on the subjects of diocesan inspection, school returns, middle schools and Sunday schools'.

The evolution of a 'general plan of inspection embracing all schools in union with the National Society' may be traced in a Minute of 6th November 1839, followed by a reported request from the clergy for some 'uniformity in the mode of conducting examinations'. On 27th January, 1840, the Corresponding Committee, or Committee of Correspondence, recommended that £200 be laid aside for the salary of such an inspector or inspectors. On 10th February a letter of invitation was sent to the Rev. Edward Feild to act in such a capacity, local boards being expected to pay his expenses. His 'brief', in the form of 'instructions', was written out in the Minutes of the Committee of Correspondence, 17th March, 1840, and despatched to him two days later. In them, the desirability of securing 'uniformity of system' was suitably stressed. Almost simultaneously, Thomas Tancred, a member of this Committee, was appointed inspecting agent, with the special duty 'to visit the several boards and confer with them, especially upon the subjects of inspection, training institutions, parochial statistics, pecuniary aid and its application'. He thus helped plan the itineraries of inspection for Feild, but achieved more prominence in his work for the Society in its relationships with the Home Office and Her Majesty's inspectors of factories, as, for example, in such matters as the siting of schools. Perhaps this was one reason for his being offered the position of Assistant Commissioner to the Commission of Inquiry into the Employment of Children, in January, 1841. His post of inspecting agent recalled S.P.C.K. experiment some hundred and forty years earlier: he drew no salary but travelling expenses were defrayed. Though no successor to him was immediately appointed, the Society did not jettison the idea; on the contrary, as pressure upon localities for increased funds grew, the need for such agents grew, and two 'organising secretaries' were authorised by the General Committee in 1856. Their main task was to arrange those 'money-spinning' sermons familiar to the early charity schools. On 2nd December, 1857, the Rev. Robert Chaffers was appointed in such a capacity for the London, Rochester and Winchester district, and other dioceses followed suit. But by

1862 only three dioceses were reported as having them, namely Exeter, Chester and Peterborough; York, Durham, Ripon, Lichfield and Worcester had all given them up.

No doubt the National Society was made more willing to allow its own inspectorate to lapse when it realised that the government was willing to meet the Society more than half-way in making choice of government inspectors for National Schools; for example, the first government inspector for these schools was the Rev. John Allen, gazetted at the same time as Tremenheere, 10th December, 1839 (their initial basic salary was not on a scale, but reckoned at £700 a year by Tremenheere shortly after). The choice could not have been bettered by the Society. In August, 1840, it was expressly declared by the Committee of Council on Education as its recognised policy:

> that before we recommend to your Majesty any person to be appointed to inspect schools receiving aid from the public, the promoters of which state themselves to be in connexion with the National Society for the Church of England, we should be authorised to consult the Archbishops of Canterbury and York, each with regard to his own province, and that the Archbishops should be at liberty to suggest to us any person or persons for the office of inspector, and that without their concessions we should recommend no person to your Majesty for such appointment.

> We further beg leave to recommend to your Majesty that if either of the Archbishops should at any time, with regard to his own province, withdraw his concession in our recommendation of such appointment, your Majesty would be graciously pleased to permit us to advise your Majesty to issue your Order in Council revoking the appointment of the said Inspector and making an appointment in lieu thereof. We further beg leave humbly to recommend to your Majesty to direct that such portions of the Instructions to these Inspectors as relate to religious teaching shall be framed by the Archbishops and form part of the general instructions issued by us to the inspectors of such schools, and that the general instructions shall be communicated to the Archbishops before they are finally sanctioned by us.

> We are further of opinion that each of the said inspectors at the same time that he presents any report relating to such schools to the Committee of the Privy Council should be directed to transmit a duplicate thereof to the Archbishop of the province, and should also send a copy to the Bishop of the diocese in which the school is situate, for his information.

Inspectors in the Early Eighteen-Forties

Naturally, the British and Foreign School Society looked for a similar agreement, the more so as they had grave doubts about the inspectorate of any government turned patron: it might form 'a precedent for bringing the influence of Government to bear . . . in a way which might at other times and in other hands be used as an engine of oppression'.[1] Then, too, the government inspector's experience and the Society's experience might lead to opposite conclusions with regard to methods of teaching in the normal schools. Publication of the former's report in such circumstances could not be otherwise than highly mischievous', the more so when 'transferred to the newspaper'. Committee of Council assurances that the inspector would do nothing which in any way could weaken the connection between the parent Society and its schools had some reconciling influence. Then came Tremenheere's report on 66 British Schools in metropolitan London, 1st July, 1842, in which he criticised among other things the monitorial system, the Society's own current policy as set down in its Manual of Primary Instruction, 1839. The Society asked that the report's application should at very most be limited to the 5 schools (out of the 66) in receipt of government aid. Had Tremenheere been more accommodating, the whole report might have been shelved (and with it, the principles involved); but in the event, as Tremenheere pithily noted in his Journal in November, 1843:

> The British and Foreign Society were not likely to work harmoniously with the Government while I continued Inspector. Yet the Government could not with any justice set me aside; they had indeed supported me throughout with the utmost steadiness. It was necessary for them to provide me with some other employment which should be a promotion, before they proposed any new arrangements for inspection to the British and Foreign School Society.

He went on:

> This they have honourably done by offering me the Inspectorship of Mines and Collieries, with an additional salary of £100 a year, and the promise of Sir James Graham that I shall have the duty of attending to the District Schools as Assistant Poor Law Commissioner pro tem

[1] British Society Letter to Committee of Council, 20th Aug. 1842.

37

adding almost in parenthesis

> how far this succumbing on the part of the Government to the
> dissenting body is politic or wise is another affair.

In the meantime, the Society turned to their own five inspecting
agents for the 'friendly' report they had been expecting from
Tremenheere. Althans' general report, 1842, was an encouraging one, and the Society noted with approval his popularity
with the crowds of parents who flocked to hear him speak. In
the course of the year he visited 382 schools, and Fabian visited
139: 'the discipline of schools,' the report added, 'is generally
improved.' It remains to add that Tremenheere's lineally
direct successor was Joseph Fletcher, whose appointment had
the prior approval of the Society: his personality, no less than
his scholarship, was sufficiently oecumenical to win general
commendation for his report on British Schools in 1846.

It should be made clear that the British and Foreign School
Society was not opposed to the principle of local inspection:
'Next to the training of teachers and provision for supplying
school materials,' declared its report for 1842, 'inspection
regular or occasional, by qualified agents, is the most important
benefit which may be rendered by the parent Society to its
branches.' What they, like the Anglicans, asked for was an
assurance that at Government level they should get the right
kind of inspector—someone in sympathy with their own ideals.
Any voluntary system of education was entitled to ask this.
But in fairness to Tremenheere, it should be noted that the
failure of his reputed 'conciliatory manners' extended only to
the lay Committee of the British Society, not to its teachers.
Indeed, Tremenheere set a precedent for all good inspection
by showing teachers first what he intended to say and asking
for their observations. In all cases, the teachers agreed with
his comments.

Similar 'concordats' were made with other voluntary bodies:
with the Wesleyan Education Committee in 1840, with the
London Ragged School Union in 1844, and with the Catholic
Poor Schools Committee in 1847. Under the last-named agreement it was expressly stated that aid would be given to Roman
Catholic schools on condition that the schools should be 'open
to inspection but . . . the inspectors shall report respecting
the secular instruction only'.

Inspectors in the Early Eighteen-Forties

These government inspectors had, therefore, to acquire authority and respect amid this welter of diverse opinions and beliefs, all of which were held with conviction, some few with a deal of truculence; some were prepared to sacrifice all hope of financial aid from the State rather than risk the loss of their denominational independence. The type of inspector to be sought therefore was 'urbanus et intellectus'; and from the beginning the Committee of Council for Education planned for them a policy of moderation, as its first 'Instructions' to its inspectors, issued in August, 1840, revealed. The strongest emphasis was laid on the fact that 'this inspection is not intended as a means of exercising control, but of affording assistance'. The aim of the Parliamentary grant was:

> the encouragement of local efforts for the improvement and extension of elementary education whether made by voluntary associations or by private individuals. The employment of inspectors is therefore intended to advance this object by affording to the promoters of schools an opportunity of ascertaining, at the periodical visits of inspection, what improvements in the apparatus and internal arrangement of schools, in school management and discipline, and in the method of teaching, have been sanctioned by the most extensive experience.

Consultation with 'the parochial clergyman or other minister of religion' was of the utmost importance in that:

> one main object of your visit is to afford them your assistance in all efforts for improvement in which they may desire your aid: but you are in no respect to interfere with the instruction, management or discipline of the schools, or to press upon them any suggestion which they may be dis-inclined to receive.

(It was in respect of this last paragraph that the British Society claimed that Tremenheere had exceeded his mandate).

To be and do all that the Committee of Council desired of them would have meant inspectors being a race of supermen, if not demi-gods. Specimen building plans, submitted to them for approval, necessitated their having surveying, architectural and sanitary training, not to mention a legal one as well. Yet this was but a third of their duties, for, in addition to inspecting 'mechanical arrangements', they had also to ascertain 'means of instruction'—entailing a knowledge of subject-teaching, books and school apparatus and 'organisation and discipline'.

The difficulties of assessing these last qualities were increased a thousand-fold if they were accompanied—as inspectors were clearly meant to be—by the members of the Committee or chief promoters of the school. But these duties were by way of preamble. In the case of all schools, inquiries must be made into the religious teaching. In schools connected with the Established Church, 'the inspectors will inquire with special care, how far the doctrines and principles of the Church are instilled into the minds of the children'. They must ascertain if there was Church accommodation, whether attendance at school was 'regular', if the children were properly behaved, if the teachers checked what the children learned—duties perhaps more in the general run of inspectorial capacity. But they must

> report also on the daily practice of the school with regard to Divine worship,

whether school begins and ends with prayer and psalmody, if daily instruction is given in the Bible, whether the Catechism and the Liturgy are explained, 'with the terms most commonly in use through-out the Authorised Version of the Scriptures'. Other details asked for are whether the children learn private prayers to repeat at home; and if there is any contact between parent and teacher to their common advantage. The moral discipline of the children has to be assessed: attendance, behaviour, obedience, what rewards and punishments appertain and with what results, 'whether their attainments are showy or substantial: and whether their replies are made intelligently or mechanically and by rote. . . . Moreover the Inspectors will be careful to estimate the advancement of the junior as well as of the senior class'. There are, in fact, 150 pages of instructions, including a questionnaire of 140 questions with an appendix of 34 more for infant departments.

Further proof, perhaps, of the wish to 'marry' Church and Government inspectors lies in a letter sent by the Committee of Council to the Church of Scotland in 1840, the reply to which (dated 19th December, 1840, and signed by John Gordon, Secretary to the General Assembly's Education Committee) stresses that the Church of Scotland already has its own 'established system of inspection', and, in turn, suggests incorporation of the two types of inspector by the Committee's 'consulting the Church on the appointment of inspectors'. The first government inspector for Scottish schools, therefore (John Gibson), was to be bound by the terms of a concordat in a similar way to Allen and Tremenheere.

By 1844 the new government inspectors had proved their worth, and their number was increased: three more were 'gazetted' for Church of England schools; Fletcher had replaced Tremenheere for inspection of British schools; and after the split in the Church of Scotland in 1843, a second appointment was made for Scottish schools. Their programme was carefully worked out: they were estimated to be able to visit 140 schools twice a year, having one day off a week to write immediate reports and two months free later in the year to write their full annual reports. They were entitled to one month's holiday a year also. The country was shaped into five areas, North, South, East, West and Midlands, each being further subdivided into five districts. The importance of their knowing the latest and best methods of teaching had also been realised. Mulhauser's manual on handwriting was familiar to them, as was Tate on arithmetic and Dupuis on drawing and Hullah on vocal music. Exeter Hall had sponsored the first 'Ministry' course for inspectors and teachers on how best to teach singing. Withal, their denominational sympathies fitted them admirably to assess religious teaching in the schools they visited.

Their early reports read like tracts for the times. John Allen's on Durham and Northumberland echoes Tremenheere's on South Wales in its laying bare the 'edge of risk' to which the country's social system had tottered. And everywhere there was shortage: 'the deficiency of books,' he says, 'was most lamentable.' Kay-Shuttleworth's remedy was to allow teachers to claim grants for buying books for themselves, and then much later (in 1853) school-teachers' associations were encouraged to apply for grants-in-aid to form teachers' libraries. But this presumed teachers knew what books to order: and in those early years they did not—hence, for example, Kay-Shuttleworth's appeal to inspectors in 1847 to submit lists of suitable textbooks in certain subjects, so that a complete list could be drawn up and circulated to schools.

Inevitably there was a certain amount of over-lapping in inspection, though both government and denominational inspectors had their own sets of instructions. The National

Society's inspection, 'emanating from one common centre, and extending over more than one diocese, may tend to promote uniformity of system and to diffuse generally such improvements as have been locally introduced'. Government inspection, likewise, aimed at securing 'a conformity to the regulations and discipline' obtaining in grant-aided schools, 'with such improvements as may from time to time be suggested by the Committee'.

National Society inspectors included in their duties that of 'collect(ing) information as to local difficulties and wants generally experienced and as to the best ways of meeting them which have been devised in particular cases'. Government inspectors likewise were required 'to collect facts and information'. Tremenheere and Allen were told in their 'Instructions' that 'reports on the state of particular districts may be required, to ascertain the state of education in such districts'; Feild likewise was expected 'to describe more at large the state of education throughout any diocese you may be commissioned to inspect'.

Yet another striking resemblance is the insistence upon encouragement of local endeavour. In both cases, managers of schools had advance information of the inspector's visit, and not only by virtue of having given written answers to the 'tabular form of inquiry' accompanying both types of inspector on their rounds. Full consultation with managers was envisaged at every stage, and in the case of government inspection managers were expressly invited to be present. In view of the later history of the two inspectorates, it is striking to note that Feild's Instructions are far more emphatic about pointing out defects than are those to Her Majesty's inspectors; but, in both cases, prior approval of managers was sought for. Against such a background, the pernicious impact of the Revised Code may be more properly assessed.

There were, however, points of difference between the two inspectorates. An important one related to emphasis, the National Society's inspector's 'most important subject for . . . investigation (being) that of religion and morality'; whereas, in the case of the government inspector, they were not required to report on the religious instruction but 'to hold themselves ready to examine the religious instruction of the school, whenever invited to do so by the parochial clergyman or other minister of religion connected with the school'. It should, perhaps, be added that, in practice, government inspectors did include appraisal of religious teaching in their reports; this was to be expected in view of their standing within their respective denominations. One other significant difference may be noted. Any school accepting government grant had also *pari passu* to accept the principle that the government had a right to inspection. The National Society's inspector(s) by contrast, were only sent to a diocese upon request by the appropriate bishop; they were thereafter dependent upon the particular itinerary he caused to be drawn up for them. Finally, Her Majesty's inspectors were expected to confine their attention to elementary schools; Feild, by comparison, could also inspect Sunday schools and any middle or commercial school by invitation.

It may be relevant to observe that at no time subsequently has the verb, 'to inspect', come nearer to its strict etymological meaning 'to look into' an existing situation together than at this time; the phenomenon could also arise of three inspectors at work in the same area at the same time; in Lichfield in 1841 there were the Rev. Henry Hopwood representing the National Society, the Rev. John Allen representing the Committee of Council on Education, and the Rev. J. Bonny representing the Diocesan Board. In one sense, all three were voluntary and could be denied entry by local managers of schools; in another sense, all three had a glimmer of gold about them, for even in the case of the only unpaid inspector, representing the diocesan board, it should be remembered that grants towards maintenance of schools from diocesan board funds were intended as subsidies for those schools in particular which were too poor to meet the government requirements. But evidence of improvement was still required from diocesan inspectors: 'no inspection, no good report, no grant. These subsidies are given on fulfilment of certain conditions, and these conditions involve the improvement of the school.'

Sometimes, on the other hand, the government inspector appeared to be carrying out the duties of diocesan inspector also, as the report presented in 1844 by the Rev. Frederick Watkins shows. His area consisted of the six Northern counties, though he could not yet visit all the Church of England schools in his area as not all were in receipt of government grants.

Inevitably, he discussed the affinity of the new Church schools to the Sunday schools, and had a good deal to say about the size and efficiency of the latter. His comments on the work done in the schools are shrewd and practicable, based on the 120 schools he inspected. In 75 per cent, he says, reading is 'easy and sensible', if lacking in expression and interspersed with 'provincial cadences' which make meaning difficult to catch. Great attention, he says, is paid to copy-writing in books, and 66 per cent of the children's work is 'neat, accurate and legible'. He queries, however, the efficiency of the so-called 'lady's' or 'running' hand, just as he queries the suitability of the material used for copying (e.g. invitations to dinner, or poetry of a questionable tendency). Steel pens, he notes, were replacing quills.

In arithmetic, 'tolerable progress' is made, five-twelfths of the work inspected being reasonably satisfactory. But he rightly condemns the system of payment for subject-teaching (with consequent discrimination among children and disruption of a time table). It has been said that there is nothing new in twentieth century methodology; certainly, Watkins' criticism that 'children are seldom instructed in the reason of a rule. They know the "how" but cannot give the "why",' has a faint echo in the Norwood Report of 1941. On the other hand he is of his age with his fondness for writing from memory and dictation. Inevitably he comes across newer practices; for example, he notes, with reservation of opinion, the use of mental arithmetic in some good schools.

Geography, grammar and the history of England were 'taught too drily and formally'. Geography laboured under a welter of terminology like 'oblate spheroid', lists of 'continents, islands, oceans, seas, isthmuses, straits, peninsulas', with parallels of latitude, degrees of longitude, and imaginary lines on the earth's surface. Grammar was 'weary words without meaning'; history, though better taught than geography and found in a third of the schools he visited, yet erred in 'overloading of memory . . . with . . . many and unconnected and therefore unmeaning dates'.

But, despite all this careful scrutiny of work done, he clearly regarded one other subject as of over-riding importance: and in this he showed most clearly why a National Society's own inspector could safely be regarded as expendable by his

Church: 'the staple commodity . . . of our schools,' said
Watkins, 'is religious knowledge, however imperfect it may be.'
It might be an old charity school or Sunday school teacher
speaking. First, he made general comments on the teaching of
the subject; for example, he found learning by heart the
besetting sin of much of it: 'they have said the catechism, but
have not been catechised'. Later in the report he investigated
the problem of religious instruction in both day and Sunday
schools far more thoroughly, and put forward tentative suggestions for improvement by giving encouragement to the
children in the form of good conduct certificates, and by arranging 'anniversaries' to keep past and present scholars in
closer touch. He also pleaded for the co-operation of parents
to improve school attendance, and stressed the need for more
and better teachers, whom, incidentally, he expected the
Church, and not the State, to train.

Chapter Five

KAY-SHUTTLEWORTH

THE evolution of the government inspectorate and its effective co-ordination with the inspectorates of the voluntary bodies
depended very largely on the genius of James Kay-Shuttleworth. The first Secretary of the Committee of Council, he
was from 1839 to 1849 the brain behind the Committee of
Council's decisions; the pupil-teacher system, as well as the
development of the inspectorate, was linked with his name; and
steadily, yet with extreme caution, he began to create a scheme
for more, and more efficient education. But he did not achieve
a tenth part of his dreams for universal education, embracing
all classes of society and administered mainly by 'local' authorities, although aided by Government grants which were made
conditional upon certain prescribed minimum standards being
attained; such education, in his plan, was to be strongly
religious though not sectarian in its character, nourished
by an adequate supply of trained teachers, and watched
over by a select body of public-spirited, high-minded inspectors.

Such was his dream: to turn even a fraction of it into a
reality needed hard work, and all his training in the art of
using facts, to convince both the government and the voluntary
societies that his ideas were right. Not the least of his achieve-
ments was the fact that the Minutes of the Committee of
Council (25th August, 1846), which aimed at the building up
of an educational system round the government inspector,
were generally acceptable to all the denominations. The
National Society, the British and Foreign School Society, the
Wesleyan Education Committee and the Catholic Poor
School Committee all expressed their approval, and that at a

time when, as Lord Brougham said, the religions 'loved education much but controversy more'.

Kay-Shuttleworth drew the facts which justified the Committee of Council's Minutes from the reports of men like Watkins, who revealed all too clearly the glaring deficiencies in the educational system, and especially in the number of teachers. From this sprang the pupil-teacher system, and this justified the existence of inspectors as no other educational formulary had done. The school managers were responsible for putting forward candidates thought to be suitable on moral grounds, but the inspector decided which of them were suitable for apprenticing and to whom. The prospective pupil-teachers had not only 'to teach a junior class to the satisfaction of the inspector', but must also pass tests in reading, writing, computation and (in Church of England schools) religious knowledge. For the next five years they underwent the annual examination set by the inspector; and the best of them were duly offered 'Queen's scholarships' to the value of £20–£25 per annum, to enable them to go to college. Stipendiary monitors were retained only because:

> the inspectors may, for some time, find in the rural districts schools in which all the general conditions required for the apprenticeship of a pupil teacher may be satisfied, but that the master or mistress of which may be unable to conduct an apprentice even through the foregoing course of instruction. Their Lordships being desirous so to adapt their regulations to the conditions of such schools, as by their improvement to enable them thereafter to provide for the training of pupil-teachers, are disposed for a few years to encourage the managers to retain their monitors, by small stipends, to the age of seventeen, without apprenticeship, but under a form of agreement with the parents, on condition that the master give each monitor extra daily instruction.[1]

(It is perhaps a sad reflection that such untrained ex-monitors were to be found in rural schools a hundred years later!) Due emphasis, however, was given to qualification and training by the award of the Normal School Certificate to successful candidates, entitling them to an augmentation grant of £20 to £25

---

[1] *cf.* also Kay-Shuttleworth, *Public Education as Affected by the Minutes of the Committee of the Privy Council, 1846–52, with suggestions as to future policy.* Appendix A.

per annum. Unqualified teachers could also sit for the examination for the certificate—which included taking a practical lesson with a class, before the inspector.

Finally, the grants awarded by 'their Lordships' to successful teachers with one, two or three years training in a normal school under the inspection of government inspectors (£15–£20, £20–£25, and £25–30 respectively) depended on

> (*a*) the trustees and managers of the school providing the master with a house rent-free and a further salary equal to twice the amount of grant:

> (*b*) their certifying annually that his character, conduct and attention to duty were satisfactory:

> and (this above all)

> (*c*) the inspector's reporting 'that his school is efficient in its organisation, discipline and instruction'.

(The same regulations applied to school-mistresses, who were awarded grants at two-thirds of the men's rate.)

Thus the inspector was brought into touch with the day-to-day work of the teachers. The implication of this ultimately was to be that inspectors must have had some teaching experience themselves, though in 1846 few in the Committee of Council would have considered this at all necessary. The inspectors might well consider themselves as the 'Intelligence Corps' of an incipient education department, embracing voluntary schools, factory schools, and the schools of the royal hospitals and asylums, of the dock yards and ships, of prisons and the Poor Law; and it was at this time that they were carving out the pattern of future development. As (Sir) Joshua Fitch outlined them at a later date:

> (The inspector's) first duty is to verify the conditions on which public aid is offered to schools, and to assure the Department that the nation is obtaining a good equivalent for its outlay. But this is not the whole. He is called upon to visit from day to day schools of very different types, to observe carefully the merits and demerits of each, to recognise with impartiality very various forms of good work, to place himself in sympathy with teachers and their difficulties, to convey to each of them kindly suggestions as to methods of discipline and instruction he has observed elsewhere, and to leave behind him at every school he inspects some stimulus

Kay-Shuttleworth

to improvement, some useful counsel to managers, and some encouragement to teachers and children to do their best. There are few posts in the public service which offer larger scope for the beneficial exercise of intellectual and moral power, or which bring the holder into personal and influential relations with a larger number of people. It will be an unfortunate day for the Civil Service if ever the time comes when an office of this kind is regarded as one of inferior rank, or is thought unworthy of the acceptance of men of high scholarship and intellectual gifts . . .[1]

Scholarship, tolerance, vision, integrity, and high personal standards—these were the qualities impressing themselves on succeeding generations of inspectors.

In his explanation of the Minutes of 1846, published in 1847 by direction of the Committee of Council, under the title, 'The school in its relations to the State, the Church and the Congregation', Kay-Shuttleworth elaborates this thesis more fully:

Every school committee will continue to hold in its own hands the power of selecting and dismissing the master; of determining the organisation, discipline, course of instruction, and methods of teaching to be adopted in the school; of selecting the books; dismissing pupil-teachers or stipendiary monitors; in fact, of regulating in all respects its affairs. In the selection of the inspector who may visit the school, the Government will consult the Education Committee or other central authority watching over the interests of the school of each religious communion. The inspector will act under instructions restraining him from all interference with the discipline and management of the school. He will have no authority to direct, and will not be permitted even to advise unless invited to do so by the school committee. With these precautions against the exactions of authority, he will not fail to be useful to all schools which he may visit, by skilfully planning under the light of a searching examination, conducted in the presence of the managers, the actual condition of the school. The results of his experience will be available for their instruction and guidance. If they desire the assistance of the Government to enable them to provide for apprenticeship of pupil-teachers, he will become the organ of an impartial communication with the Committee of Council. If the master desires to present himself for examination for the certificate necessary to an augmentation of his salary, the Inspector will inform him what are the studies to

[1] J. G. Fitch, *Thomas and Matthew Arnold.* 1897, p. 169.

49

be pursued, and the standard of requirements to be attained, in order to procure this benefit for himself and for the school. If the augmentation of salary be granted, it will be withdrawn in any year in which the Managers refuse a certificate of their satisfaction in the conduct of the master and of his attention to his duties . . .

The debt of English education to Sir James Kay-Shuttleworth is great on several counts: but one of the most important is his belief in the power for good of inspectors in all types of school. At his retirement, the strength of the inspectorate was eight for National schools, two for British and Wesleyan, one for Roman Catholic; and one (Allen) had been Inspector of Training Schools since 1847. In a time of great social tension, and faced by the seeming irreconcilables of compulsory State inspection on the Prussian or Dutch model and a voluntary one by the churches, he achieved a working compromise from which something could grow. He had plumbed the depths of the new proletariat and had no fear of chaos overtaking England's traditional social patterns, provided that there were enough elementary schools and sufficient teachers of the right calibre to staff them; and these, in turn, necessitated an inspectorate 'hand-picked' for their job. From an inspectorial point of view, perhaps, the greatest vindication of this selection-procedure was the relative ease with which they survived the quarrel between Committee of Council and local school over the 'management clauses'. Archdeacon Denison might go so far as to threaten to throw government inspectors into the horse-pond if they came near 'his' schools; but in the main, the question of administrative loyalties on the part of inspectors was not raised; nor was their independence of testimony brought into dispute.

Chapter Six

MID-CENTURY DEVELOPMENT

BY 1850 the number of Government inspectors had risen to 23, and the National Society inspectorate had completely disappeared, although diocesan inspectors were still very active in their own areas. Government inspectors continued to be 'gazetted' to particular denominations, and, as the number of schools continued to multiply, 'assistant' inspectors had to be appointed at a salary of £215 per annum: the first two were appointed in 1850, two more in each of the following two years, and by 1860 there were 19 of them in Church of England schools and three in the schools of the Established Church of Scotland.[1] Other denominations were making equally determined efforts though on a smaller scale; for example, the Episcopal Church in Scotland had set up enough schools to warrant, in its opinion, an inspector of their own denomination. Accordingly, they asked 'My Lords' for one (12th June, 1852) and one was appointed. The Committee of Council, in fact, was beginning to realise how much it depended on its 'eyes and ears', the inspectors, one of the very rare compliments ever made to 'Civil Servants' in any age being paid to them in 1852: '(The inspectors' reports) constitute the foundation of the whole system (of education)'.[2]

As the number of inspectors grew, so did the scope of their duties again, and one learns much of the development of the work required of a Government inspector from the various reports made by the Rev. Frederick Watkins at this period. In 1843 the inspection of schools had been his sole duty; by 1851 it was only half, and that included the inspection of

[1] F. W. Watkins, *Letter to His Grace, the Archbishop of York, 1860.*
[2] Circular Letter to Her Majesty's Inspectors, 1852.

training schools. In addition, he had to set, supervise and mark all the examination papers of teachers, teachers-in-training at normal schools, and pupil-teachers. He was responsible for the award of certificates of merit to teachers and of retiring pensions. In 1853, when the principle of capitation allowance was established, registers and voluntary subscriptions had to be checked by the inspector before the allowance could be granted or the children inspected. As a result of this close contact with the schools, the inspectors became very much aware of the deficiencies of the educational system and pleaded eloquently for improvements—for more assistant inspectors to improve the standard of the work in schools, for more and better-paid pupil-teachers to improve the standard of entrants to the teaching profession. Over and over again the reports speak of irregular attendance, the conflicting claims of labour and the lack of parental interest in education; albeit the last-named might be due in many cases to parental poverty; school pence (twopence or threepence a week) took some finding, particularly if the family was large, and it must have been very tempting to put the children to work, when a child's earnings of three or four shillings a week made a very valuable increase to family income. 'The small age of the school-children' was another theme in the inspectors' reports: Watkins, for example, says that in the North of England only $3\frac{1}{2}$ per cent of school children were over $13\frac{1}{2}$ years old, and $32\frac{1}{2}$ per cent were under the age of seven. Hand in hand with criticisms come equally pertinent recommendations, recommendations, indeed, which have a forward look about them. Firstly, he wants a higher school leaving age, and more night schools under more experienced teachers. Then he would also like more thorough-going diocesan inspection, though the old bogey of lack of funds is already visible, and what money was available was being used in other directions. The National Society's Report for 1860 mentions the award of exhibitions to (student) teachers at training institutions, the cost being halved by the National Society and the local diocesan boards. Organising masters were also appointed in five dioceses to help in the schools. Watkins goes on to urge that more attention be paid by managers and teachers alike to the great task of fitting the children of the labouring classes for their work in life. His conclusion has a familiar echoic sound:

We want the few elementary subjects more fully and more practically taught ... little more than the old trio of attainments, if the term be rightly interpreted.

It is clear, therefore, that government and diocesan inspections were regarded as complementary, and also that the demise of the National Society inspectorate was regretted.

How the advantages of local forms of inspection were being fully explored at this time may be summed up in the prolegomena of the Chester Board of Education, September, 1839; schools 'will be subjected, with the consent of the managers, to inspection by qualified and authorised examiners. Of this inspection and examination, the benefits may be estimated as great. It will tend at once to raise the character and quicken the zeal of the teachers, to stimulate the energies of the scholars, and by these means to improve the general quality of parochial education'. After the ending of the National Society of its own centrally appointed inspectorate in 1842–43, and its variegated acceptance of Her Majesty's inspectors as 'a most powerful ally', the possibilities of local inspection became much more important to the Society. The reports of diocesan and district boards, with lists of office bearers, were still valuable, even when summarised in the form of appendices to the Society's Annual Reports; and after 1847 the Monthly Paper also began to include such summaries, usually in more popular form. The difficulties inherent in such localised inspectorial units may be deduced and summarised thus:

1. Should schools know beforehand of the diocesan inspector's visit?

2. What subjects should he include in his inspection; and should staffs of schools be informed beforehand?

3. How soon after or before Her Majesty's inspectors' visits should diocesan inspectors' visits be? What weight should be attached to the suggestions of the former vis-à-vis the latter? What, in fact, was the relationship between the two sets of inspectors?

4. What was the total effect of the cherished diocesan inspectors' 'extensive and well-digested prize scheme', or other variants upon examination of several schools together? How did this examination compare with the examination papers set by government inspectors—criticised as too difficult by some?

53

E

5. What should or could be done about the many schools not visited by diocesan inspectors? Conversely, what of those schools not yet subject to government inspection, including the occasional central school in the provinces, where the vexed question of subsequent 'recognition' was involved?

6. In the interests of a uniformity of assessment which at the same time should not be oppressive but a preliminary to ensuring over-all national efficiency, what steps should be taken? 'Judicious instructions . . . given in manuscript to the inspectors' were hardly enough, and contrasted strongly with some forms used by Her Majesty's inspectors of schools. Was even joint-consultation on a larger basis enough? Had statistical enquiries conducted at local level any comparative value? Earlier ones, in any case, were made imperfectly. Circular letters urging union of local schools with the local board were a useful expedient but depended so much for success upon the power of public persuasion of the diocesan inspector(s). Yet again, individual types of reporting admirable though they might be, did not always allow of customary abridgement.

7. One other difficulty arose from the tendency for a locality to begin to see its own educational efforts 'through rose-coloured spectacles'. Could the diocesan inspection, in fact, become feeble because it was friendly, as the Report of the Diocesan Board of Bath and Wells suggested in 1854?

Answers to several of these problems may be now self-evident, but then there was by no means a common agreement. Even the Archbishop of Canterbury himself would appear to be dragging his feet in his reference to government inspection—it certainly delayed development of working arrangements with diocesan inspectors in the province. There could be no doubt about its beneficial effects, as a letter to the Monthly Paper in December, 1850, pithily expressed, lending strength to the Society's confident claim in 1850 that diocesan inspection was gaining ground. It was, therefore, fortunate that in the Annual General Meeting of the Association of Secretaries of Diocesan and District Boards the parent Society should annually be prodded by a well-organised agency into formulating the needs of represented localities. The greatest one in relation to inspection was a standardised form for assessment. In 1847 the Association was engaged upon the problem: in 1849–50, specimen forms of questions were being circulated to several diocesan boards. By 1854 a memorandum had been drafted on the possibilities of such pro-formae, and, as revised five years later, it had become a really helpful document both for teachers in Church of England schools and for those inspectors who had always to rely upon voluntary co-operation from teachers and managers.

Two practical suggestions were made (and they were no more than suggestions):

'1. As to the appointment of diocesan inspectors. In Canterbury diocese, the work of diocesan inspection is confined to a single inspector, who pays a *biennial* visit to every school under inspection, and receives a salary for his services. This arrangement is preferred in that diocese, on the grounds that it tends to secure a regular and uniform performance of the duties of inspection; that it subjects school-education throughout the diocese to the oversight of a single mind; and that it promotes the efficiency of the inspector by furnishing him with a large and varied experience. In other dioceses, the funds at the disposal of diocesan boards have been found too scanty to furnish salaries sufficient to secure the permanent services of an efficient single inspector. It is also by many considered as an objection to the employment of a single inspector that he cannot, of course, inspect all the schools in a diocese at the same time of the year; and that a biennial visit at an irregular period can have little practical effect on the progress or efficiency of schools where the average duration of the attendance of the children is very short. Most other dioceses have, therefore, in preference adopted the appointment of district inspectors, at the rate usually of one for every rural deanery.'

Three-yearly 'tours of duty' were suggested, no salary being paid but all travelling expenses being met. A summary report was also suggested, compiled by one of the inspectors, for which he might be paid, half being offered by the Sub-Committee of Inspection up to a maximum of £20 yearly.

'2. The Committee venture very strongly to recommend that each inspector should be furnished with a copy of instructions . . . that, as a general rule, the schools in each diocese should be inspected at the same time of the year.'

A uniform and intelligible report was also to be secured by recommending all to use the 'forms of return prepared by the National Society'. The Committee further recommended 'the annual issue of a list of fixed subjects for examination', with the expressed intention of introducing 'order and system into all schools'; the practice of an old friend, H.M.I. the Rev. F. C. Cook, was quoted by way of supporting evidence.

As might be expected, diocesan inspection varied very much in quality from diocese to diocese; and opinions concerning the duties of diocesan inspectors varied almost as much: the fifth Annual Report of the Northampton Society for promoting and extending education in the principles of the Established Church describes such inspection at its best:

> With the special business of the government inspectors, so far as we understand it, we have nothing to do. We do not go to make inquiries whether the conditions attached to certain liberal money grants have or have not been fulfilled. The sole object of a diocesan inspector is to improve the school which he is visiting. He will, therefore, not be content with pointing out defects; he will offer advice as to the best way of supplying them. He will notice any plan as regards either discipline or instruction which he finds working advantageously in a parish, and will suggest it in the next school he visits. Sometimes where the teacher is untrained, and some one branch of the children's work is unusually backward, he will sit down himself and give, in the presence of the master or mistress, a model lesson. If there is a deficient supply of books or maps, or other school apparatus, he will, where he thinks a case a deserving one, himself apply for a grant from the joint fund of the National and Northamptonshire Societies, and will offer his advice as to the best way of laying out the money. He will try to encourage the master in his difficult and often disappointing work by a friendly manner, and by a ready offer of such assistance as it may be in his power to give. He will keep up a correspondence, as often as occasion calls for it, with the Managers of schools lying in his district. Above all, as the Bishop's officer, he will give a special prominence to religion, not only assigning to it the chief place in his examination, but also watching for any little signs by which it may appear how far the character of the children is practically influenced by the solemn truths they learn. Such is our aim. We are sadly conscious indeed that we fall short of our mark, but we wish to be allowed once for all to state the real end we have in view when we write to the managers of any school and offer to inspect it.

Had such maturity been common to diocesan inspectors over the whole country, a good deal of current criticism might have been silenced—and let it be granted to the lasting credit of the Established Church that much of that criticism came from within. The Rev. Francis Close, incumbent of Cheltenham for so long, wrote in 1852:

> The great advantage of a central system of inspection over one that is local, diocesan and voluntary, is obvious. The government inspectors devote their whole time and talents to this work; by practice they become expert in their business; they discover defects in a school at a glance, and are equally ready in supplying remedies. Local inspectors, having other and more pressing engagements, can devote only a portion of their time to this difficult and important work, and they labour under the great disadvantage of a want of that mutual conference and comparison of labour which the government inspectors enjoy, and which, necessarily, gives a unity and idiosyncrasy to their labours, which can never belong to miscellaneous inspectors.[1]

Another moderate Churchman, the Rev. Richard Dawes, said categorically in 1850 that, 'if education should fall entirely into the hands of diocesan associations and committees, where rural deans are appointed inspectors, it will be almost good for nothing. Such diocesan inspectors will effect but little good.'[2]

Closely linked with the development of diocesan inspectors was the use of organising masters, appointed by the National Society, to improve the standard of education in Church schools. Many of these men were outstanding both as teachers and organisers, and several of them became inspectors in later life. Some organising masters held government certificates of merit and were paid accordingly; they were all well qualified 'to suggest improvements, and work for a time in schools in friendly co-operation with the regular teachers of the school';[3] and the allowance made them by the Society for books would indicate that they were expected to use them. To sum up: at this period the essential characteristics of organisers and organisation were being formulated. The job offered to young teachers an opportunity for gaining experience quickly of different types of school as well as the teaching situation in

[1] F. Close, *National Education. The secular system, the Manchester Bill and the government scheme contrasted*. 1852, pp. 28–29.

[2] R. Dawes, *Remarks Occasioned by the Present Crusade against the Educational Plans of the Committee of Council on Education*. 1850, p. 10.

[3] National Society *Annual Report*, 1846, p. 4.

them; they could rapidly enrich their knowledge of 'man-management'; their social contacts were many, at many different levels. The avenues of promotion from the post were attractive, a point of some importance. The basic requirements, apart from being of the right religious persuasion, were ability to teach well enough to win other teachers' respect and confidence; to present advice for improvement in palatable fashion; to be good at getting on with folk: all these, incidentally, being qualities highly valuable in an inspector.

It was only to be expected that schools might tend to regard the organising master as a deputy, if not an alternative, inspector: in fact, the National Society in 1841 recognised such a possibility:

> In addition to their peculiar duty of bringing schools under proper discipline, organising masters may sometimes be employed under Diocesan or District Boards, in a capacity somewhat resembling that of inspector—to make a tour through a certain district, visiting schools and suggesting improvements. Such a plan would unite usefulness with economy.

The General Committee proceeded to make their point:

> The chief difference between an inspector and an organising master would be that the former possesses higher general qualifications, and is required to report upon the schools he visits; while the latter, with an equal, or perhaps a greater degree of practical knowledge, excites no alarm by the prospect of any report, and not only explains what should be done but remains long enough to assist in doing it.

However, it was stressed from time to time that the two were not equal in status, but that the work of the two was complementary; the National Society's Report for 1842 makes this abundantly clear:

> Nearly connected with the organisation of schools is inspection, for which it is a useful preparation, in order that the report of the inspector may be as satisfactory as possible, both to the parties visited and to the public. After the best arrangements have been made in the school-room, and the best books and time-tables, with other school apparatus, introduced, the inspector's report will of course be much more favourable and encouraging than it would have been without those aids.

Mid-Century Development

The differences between organiser and inspector were thus clearly formulated by the middle of the nineteenth century. By one of the odd inversions of time, whereas the inspector was the 'specialist' and the organiser 'general', today the reverse applies. Perhaps most interesting of all was the combination of some of the duties of both in the person of Her Majesty's inspector as conceived by Kay-Shuttleworth. Though very definitely expected to take the large view of the well-educated man, they were also expected to acquire a knowledge of schools ranging 'from brains to drains'. From the first they were the paid experts, too, contrasting strongly with the usually unpaid diocesan inspector doing the job in what spare time he could afford.

Although the National Society had abandoned its own inspectorate in favour of spending the money on organising masters, and relying, for the inspection of its schools, on the activities of diocesan and government inspectors, other voluntary bodies were by now active in the inspectorial field. The Roman Catholics had developed their educational work very rapidly since 1829, and by 1850 17,000 children were estimated to be in attendance at Roman Catholic schools. By 1857 the Committee of Council had appointed three inspectors for their schools. Their system of school administration was analogous to that of the National Society: the parent society, the Catholic Poor School Committee, made grants to, and kept in touch with, the local committees, whose work was similar to that of the Anglican diocesan boards.

The early reports of inspectors on Catholic schools make much the same critical comment as did inspectors of other denominations. H.M.I., Mr. T. W. M. Marshall's report in 1849 commented on the absence of a Catholic normal school, and on the paucity of infant schools. The first of these points was answered by the opening of St. Mary's Training College at Hammersmith in 1851: Marshall's report on it in 1853 echoes much of what had already been said about other denominational colleges, his most telling remark being that the students were really only just beginning their own education instead of completing it at college.

But the Roman Catholics, no less than the Anglicans, were much taken up with the question of the diocesan inspection of Religious Knowledge by their own officers. *The Catholic School* (published by the C.P.S.C. since 1848) made reference (14th October, 1854) to the fact that their Church had no officers of her own 'especially charged in each diocese to visit and examine schools and teachers, and compare the best methods of instruction and to view the whole subject of the education of the poor', for 'this part of the episcopal office has not hitherto been delegated to anyone'. Subsequent annual reports of the C.P.S.C. show increasing sensitivity to the problem. The eighth, in 1855, voices a fear that Religious Knowledge might easily get pushed into a corner. In 1856, however, four paid inspectors of their own were appointed, with an intention to add three more. The elaborate system of rewards for proficiency— a silver medal for pupil-teachers at the end of their course, a bronze one to scholars on a basis of one for every 50 children— is again analogous to Anglican practice. After 1870 these inspectors were to play an increasingly important part in assuming full responsibility for the inspection of Religious Knowledge in Catholic schools.

The Wesleyans, too, appointed their first inspector in this period, although their Education Committee declared that the general oversight of schools was part of the minister's duty:

> The regular visitation and inspection of day schools is justly regarded as a point of great importance, both with respect to general and local objects. This work, as the Committee would fain hope, is now therefore reckoned, by the Ministers of the Circuits in which such schools are established, as a regular and indispensable branch of ministerial duty, and is attended to accordingly.[1]

The first Wesleyan school inspector was appointed in 1844,

> representing, in personal intercourse, the spirit and maxims of Wesleyan education.

For the next twenty-one years, Mr. H. Armstrong was their tireless agent-cum-inspector, inspiring teachers and local committees, encouraging further building of schools during this tremendous upsurge of Wesleyanism throughout the country, offering advice in planning and constructional

[1] *Report* of the Wesleyan Education Committee, 1847, p. 13.

details, and faithfully reporting progress to the parent Committee in London.

The British and Foreign School Society's inspectorate developed steadily during this period. By 1847 the Society had half a dozen inspecting-agents, was spending upwards of £1,350 a year on their salaries, and had 'zoned' the country, so that each inspector was responsible for a specific area; the whole scheme was controlled largely from the Society's central office. The Society's report of the following year (1848) stresses that they retained the right to close the doors of their central or normal schools against the Government inspector, 'should such a course ever be necessary'. The comments upon the schools made by the Society's inspectors are in the same strain as those of the inspectors of the other voluntary bodies: some schools were short of supplies; attendance was very variable; there was much room for improvement.

The strength of a school is in direct proportion to the strength of its management; and perhaps no better example at the time could be quoted than the ragged school. Entirely local in inspiration, the product of a developing social conscience, it epitomises the whole strength and weakness of nineteenth century voluntary effort. At no point can inspection of these schools be severed from the broader aspects of organisation generally; and any interpretation of inspection as a process concerned exclusively with 'testing the intellectual life of the school' would be entirely inadequate. Far from assessment in any objective, dispassionate sense, it was personally involved in nourishing the life of the school, encouraging and supporting it in every way; intellectual life was relatively less important than actual physical well-being and social training. The dominant theme of the many public exhortations for funds is to help save the children from a moral suicide in adulthood.

Early examples of the group-principle of supervision are manifest in the up-springing schools of industry at the turn of the eighteenth century. In the case of one in Birmingham, founded in 1797:

> The Committee, five in number, meet once a week at the Asylum for the regulation of the accounts, and for the general superintendence of the whole. Each takes a Department in providing the various supplies; making himself responsible for the quality, quantity and terms on which the articles are purchased. Thus,

the children are better kept, and with more economy, than by any preceding plan.[1]

In the school of industry at Croston (Lancs.), four trustees were appointed from the subscribers; at their quarterly meetings, enquiry was to be made into the conduct of teaching staff and the behaviour and proficiency of children. In case of a divided vote upon any issue, the rector of Croston had a casting vote. Two of the trustees were regarded as a quorum. Local clergy were a natural choice for visitors to these schools. One at Fincham (Norfolk), opened in 1802 with 64 children on roll, was

> very frequently visited by the Rev. Mr. Forby, the vicar of Fincham. He very kindly allows himself to be referred to, as a kind of judge or arbiter, upon any matter arising in the school; and, in case any of the children have been neglectful and in-attentive, he makes use of his influence to amend and improve them, and to prevent a repetition of the cause of complaint.[1]

Such is the 'white radiance' of some of the early public meetings locally in support of ragged schools that they partake almost of religious assemblies. The first annual meeting of the Hull Ragged and Industrial Schools in 1848 was punctuated by 'loud and continued cheering!' At the conclusion, the Mayor of Hull 'most earnestly invited his fellow-townsmen (and strangers also) personally to visit the schools'. Any subscriber or donor, in fact, to the cause generally was not only automatically a 'visitor'; he was eligible for membership of the local committee, and a large donor might well expect to be actively canvassed to that end.

Subscription carried with it the privilege of nominating children for admittance to the school: the only limiting factors would seem to have been the number of places available, and the suitability of the child, who was presumed to be from the most destitute classes (e.g. 'mendicants, thieves, vagrants— those, in short, who (were) shut out from every other school').

As public support was so desperately needed, however fickle

---

[1] *Society for Bettering the Condition of the Poor, Report No. CXXIII and No. CXII.* The decline of schools of industry *per se* is well illuminated by the Central Society of Education's pamphlet, "Schools for the Industrious Classes", 1837. For other difficulties *v.* Mrs. Heaton, *Memorandum on Schools of Industry.* Committee of Council Minutes, 1855–56, pp. 770–772.

a jade she was to prove, visitation was actively encouraged, and the Visitors' Book placed at their disposal. The invariably hortatory comments were needful. In the book for 'The Refuge' in Old Pye Street, Westminster, one distinguished visitor follows another with all the permutating clichés of commendation. There was, however, an obverse to them, less emphasised for very valid reasons. A visitor to the not inappropriately termed World's End Passage Ragged School (Chelsea) wrote:

> The boys broke the panels of the door, forced an entrance, and then be-spattered the teachers with mud.

In addition to any such natural hazards, there was the filth, the risk of contamination, 'the difficulty', as Lord Ashley said, 'of infusing into these wanderers a sense of shame, and delicate notions of "meum" and "tuum".' The visitor moreover, as in other types of schools at this time, was expected to reach into his pocket: at Stoke Newington, for instance, the members of the Committee added a sum equal to that paid by the children into a clothing club. Actual teaching was also sometimes looked for on Sundays, though this was not limited to the Committee but to any kind friends, including ladies.

Such activities, it may be added, required courage as well as philanthropy. The reaching out towards union on a wider, though still very local, basis was to be expected. Wider publicity, pooled experience, possible additional financial help from the centre—these were all advantages of a tangible kind. London Ragged School Union for example was formed in April 1844, its first annual report appearing in June the following year. Associations founded on similar principles were also formed in cities like Liverpool, Manchester, Newcastle, York, Bath, Glasgow, Aberdeen and Edinburgh. It might have been supposed that such centralising agencies would seek a general supervisory control; in practice the reverse obtained: e.g. one of the Articles of the London Ragged School Union expressly stated:

> that this Union shall not interfere with the financial concerns or the internal management of particular schools.

Where a school faded out completely, as happened at Turk's Head Yard, it could only urge that a new local committee of management would prosper more. Nevertheless, the life-giving grants to schools did imply something more than a passing interest; and they were 'visited' by the Union's own inspector and sub-inspector. These two were paid agents of the Union, and their salaries were duly shown in the annual balance sheet. It is perhaps one further example of the consummate tact the 'parent' Union extended to its 'daughter' schools that, when cataloguing the schools visited by its inspectors, it should add at the head:

> These schools are under the management of independent and local committees.

The third Annual Report of the Union stressed that 'in addition to frequent inspection, two delegates are summoned once a quarter from every school to meet the Committee and report how matters go on;' 40 delegates, stated the Report, had been at the last quarterly meeting of this kind.

Though voluntary, gratuitous supervision of an external kind was relied upon by individual schools (whose funds, in any case, would hardly have allowed of more), there was one other official in the catena of inspection who served as a co-ordinator of policy and its implementation between committees of management and their schools. The superintendent was part principal, part administrator, part liaison officer. As in any local organisation depending so precariously upon local support, duties varied according to local circumstances and local interpretation of them. The relatively small East London Shoe Black Society, established in 1854, had a small 'Refuge for homeless and destitute boys of the East London Ragged Schools' Shoe Black Society'. There were 40 boys in the Shoe Black Society, 20 of whom were homeless and destitute: sleeping accommodation altogether was for 21 boys. The staff consisted of a superintendent and inspector, a matron and assistant. Here, then, was a superintendent in charge of a single 'school'. At the other antipodes was the superintendent of the big Ragged School Unions like Liverpool with twenty or more schools in union. A full definition of the duties of such a paid official was given by a Committee of Management of the Edinburgh Original Ragged or Industrial Schools:[1] from which it may be seen that he was primarily an administrator, attending all committee meetings and writing up their minutes as

[1] T. Guthrie, *et al.*, *On Ragged Schools*. 1848.

well. Apart from deputising for any absent teacher, he took no, part in the teaching programme, nor could he interfere with it in any way, unless so directed by the Committee of Management. He was however expected to exercise a general oversight of the work department(s) of each school. Here in fact may be traced the growth of an idea visible in later school board and county/county borough council history that the administrative education officer—the one more nearly concerned with implementing Committee decisions and translating them into action—is superior to the education officer who simply reports upon schools to the Committee. Both types of officer may make recommendations to the same Committee of Management, both may preserve the fiction of seeming only to advise; but the former is in more regular contact with his lay-masters than is the latter, and so comes to exercise executive power more directly.

Some of the bye-laws for management later incorporated more fully the idea of group supervision. Thus, after the amalgamation with the Humber Industrial Ship in 1868, the Hull Ragged School expressly provided for supervision by an executive committee which had to visit the *Southampton* at least once every three months. In addition there was to be one visitor or more for each month who 'shall visit once at least during his term of office, to see that the admissions are in accordance with the Orders of the Executive Committee, and the general arrangements for the management carried out. At his last visit he shall make an official report in the form provided by the Committee.'

Despite all this rather attractive pattern of supervision within and without the local ragged school, it could not withstand 'the world's slow stain' affecting all voluntary agencies in the mid-nineteenth century. Apathy, local prejudice, shrinking financial support throwing an intolerable burden for maintaining the schools on to the faithful few; the vicious circle of crippling shortage of funds leading to insufficiency of material equipment and discouragement of effective teachers. Volunteer teachers like these were in any case hardly likely to have the highest qualifications, though no praise can be too high for these successors to John Pounds. But more than any of these weaknesses was the absence of complete supervision extending beyond the confines of the school to the 'seamy side' wherein they lived. Some of the best ideas—infants classes and Mothers' classes—wilted all too quickly when the school doors were left behind.

The report of Her Majesty's inspector, D. R. Fearon, on schools for the poorer classes in Liverpool included one sentence 'prophesying doom' upon all ragged schools for so long poised on the razor-edge of a bankrupt local effort:

> Such a society (he said) has not sufficient power, not enough weight and influence, and does not stand on a sufficiently authoritative basis to organise the whole of the efforts which are, or might be made in Liverpool for the education of this section of the community.[1]

Much the same could be said of London. The increasing attendance figures shown in successive annual reports look well until it is added that for every child in a ragged school, at least four remained without who could have been brought in had funds been available. The total effort therefore still left room for improvements like those outlined in the Morning Chronicle 25th April, 1850: zoning of schools for example with an inspector and one or more industrial schools for each (district), such schools to be open to all; ragged schools with better order and under more strict discipline than before.

It is quite obvious that at this time inspectors tended to work in a kind of professional vacuum, shut off from contact with each other by differing denomination and district. Very early, varying approaches to schools were apparent. Matthew Arnold, one of the most outspoken of the early inspectors, touched on it in his report for 1854. After mentioning how some inspectors, to avoid discouraging voluntary effort, are 'silent respecting the deficiency of schools', he says appositely:

> Inspection exists for the sake of finding out and reporting on the truth, and for this above all. But it is most important that all inspectors should proceed on the same principle in this respect—that one should not conceal defects as an advocate for the school while another exposes them as an agent for the government.

There was no established system of training, either before or after inspectors were gazetted; in fact, it was hardly considered necessary. The first few courses on method for inspectors in

[1] *Returns.* Schools for poorer classes in Birmingham, Leeds, Liverpool and Manchester, dated 18th March 1869, printed 2nd March 1870, p. 172.

the very early years had not been widened out. Opportunities for meeting together to discuss common problems like minimum standards of satisfactory work in schools were fleeting, but were there until Adderley saw fit to terminate them in 1858. Even minimum building and accommodation standards were not clearly formulated for inspectors as a whole body. Finally, there was no superior inspectorial authority, and the consequence was that it was almost impossible to effect any proper co-ordination of the standards adopted by the inspecting staff—such an authority did not exist until 1890.

It was indeed fortunate, therefore, that inspectors, by virtue of early academic training, tended to have similar ideals and aims. The majority of them, as clergymen, were well fitted to urge on schools a conception of education probably best described as 'handing on the spiritual possessions of the race'. Had they been methodologists, the lack of common meeting-ground to discuss a common policy might have been felt more keenly. As it was, their role of the honest friend, removed from the realm of immediate practice, delivering 'a round, un-varnished tale' to managers and teachers, praising the good but pointing out the bad—this was a role that they accepted easily. They could also explain the intricacies of educational administration, and bring 'My Lords' a little more into the ken of teachers.

Perhaps one can conclude with a typical 'inspection' of the period, reported by Matthew Arnold in 1863:

> Inspection under the old (pre-1862) system meant something like the following. The inspector took a school class by class. He seldom heard each child in a class read, but he called out a certain member to read, picked at random as specimen of the rest; and when this was done, he questioned the class with freedom and in his own way, on the subject of their instruction. As you got near the top of a good school, these subjects became more numerous; they embraced English grammar, geography and history, for each of which the inspector's report contained a special entry, and the examination then often acquired much variety and interest. The whole life and power of a class, the fitness of its composition, its handling by a teacher were well tested; the inspector became well acquainted with them and was enabled to make his remarks on them to the head-teacher; and a powerful means of correcting, improving and stimulating them was thus given.

Chapter Seven

THE EIGHTEEN-SIXTIES

IN the following decade the pattern of inspection was much the same, the voluntary bodies' inspectorate fluctuating in proportion to their financial balance. Diocesan inspectors, in particular, were active, notably in the inspection of middle-class schools, an activity proposed by the National Society for its own inspectors as early as 1838, but only just accepted in principle by the schools, and then only in certain dioceses. The Corresponding Committee of the National Society encouraged the idea, Her Majesty's Inspectors approved, some diocesan boards were interested, and some experiments were made:

> The one thing which the middle-classes want, and which they cannot get without help, is organisation. Let the schools remain self-supporting, but the systematic action introduced by the government into the working of elementary schools be extended to theirs; let inspectors visit and examine; let exhibitions and scholarships be founded; let first-rate teachers be distinguished; let the nation give as much money as will organise schools into a system; and £50,000 a year would completely do it, and the middle-classes can do the rest for themselves.[1]

But it was not until the National Society gave a more definite lead in the mid 1860s that the question of principle to be adopted in supervising these schools finally was answered. A sub-Committee 'on the education of upper divisions of poorer classes' was authorised by a minute of the General Committee, 1st November, 1865:

> It was agreed to appoint a sub-committee to consider and report

[1] National Society *Annual Report*, 1841, p.26.

whether the Society can assist and if so how best in promoting the education of the children of the class of poor just above those who usually attend the National schools.

Nine days later it met, and on 2nd May, 1866 it unanimously accepted seven resolutions, of which the last was most important:

> that a perpetual right of inspection shall be reserved to inspectors, to be nominated from time to time by the Committee.

This emphasised the Society's right of inspection; no less important, it did not allude specifically to inspection by local clergy as a duty. On 16th January, 1867, the new title of the Sub-Committee first appears as the Middle Class Schools Committee, and immediately clarified its conditions of working. Article II stipulated that the Committee should further its object

> by receiving into union, *after inspection*, schools of the class contemplated, security being taken that such schools shall be—
>
> (a) conducted on the principles of the Established Church;
>
> (b) open to visits of inspectors appointed by the Committee.

Article III further dealt with supervision, the Committee planning to establish 'as soon as is practicable, a system of inspection and examination for schools in union'.

As elaborated, inspection was, in fact, in the form of examination, as asked for by schools, £5 being offered initially for rewards and prizes. Later the Rev. F. L. Bagshawe was voted up to ten guineas for conducting an examination of three middle schools and making a brief report on them for the use of the Committee. A later Minute, 24th June, 1868, directed that Mr. Bagshawe's 'special attention be drawn to the inspection of schools in union with this Society, and that for the present his examination of such schools be limited to adjudging prizes to the boys who exhibit the best knowledge in Holy Scripture and the Prayer Book. The particular points in which such examination (at Christmas, 1868) is to be held, to be published by Mr. Bagshawe in an early number of the Society's Monthly Paper and in such other periodicals as Mr. Bagshawe may deem expedient'.

F

Nearly a year later, the Minutes record:

> that it is desirable to inspect all schools in union through competent persons appointed by the Committee, and that at present a sum of not less than £2 2s. 0d. with the addition of travelling expenses be allowed for the inspection of each school; such inspection to include secular as well as religious knowledge.

Two principles were thus adumbrated: that an inspector should be paid, and that he should not confine his inspection to religious education only.

The examination covered a wide range of subjects 'chosen upon the basis of the recommendations for schools of their grade, made by the Middle Class School Commission and of the requirements of the Oxford and Cambridge Local Examinations. Prizes will be given according to the report of the Examiner'. The close connection of the examination with inspection was also expressly stated:

> A favourable report on the general efficiency of the school and of its bona fide connection with the Church of England from the inspector appointed by the National Society is required previous to the Examination.

The scheme lasted until 1878, and it appeared to meet with reasonable success: it only came to an end when examinations of a more national character were becoming common. In any case, its use illustrates a principle often expounded later, that in the secondary stage of education examination is preferable to direct inspection.

This interest in the middle class schools did not mean that the diocesan inspectors neglected their chief task, which was inspection of elementary schools for the poor: this work went on as thoroughly as ever. Similarly, the inspectors of the Catholic Poor School Committee, the Wesleyans and the British Society were also very active. In fact, so popular did the idea of inspection become that several of the Unions of Mechanics' Institutes raised funds to pay for an organising-inspector, who would be expected, according to the Yorkshire Union of Mechanics' Institutes as early as 1849:

> to deliver lectures, to assist in the formation of new institutions wherever openings present themselves; and to visit committees when invited by them for the sake of suggesting improvements in

the constitution and management of the institutions, or to assist them at their annual meetings.[1]

Later it was suggested that two types of official might be appointed by the government:

1. One or two inspectors to inspect and report on the institutes, grant-in-aid being conditional upon the satisfactory nature of such reports. (A resemblance may be observable to Revised Code government inspection of evening schools.)

2. A staff of some forty lecturers, at salaries of £300 a year, appointed initially for a seven year period, to raise standards of performance in institutes, and where necessary, show how this could be done. (These were, thus, more akin to L.E.A. organisers of "further education" in this century.)[2]

Although this remained purely theory for many years, it shows clearly that the Mechanics' Institutes were grappling intelligently with the problem of organisation at local level with a view to inspection for the life-giving grants-in-aid from central government level. It is equally clear, from the records of the various Institutes, that ample and effective use was made of any available organising masters: for example, the records of the East Lancashire Union of Institutes in 1863:

> Any evening school in Union can also secure the advantage of the Organising Master's services on one evening every week throughout nine months in the year, by the annual payment of £15. The aid to the limited teaching-staff ordinarily at the command of managers and teachers would be of the greatest value in enabling the master to carry on the classes in a thoroughly satisfactory manner—to establish an efficient system of *local* and *candidate* teachers—and also to connect science classes with his school.

It is from this pioneer work that the present-day pattern of 'Evening Institute' classes has evolved.

During this period the government inspectors were as active

---

[1] *Annual Report*, 1849.
[2] A. Kilgour: *Mechanics' Institutes;* Smith & Elder, 1853.

as the local ones, and were often very much in demand, as upon their favourable reports depended the grants-in-aid which gave life to the schools and institutions. Education, in fact, was becoming a very large item in the government budget, and already inquiries were being made about the spending of these grants: was the country getting value for its money? It fell to Robert Lowe to try and answer this age-old question, and the results of his work have been alternately praised and deplored for the past century. H. S. Tremenheere, who was not dissimilar in temperament, termed him 'a man of varied learning and great cleverness', adding 'but he had crotchets of his own which injured his value as a statesman'. Certainly, Lowe liked scholarship able to give an account of itself in the examination room; for any other kind he had neither time nor patience, and it was certainly not worth spending money on.

To the intellectual pride of the old humanists he added an administrative one when it came to dealing with school inspectors. He disliked their 'taking refuge in', as he called it, such vague inexactitudes as 'moral tone', their readiness to resort to general observations—including those of a sociological kind—instead of 'confining themselves to the state of the schools under their inspection and to practical suggestions for improvements'. As for the growing practice of inspectors to meet annually to discuss common problems, he could not agree more with Adderley's "putting a stop" to such "a sort of Parliament in the office". This hardness of heart, which Lowe might call administrative acumen, made him out of sympathy at the start with those on whose behalf he administered.

Lowe's reading of the Newcastle Commission's Report was one that might have enabled him to bring to reality the favourite pipe-dream of every administrator—a scheme whereby the education of the masses can be measured reasonably in terms of pounds, shillings and pence. For the Report had, while stressing the continued need for 'discipline, efficiency and general character' in schools, expressed dissatisfaction with the existing methods employed by inspectors in ascertaining them. In particular, inspectors had

> neglected the examination of the lower classes in the three Rs, and had based their reports on the examination of the highest classes only.

But the sentence which could not fail to arrest Lowe's attention was that stating:

> There is only one way of securing this result (i.e. efficiency in the teaching of every scholar) which is to institute a searching examination by competent authority of every child in every school to which grants are to be paid, with a view to ascertaining whether the indispensable elements of knowledge are thoroughly acquired and to make the prospects and position of the teacher dependent to a considerable extent on the results of this examination.[1]

Here was the main-spring motivating the action of the subsequent 'twice revised' Code and—to extend the metaphor—the despised inspectorate became the axis on which it rotated. As might have been expected, Kay-Shuttleworth, who saw the aims and functions of Her Majesty's inspectors metamorphosed almost overnight, criticised the extent of the new status:

> Even the Department itself has never exercised any authority so large as that with which it is proposed to charge the inspectors.

Under Article 40 of the Code, the Managers of schools may claim at the end of each year, as defined by Article 17:

(*a*) the sum of 4*s.* per scholar according to the average number in attendance throughout the year at the morning and afternoon meetings of their school, and 2/6*d.* per scholar according to the average number in attendance throughout the year at the evening meetings of their school.

(*b*) for every scholar who has attended more than 200 morning or afternoon meetings of their school:

> (i) if more than 6 years of age, 8/- subject to examination;

> (ii) if under 6 years of age, 6/6*d.* subject to a report by the inspector that such children are instructed suitable to their age, and in a manner not to interfere with the instruction of the older children.

(*c*) for every scholar who has attended more than 24

---

[1] Newcastle Commission's *Report*, Vol. VI, p. 156.

evening meetings of their school, 5*s.* subject to examination.

Under Article 44, every scholar attending more than 200 times in the morning or afternoon, for whom 8/- is claimed, forfeits 2/8*d.* for failure to satisfy the inspector in reading, 2/8*d.* in writing, and 2/8*d.* in arithmetic. Under Article 51, the grant is withheld altogether:

(*a*) if the school be not held in a building certified by the inspector to be healthy, properly lighted, drained and ventilated, supplied with offices, and containing in the principal schoolroom at least 80 cubical feet of internal space for each child in average attendance;

(*b*) if the principal teacher be not duly certified and duly paid;

(*c*) if the girls in the school be not taught plain needlework as part of the ordinary course of instruction;

(*d*) if the registers be not kept with sufficient accuracy to warrant confidence in the returns;

(*e*) if on the inspector's report, there appears to be any prima facie objection of a gross kind. A second inspection, wherein another inspector or inspectors takes part, is made in every such instance, and if the grant be finally withheld, a special minute is made and recorded of the case;

(*f*) if three persons at least be not designated to sign the receipt for the grant on behalf of the school.

Article 52, Sec. (*a*) also adds that the grant is reduced by not less than one tenth nor more than one half of the whole, upon the inspector's report, for faults of instruction or discipline on the part of the teacher, or (after one year's notice) for failure on the part of the Managers to remedy any such defect in the premises as seriously interfered with the efficiency of the school, or to provide proper furniture, books, maps, and other apparatus of elementary instruction. Articles 55–6 deal with the keeping of log books by schools. Section 73 deals with candidates for certificates (as qualified teachers) who must, beside passing this examination also as teachers continuously engaged in the same schools, obtain two favourable reports from the inspector with an interval of one year between them.

Article 79 laid upon Managers the duty of reporting on a teacher's conduct and attention to duty, whilst under Article 80,

the inspector must annually report whether the teacher's school is efficient in organisation, discipline and instruction.

Articles 81 to 90 were, perhaps, the most unfortunate from the pupil-teacher's point of view: his five-year 'contract' could be terminated at any time; and the teacher received no extra allowance for coaching him. The inspector was still responsible for approving their selection academically (the Managers presenting candidates suitable in moral character), and examining them annually. By Section 93, assistant teachers were left to make their own terms about wages and working hours with the Managers.

'The Instructions to Her Majesty's Inspectors of Schools', issued in September, 1862, were a lengthy commentary on how the Code was to be interpreted:

The grant to be made to each school depends as it has ever done, upon the school's whole character and work. The grant is offered for attendance in a school with which the inspector is satisfied. . . . You will judge every school by the same standard that you have hitherto used, as regards its religious, moral and intellectual merits. The examination under Article 48 does not supersede the judgement but pre-supposes it. That Article does not prescribe that, if thus much is done, a grant shall be paid, but unless thus much is done, no grant shall be paid. It does not exclude the inspection of each school by a highly educated public officer, but it fortifies this general test by individual examination.

Two points rise immediately out of this. One is that up to one tenth of the grant could be deducted for poor religious instruction, though it would appear that such a deduction was rarely made. In fact, religious instruction as a subject tended to be pushed into the background, along with other subjects (e.g. Science) as compared with the more easily examinable 'three R.s'. That there was much current misapprehension by diocesan inspectors and clergy is evident in the Rev. T. W. Sharpe's report on Yorkshire schools (1862), for he is at great pains to stress that Her Majesty's Inspector must be satisfied with the state of the religious instruction before he proceeds with the rest of the examination.

The second point is that nowhere is it stated that subjects other than the three R.s should not be inspected. Mr. D. R. Fearon, Her Majesty's Inspector, in his book on *School Inspection* (1875) was keen to say so:

> The Minutes issued to the inspectors in September 1862 after the introduction of the Revised Code show that such instruction (in English grammar, geography and history) was always in-tended to be kept up in elementary schools, and to be tested and reported upon by the inspectors. It is no doubt the fact that such instruction was largely dropped in the schools on the introduction of the Revised Code, as is admitted in the Report to Her Majesty of the Committee of Council for Education for the year 1874 . . . and it is also no doubt true that in many schools in which these subjects were efficiently kept up, they were not much noticed by the inspectors, after the introduction of the Revised Code.

Fearon makes it quite clear that in many schools it was not possible to teach these 'extra' subjects and, at the same time, do justice to the elementary and essential subjects:

> And in so far as the Revised Code forced such schools to give up their more tempting and showy work and apply themselves to the drudgery of the essentials, it did good service.[1]

At least some inspectors and some parents, if not the majority that Lowe claimed, were in favour of 'payment by results'. The Rev. W. H. Brookfield, the Rev. J. P. Norris, and the Rev. F. C. Cook also (at first, at any rate) inclined to suggest that the government grants be based on examination of individual scholars. It was, in fact, Cook's estimate that a school of 150 children could be examined in this way in an hour and a half (later amended to six hours) which influenced the Newcastle Commission so much. The Rev. W. H. Bellairs and the Rev. J. H. Brodie were both out-and-out 'coders': and a survey by the Education Department in 1864 of educational progress quoted the remarkable figure of 23 out of 26 reports by inspectors expressing approval of the Revised Code. Reporting on Yorkshire schools in 1863, Watkins says:

[1] D. R. Fearon, *School Inspection*, Sect. 26(a).

I do not remember that I was ever better satisfied with their general progress and actual condition.

and notes 80 per cent of passes under the Revised Code (i.e. 240 out of 300 schools). In the same year, H. J. Lynch, reporting on Roman Catholic schools, confidently anticipated better instruction and increased grants. The two previous annual reports, however, of the Catholic Poor School Committee were far less optimistic. Of course, the full effect of the principle of 'payment by results' had not yet been felt, but occasional comments indicate that some schools did well under it; e.g. the Vicar of Adwick-le-Street says of the mixed school of 50 children in his parish and in receipt of government grants: 'every child has passed in every subject for four consecutive years'.

Then, too, some less bright children, at any rate, did receive attention (if not too backward!); and inspectors had to examine all classes of children over 8 years, not only the top few, as was alleged happened previously. Another important immediate result of the Revised Code was to bring school-managers into much closer touch with the inspector. (There is, of course, an obverse side to this, in that the managers *had* to meet him only because on his assessment for grant purposes depended how much they could pay their teachers. This was one reason why so many Boards of Managers petitioned against the introduction of the Code originally.) Managers, therefore, could hardly help feeling a new sense of importance in their relationships with the inspector, even if those with 'My Lords' were to be more exasperating and less happy. Their physical presence alone during the inspector's summing-up gave them a 'raison d'être'. In theory, of course long before 1862 the managers had accompanied the inspector on his round of the school. But from 1862 to 1870 (the year when inspectors ceased to announce their visits beforehand) and even after then though to a less extent managers were important people. They appointed and dismissed their teachers just as they ordered slates in preference to copy-books or vice-versa. Some shrinking of their area of responsibilities after the Act of 1902 took considerable incentive out of local effort and enterprise in education in certain country areas.

On paper administrative order had been introduced. One

block grant was now to be doled out, instead of three, and the inspectors were, as before, the field workers, sending up their reports and pass-lists to the Education Department which appointed

> committees of inspectors and examiners to look over specimens and determine the means of fixing the minimum of each standard.[1]

The government, it would appear, could not lose; if the million pounds expenditure remained, greater efficiency would result; if expenditure fell, a saving, at least, in spending of public money would be achieved. Robert Lowe, too, was in a tradition which looked back to Adam Smith and to Wordsworth, that public education should be provided for the poor—but only at very small expense. It is not without its irony that the Church of England had been faced with a somewhat similar choice in 1840: then it had to decide whether it appointed and paid inspectors, or whether it let the government pay its own inspectors to do the job. The Revised Code was a parallel attempt to cut the cost of education without impairing unduly the work already being done: administratively this is always a good potential (paper) solution. Costs, indeed, did fall, for smaller grants were made to schools, fewer pupil-teachers were forthcoming, and so grants to training colleges dwindled.

Lowe always maintained that he was not responsible for the subsequent development of payment by results, particularly as it affected other subjects:

> The idiots who succeeded me have piled up on the top of the three Rs a mass of class and specific subjects which they propose to test in the same way.[2]

Nor, perhaps, could he foresee how quickly prescribed minimal standards would become maximal.

Although the opposition case to payment by results was nowhere better stated than by some of Her Majesty's Inspectors themselves, inspection of schools was not suddenly transformed 'over-night' as it were. The general tenor of reports

[1] *Instructions to Inspectors*, September, 1862, sect. 20. *cf.* further, *History of the Appointment of Inspectors and Examiners Under the Education Department*. Royal Commission on Civil Service 1912–14, Second Report, Appendix IX.

[2] Quoted from Lord George Hamilton, *Parliamentary Reminiscences and Reflections*, 1868–85, Vol. I, p. 158; cf. also p. 157.

after 1862 is, at first, much the same as before. The Rev. H. Sandford's report, for instance, on church schools in the North and East Ridings of Yorkshire for 1864–5 might be for any year. Halifax and Beverley schools please him; some of the sea-coast towns like Scarborough and Bridlington—with their seasonal fluctuation in attendance—do not please him. He quotes with approval the fact that in good schools 39 per cent of the children are over ten years old; whereas in Middlesbrough it is only 16 per cent. Again, he notes with regret, without laying blame anywhere, that only 69 out of 195 East Riding schools are recognised for grant purposes: one must lay alongside this the pathetic comment by the Vicar of Goathland in 1868:

> We can never raise money in the parish to meet the conditions required by the Government codes.

The most serious fault in payment by results was the sheer futility of attempting to regulate education by economic laws. Any country at any time gets the teachers, the pupil-teachers, the inspectors it is prepared to pay for, and grave deterioration in many aspects of education is obvious in the 1860s. This is particularly noticeable from inspectors' reports during those years; in them, all too frequently, emphasis is laid on the wrong things: the fact that a child was too cold in school to be able to hold his pen is of less importance than the fact that he was accidentally marked present in the register on a day on which he happened to be absent; lack of light, ventilation and sanitary facilities in schools would seem to weigh less with inspectors than the performance of children on examination day. Within a very short time after the institution of the Revised Code, education may have been cheaper, but it was certainly poorer than before, and the quality of inspection was poorer, too. Matthew Arnold, an experienced inspector and outspoken opponent of the Revised Code, forecast this deterioration in the quality of inspection in his general report for 1863:

> The new examination groups children by its standard, not by their classes; and however much we may strive to make the standards correspond with the classes, we cannot make them correspond at all exactly. The examiner, therefore, does not take the children in their own classes.

79

This, in itself, was retrograde, because, as Arnold goes on:

> the life and power of each class, as a whole, the fitness of its com-
> position, its handling by its teacher, he therefore does not test.

It is true that the inspector:

> hears every child in the groups before him read, and so far, his
> examination is more complete than the old inspection. But he
> does not question them; he does not as an examiner under the
> rule of the six standards, go beyond the three matters—reading,
> writing and arithmetic—and the amount of these three matters
> which the standards themselves prescribe.

Arnold then lays his finger on the shrunken curriculum by
saying:

> > Indeed, the entries for grammar, geography and history have now
> altogether disappeared from the forms of report furnished to the
> inspector. The nearer, therefore, he gets to the top of the school
> the more does his examination in itself become an inadequate
> means of testing the real attainments and intellectual life of the
> scholars before him. Boys who have mastered vulgar fractions and
> decimals, who know something of physical science and geometry,
> a good deal of English grammar, of geography and history, he
> hears read a paragraph, he sees write a paragraph, and work a
> couple of easy sums in the compound rules or practice. . . .

His summing up is the clue to the changing status of the
inspector:

> The whole school felt, under the old system, that the prime aim
> and object of the inspector's visit was, after ensuring the fulfil-
> ment of certain sanitary and disciplinary conditions, to test and
> quicken the intellectual life of the school. The scholars' thoughts
> were directed to this object, the teachers' thoughts were directed
> to it, the inspectors' thoughts were directed to it. . . . The new
> examination is in itself a less exhausting business than the old
> inspection to the person conducting it, and it does not make a
> call as that did upon his spirit and inventiveness; but it takes up
> much more time, it throws upon him a mass of minute detail, and
> severely tasks hand and eye to avoid mistakes.

What he saw on return to England in 1867 had not caused him
to alter his opinion: he writes in his general report for that
year:

> The inspection, therefore, is not now that stimulus to the whole

school which it was when a proportion of each class, picked at random by the inspector, were freely examined by him.

One should add that this earlier system had had its weakness (how often will an inspector pick upon the worst boys and girls in a class!). The new examination was at least objective—some few teachers today would prefer this system of inspection. But there can be no gain-saying Watkins' comment in 1869:

> The country needs education and must have it, real, sound practical education, not merely instruction in the elementary subjects . . . from the nature of (this) examination, which is entirely formal and mechanical, only mechanical results can be expected.

The greatest evil of all, perhaps, was the elevated status of the inspector, deriving from his increased powers: he could no longer be a friendly critic, for on the nature and results of his examination, the life-blood of the school depended. As Kekewich said bitterly:

> Imagine the feelings of the unfortunate teacher when he looked over the inspector's shoulder and saw the failures being recorded wholesale, and knew that his annual salary was being reduced by two and eightpence for each failure.[1]

The teachers and managers could not make nice distinctions between 'their Lordships' and their inspectors—all were synonymous with a department which

> was always on the watch to find something which deserved a lecture or chastisement, but never ready to help, guide or sympathise.

Instead of being a constructive adviser the inspector had become the harsh dispenser of an all too meagre government grant whose size he determined.

Such a burden of responsibility was both unfair to the inspectors and unwanted by most of them. The best must have wondered why such care was taken in choosing them when, after appointment, they were set down to the dullest routine work, not calculated to edify anyone. Sneyd-Kynnersley, one of the newer inspectors in action when the Revised Code was

[1] G. W. Kekewich, *The Education Department and After*, p. 10.
[2] G. W. Kekewich, *The Education Department and After*, p. 11.

at its height, gives a vivid sketch of the dreary inspection-cum-examination day so dreaded by the schools:

> Our plan of campaign was delightfully simple. Most of the children were in the two lowest standards. These were supplied with slates, pencils and a reading book, and were drawn up in two long lines down the middle of the room. They stood back to back to prevent copying, and did dictation and arithmetic, sometimes dropping their slates, sometimes their pencils, sometimes their books, not infrequently all three, with a crash on the floor. When we had marked the results on the Examination Schedule, all these children were sent home, and the atmosphere was immensely improved. Then we proceeded to examine the rest, the aristocracy, who worked their sums on paper. As a rule, if we began about 10, we finished about 11.45. If the master was a good fellow and trustworthy, we looked over the few papers in dictation and arithmetic, marked the Examination Schedule, and showed him the result before we left. Then he calculated his percentage of passes, his grant, and his resulting income; and went to dinner with what appetite he might. But if the man was cross-grained, and likely to complain that the exercises were too hard, the standard of marking too high, and so on, he would be left in merciful ignorance of the details. Half an hour in the evening sufficed for making up the Annual Report, and the incident was closed.[1]

As time went on, examination day became more of a torment in schools, and the inspectors themselves became slaves of the examination machine, filling in forms, visiting schools and writing reports. Kay-Shuttleworth added his criticism, oblique but pungent:

> All inspectors are not perfect either in manner, utterance, choice of words for poor children, method of examining them; nor in the skill, kindness and patience required to bring out the true state of the child's knowledge.[2]

The Instructions to Her Majesty's Inspectors of Schools upon the administration of the Revised Code abolished the office of assistant inspector, and sub-divided the districts in which they had been employed. It was claimed that in this way economy of time, of money, and of personal fatigue in travelling

[1] E. M. Sneyd-Kynnersley, *H.M.I. Some Passages in the Life of One of Her Majesty's Inspectors of Schools*, p. 59.
[2] Letter to Lord Granville, 4th Nov. 1861.

would be achieved. In practice the government saved a good deal in salaries, but the inspectors were left with thousands of scripts to mark, a task for which they must have assistance. A Minute of Committee of Council (19th May, 1863) gave details of the form this assistance should take. After obtaining appropriate sanction from the Department an inspector could, if he so wished, choose from his locality an elementary school head-teacher whom he considered outstanding at his job to help him with the routine of examining. They were not appointed, as inspectors were, by Order of the Queen in Council, they had to pass a Civil Service examination, and their annual salary was £100 rising to a maximum of £250. (By one of those delicate Victorian social distinctions, they were also referred to in official lists as Mr., never Esquire, which gave them cause for concern.) Kay-Shuttleworth in his evidence before the Newcastle Commission had agreed that extension of the inspectorate could be effected cheaply by employing first-class school-masters as helpers (under assistant-inspector and inspector). Seymour Tremenheere had also suggested using local effort to cut back the growth of Her Majesty's inspectorate.

Sanction to their appointment having duly been given by the Education Department, these new assistants could then accompany the inspectors, examining the children in 'the elements' under supervision of their inspector. Later, this developed into his inspecting the girls whilst the inspector examined the boys, and vice versa. 'Their Lordships' were in no two minds about the inferior role of the assistant:

> It is only by your thoroughly comprehending the limited and subsidiary character of the assistant's duty that you will repel the imputation of setting a young man to judge his elders, and often his superiors, in the art of school-keeping.

Some qualms did arise in certain quarters: as the Rev. J. G. Londsdale noticed in his evidence before the Select Committee on Education of 1865, there was locally 'not exactly dissatisfaction but rather apprehension I should say, as to what might be done' by teachers promoted to inspectors' assistants. Clergy and managers feared they might come into a school under a simple written order of an inspector and examine the children in all subjects, including religious knowledge, thus violating the spirit of the concordat of 1840. (Later, however, Londsdale says he has been re-assured by inspectors on this very point.) In practice, the assistants never recommended deductions of grant, nor did they report direct to the Education Department, but always only to their own immediate inspector. They were generally limited to the examination of reading, writing and arithmetic—and lower down the school at that. How much they were appreciated and used by inspectors may perhaps be judged from Fearon's comment in 1875:

> (inspectors) were expected to inspect as many schools in the week under the Revised Code as they had inspected under the old Code, and yet were told to do it in a way which took them three times as long and tired them incalculably more. If all inspectors had been from the first supplied, as they are now, with certificated teachers as assistant inspectors to help them in conducting the individual examination in the elements, which was required by the Revised Code, and thus to relieve them of some of the mechanical drudgery of their work, they would gladly have applied themselves to instruction in higher subjects.

Although, even after 1862, Her Majesty's Inspectors still inspected religious instruction and could withhold the government grant if it were not satisfactory in any school, it was increasingly clear that government inspectors were becoming, more and more, secular officers and that the dioceses ought to clarify their positions as guardians of education. On paper, at least the diocesan boards were flourishing and some had their own inspectors, who in general did not clash with Her Majesty's Inspectors. They aroused less animosity among school managers and teachers than did the government counterpart, probably because they entered the schools more permissively. Their reports, on the whole, were less condemning than those of Her Majesty's inspectors; possibly because they accepted lower standards of work and performance. What was clearly needed was some kind of liaison between the two, and several suggestions were made. The possibility of using local clergy as part-time inspectors' assistants was explored; as they were only part-time, the help they could give was bound to be small, and besides they were restricted by their denominational character. Perhaps the most sensible and positive contribution came, not from any Select Committee, but from Mr. S. J. G. Frazer,

Her Majesty's Inspector of Schools in Hampshire and Wiltshire. In his report for 1869 he points out that half the schools do not apply for government grant, yet diocesan inspectors visit this half. Why not, therefore, establish liaison with each other as they had, to his knowledge, done in Lichfield? The diocesan inspector accepts without question the results of any examination-cum-inspection of secular subjects by government inspectors, who, in turn, leave inspection of religious knowledge entirely to the diocesan inspector and accept his opinion as final. He adds that others of his colleagues have done likewise; why should not a similar arrangement be made on a national basis?[1]

[1] *Minutes*, Committee of Council, 1869–70, p. 125.

Chapter Eight

SCHOOL BOARD INSPECTION

DESPITE the ideas for amalgamating the various inspectorates with a view of greater efficiency, and despite the almost savage administration of the Revised Code towards the same end, English education in 1870 was still in a chaotic state. There were still far too few school places for the children who required them, and attendance figures were pathetically meagre compared with today. Some 40 per cent of the nation's children were reckoned not to be attending a school of any kind, largely because there were no schools for them to attend; especially was this so in the rapidly growing industrial areas of the North, where even the Church of England's parochial system became temporarily disorganised. The twin ideas behind the Act of 1870 were that a local rate should be levied to provide local elementary education where none existed or was insufficient; and that an ad hoc local body should have control over the spending of this education-rate. By 1902, there were no fewer than 2,214 such school-boards in England, and they varied enormously in size and efficiency. At their puniest, where the product of a penny rate might produce under twenty shillings, they could be hopelessly ineffectual: at their biggest, where the precept might run into thousands of pounds, they could amply sustain the claim made for them as local educational parliaments.[1] The procedural pattern and whole ethos of local educational administration today stem directly from such boards. Resting as they did upon direct personal contact between Board members and schools, they humanised policy, sensitising it to every change of local opinion.

Month by month these Boards met, carefully recording all transactions and regulating their proceedings in accordance

[1] *cf.* R. H. Mair, *School Boards, or Our Educational Parliaments*, 1872.

with that vital Third Schedule of the Act. Small decisions lie alongside big ones. A constant stream of letters went out in all directions; those to 'their Lordships' received less prompt replies, it seemed, to the frequent exasperation of many, to the secret delight of the few. Their motives were genuinely altruistic—'the welfare of the poor' educationally. They had their critics and their defenders; notable among the latter was Huxley, who first urged on the Education Department devolution to the Boards of inspectorial functions.[1] Inevitably, some arrogated to themselves many of the functions since more properly delegated to heads of schools! These were problems to be solved only by living and working together.

The task facing the new town school boards was an Augean one, and much time was to be given up by lay members of that voluntary, unpaid kind, in the best traditions of English local government. The scope of their problem is seen in the monthly minutes and agenda. The bigger boards had first to estimate how many children should be attending school and how many places there were for them; thus, the Leeds Board's census revealed 48,787 children needing places, with only 27,329 places available. Yet, just over thirty years later, this same Board handed on to its successor 157 elementary school departments, 2 higher grade schools, 4 industrial schools, 5 'special' schools, a pupil teacher centre and nearly 60 evening schools.[2]

The classifying of schools already in existence also presented problems from the point of view of efficiency generally. Bradford School Board, for example, listed the schools in the city as follows:

32 efficient schools, receiving government grant
10 efficient schools not receiving government grant but about to make application
7 efficient schools not receiving government grant and not applying for grant
24 efficient "private venture" schools not eligible for grant
16 "private adventure" schools with efficient teaching but inefficient premises
25 "private adventure" schools with both inefficient teaching and inefficient premises.

[1] *cf.* his article, "The School Boards: what they are and what they may do", *Contemporary Review*, 1870.
[2] *Education in Leeds; A Backward Glance and a Present View*, 1926, p. 13.

The large town boards through their Sites (and Buildings) Committee had to find sites for new school premises, if no buildings could be leased (a measure judged expedient on grounds of speed and economy). Only rarely were premises offered, as in Bradford, though non-conformists on the whole were well-disposed to the Boards. As none of the more modern methods of forecasting a rise in population existed, schools were planned to house existing numbers of children, with inevitable results. Areas of sites selected varied greatly; but once approved by the Education Department, usually through ubiquitous inspectors who once more 'brushed up' their architecture, tenders could be asked for, the lowest selected and a loan negotiated with the Public Works Loans Commissioners. These stages of getting a school built fell more properly within the purview of the all-important Finance (and General Purposes) Committee. It was this Committee that authorised payment of any bills, requisitions for apparatus, books or stationery. Other duties devolved upon the School Management Committee for example, teaching posts had to be advertised, and candidates interviewed on short-lists. Salary scales had to be drawn up for both teaching and non-teaching staff, and lists of duties. The other large Committee was usually an Attendance Committee. As Board Schools depended for maintenance on government grant besides rate aid and perhaps school-pence, and as one-third of the government grant was for attendance, the boards were at great pains to inculcate the school-going habit among 'the dirty infantry of the streets'. Bye-laws were drafted very early on, and managers encouraged in the habit of going into school to check the registers. Larger boards also appointed School Attendance Officers, better known locally perhaps as 'kid-catchers'.

Already existing schools could apply to come under the Board, and board members could be brought into immediate managerial relationship with such schools. Leeds Zion School provides a good example in this respect, as both the Board's 'Committee on Zion School transfer' and the Zion School Managers' Minute Book have been preserved. Five Board members, two of the erst-while Managers, and two ladies were nominated Managers by the Leeds Board under Section 15 of the 1870 Act. The offices of Chairman and Treasurer were accorded to two of the Board Members for the ensuing twelve months; and the Clerk of the School Board was appointed Secretary to the Managers. In the manner by now customary from long-established voluntary school practice, the Managers further resolved that they themselves, along with three ladies, should act as visitors to the school for the next twelve months; it was further resolved:

> that such visitors be appointed in rotation to visit the schools for one week at a time, the order of visitation to be entered in a Visitor's Book, and that it be the duty of each visitor to attend the school at least twice during such week of visitation; and to enter in the Visitor's Book the dates of visits, and any remarks which the state of the several departments may call for: the Book to circulate among the visitors as required, and to be produced at the monthly meetings of the Managers.

If it be added that the new managing committee of the school could not spend more than £10 at any one time without prior School Board approval; and that the committee held its monthly meetings at the Board Offices (at 9 a.m.!) it is abundantly clear that supervision of school life was indissolubly linked with the larger administration of school affairs in general.

The bigger school boards, spending rate monies rather than their own (and critics were always at hand to remind them of the fact) were quickly faced with the acute problem of just how much supervision they could exercise over their growing number of schools, some built by the Board, others coming over to 'Board status' from being formerly voluntary—ragged schools, and Wesleyan and British schools in particular. It had all been very easy at first; Board members could get into the Board's schools without great effort. Even if the number of schools to be so visited increased steadily, a system of grouping of schools could be worked out so that information could regularly be shuttled up to the Board's Committees and conversely from them to the schools. Thus, the 'Scheme of Education for the control of the schools of the (Leeds) Board', 20th November, 1873, included the following resolutions:

> 1. That every Board school shall be conducted in compliance with the regulations of the Education Department for gaining annual grants.

2. That the schools of the Board shall be under the direct management of the Board through the Education and Management of Schools Committee.

3. In order to provide for the complete supervision of the schools, in addition to official visitation, there shall be appointed Visitors for the schools.

4. For this purpose the schools shall be grouped or otherwise on the recommendation of the Committee, and there shall be appointed as visitors any members of the Committee or the Board who are willing to undertake the duty, and such persons, not being more than three for each school or group, as may be approved by the Board.

5. The schools shall be visited from time to time, and there shall be kept in each school a book in which records of visits and recommendations shall be made, having reference to the entire management of the schools, including premises, fittings, teachers, instruction, cleaning, and evening schools.

6. The Visitors' Books shall be statedly brought before the Committee, in such order as the Committee may direct, and the recommendations and notes considered.

The blend of administrative and educational supervision was apparent from the questions Visitors had to answer; the Norwich Board's read thus:

VISITOR'S BOOK

.... School.

.... Department.

Question.
1. Name and Address of Visitor?
2. Date and hour of Visit.
3. Is the attendance of Teachers regular and punctual?
4. Is the Staff complete and efficient?
5. Are the Pupil Teachers and Monitors regularly instructed and when is instruction given?
6. Is the Time Table duly observed?
7. Do you observe any defect of discipline or organisation in the School?

8. Is the average attendance satisfactory, and the attendance of Scholars punctual and regular?

9. Are the Books appointed to be kept by the Teachers in order, and entries duly made therein?

10. Are the School and Class Rooms clean, and well warmed and ventilated?

11. Is the Caretaker attentive to his duties, and careful of the property of the Board?

12. Are the Books, Apparatus, and General Appliances of the School sufficient, and in good order?

13. Is the condition of the Playground, Yards and Offices satisfactory?

.....................*Signature of Visitor.*

So schemes of general visitation were evolved; but as two-thirds of the government grant to board schools, as well as to other inspected schools, depended on the result of examination under the still flourishing Revised Code, the emergence of more definite local inspection was only to be expected. London led the way, appointing the first local inspector in January, 1872. At first the duties of the London School Management Committee had been defined as being:

> to deal with all business relating to the management and discipline of the Board Schools, and to the instruction given in them: to consider and report to the Board upon the appointment and removal of managers and teachers, and upon the fees to be paid by scholars; in all matters in relation to Industrial Schools, to superintend the Industrial School Officers; and to administer the bye-laws relating to compulsion and to appoint one or more sub-committees to deal, in the first instance, with the several parts of its business.

The School Management Committee's first task was to determine what should be the nature of its administrative relationship to schools. By a Minute of 18th October, 1871, it recommended in relation to four schools that

> the Clerk be instructed to write and say that the Board are about to appoint a body of eight managers, under Section 15 of the Elementary Education Act (1870); that four of the new managers would be nominated by the existing body for appointment by

the Board, and four would be appointed directly by the Board themselves.

On 1st May, 1872, when a second Board Inspector had just been appointed, the Board showed signs of amending this policy; it was moved:

> that in future, no managers be appointed for new schools established by this Board, but that the schools shall be managed by the inspectors who shall visit each school periodically at the discretion of the School Management Committee; . . . that it be referred to the School Management Committee to consider what additional staff of inspectors will be required for this purpose; . . . that it be referred to the Finance Committee to consider whether, in the case of these schools, the payments for salaries and other expenses cannot be made by cheques made payable at the offices of the Board, authority being given for each payment by the inspectors.

These were large claims for any inspectorate and, had they been adopted, would powerfully have modified subsequent development of 'Clerks' or 'Secretaries' or 'Directors' to local authority education committees. But on 29th May, 1872, the School Management Committee:

> in answer to the reference beg leave to report that in their opinion it is not desirable that the Board should manage their schools by inspectors, but they think it desirable, where practicable, to have several schools under the same managers, especially when they are grouped so as to comprise various kinds of schools.

These were wise words, and, indeed, a development of this idea of a group of managers being responsible for the several schools of a locality has characterised the educational development plan of many local authorities, some as early as 1902, others since 1944. 'Dual management' by the School Management Committee acting in close co-operation with bodies of local managers was in keeping with the slowly forming tradition of school boards being local educational parliaments. In this connection it is revealing to note yet again the pressure of the microcosm within the macrocosm. Local managers were never content merely to rubber-stamp policy from above; rather they wished to have a hand in deciding it, and, in the case of London, memorialised the Board to that effect. A Special Committee on the constitution and powers of managers of board schools sat from 5th July to 16th November, 1882, and the evidence taken clearly indicated that joint consultation was essential between School Management Committee and local boards of managers. It was not good enough for the former to act upon communication not made by the latter, without, at least, giving the managers themselves the opportunity of expressing opinion (except, of course, in cases of urgency). Again, complaints against teachers in their schools should, at least, be made known to the managers before executive action had been taken after due investigation. No better cases could be made out than this Sub-Committee's findings for local inspectors acting as liaison officers—but certainly not in place of managers.

Other school boards were thinking along similar lines to London. Nottingham, for example, zoned its schools, appointing local managers, but, at the same time, nominating two elected school board members to serve with them as co-adjutors. These boards of managers made recommendations to the School Management Committee of the Board, consisting of four Board members and the Board Chairman and Vice-Chairman ex officio. Their local responsibilities were considerable and left scope for exercise of initiative as well. A much bigger board adopting the same system was Liverpool, the General Instructions to School Managers being carefully worded:

> The new managers will be responsible to the Board and they will manage the school in conformity with the regulations of the Board under the Elementary Education Act. The new managers will be requested to elect one of their number to act as Secretary and another as Treasurer, and to notify to the Board such appointments as soon as made. The managers will be required to visit the school periodically, and see that it is duly provided with furniture, desks, maps, books and apparatus; to receive and examine all tradesmen's bills, to receive from the teachers the fee paid by the scholars, to keep the accounts, to recommend teachers for appointment, and advise, when necessary, their dismissal, to make the half-yearly reports on the general efficiency of the school, and, in short, to act as representatives of the Board, subject to the regulations to be hereafter presented.

A much more elaborate form of this was operated by the Bristol

School Board, the following resolutions being adopted, 18th May, 1888:

> That three or more visitors be appointed to each school.
>
> That they be appointed to each school for a calendar year.
>
> That each visitor shall have notice by rota list of the months when specially responsible for visiting: but all shall be at liberty to visit the school whenever they please.
>
> That each visitor be requested at the conclusion of the month to report to the Clerk of the Board on a form to be supplied.
>
> That each visitor be notified, by the head teacher, of the annual prize distributions.
>
> That half-yearly meetings be held in June and December of all the visitors of each school, and the member of the Board who is the visitor for the month. Also that the said Member of the Board shall be chairman of the meeting.
>
> That there be a General Annual Meeting early in the year of all the members of the Board and all the local visitors. The chairman of the Board to be chairman of that meeting.

All these schemes were group-versions of a local, and at least semi-official, inspectorate. Birmingham, on the other hand, had quite a different scheme (one much more closely related to the inspectorates of the present day), best expounded by Joseph Chamberlain in 1876:

> there are, of course, two systems of inspection, and for my own part I am prepared to admit that either of them may be very good. There is a system, which is adopted in London and Liverpool, of establishing a voluntary management committee outside the Board, and in connection with each of the Board schools. I have no doubt that future Boards, from time to time, will re-consider the whole subject, and if they see fit they may adopt this system in preference to that we have chosen. We have thought such a system objectionable on two grounds; in the first place because this voluntary inspection tends in a great number of cases to become perfunctory and inefficient; and because, in the second place, it is likely to lead to clashing of authority between the committee outside the Board and the Board itself. We have, therefore, preferred to appoint an efficient inspector, who is himself a master of considerable attainments, and who makes a periodical report of the most elaborate character concerning all the schools, which reports are in turn examined by the Educational and School Management Committee, and any defect discovered, or recommendation made, receives prompt attention. We have,

in addition to this, an inspector of school accounts, statistics of attendance, and other matters of a similar kind, and we have an inspector to give special attention to the singing, and also an inspectress of needlework. These two latter travel from school to school, and occupy their time in superintending these two important departments.[1]

Ten years later, Birmingham was still persisting with this policy, examination of children individually and general inspection of the condition of a school being performed by separate inspectors. Their reports

> come regularly before the committee with a very perfect and systematic analysis of the work of the teachers and of the condition of the schools. In that way, the School Management Committee have in their possession in the course of the year accurate reports of their schools twice over from two authorities, apart from the government inspector: they form the opinion of what is going on in the schools; they take measures to appoint teachers or to add to the staff, or what not, as may be necessary, based upon these reports and upon personal examination of the schools.[2]

It was not by chance that the managers of ragged schools were among the first, and in by far the greatest number, to ask to come under the new school boards after 1870. London School Board, by a Minute of 10th May, 1871, announced its readiness to receive applications from managers wishing to transfer their schools to the Board. Nearly two months later, on 5th July, 1871, it resolved:

> that it be an instruction to the Committee on the Scheme of Education to consider and report what arrangements should be made by the Board, provisional or otherwise, to provide education for the class of children now attending ragged schools, and to consider whether or not it would be necessary for this purpose to establish free schools.

In the very first list of schools shown as willing to be taken over, there were no fewer than 24 ragged schools.

[1] *Six Years of Educational Work in Birmingham*, pp. 21–22. Birmingham School Board Minutes record the appointments: G. C. Lloyd, Board Inspector, 1st Sept. 1874; H. Rudge, Inspector of Registers, 6th July, 1876; W. Dobson, Superintendent Teacher of Singing, 13th Jan. 1876; Mrs. C. Buncher, Inspectress of Needlework, 8th Oct. 1875.

[2] Rev. H. W. Crosskey, *Evidence*, Cross Commission, Second Report, Q. 31238–43.

There were other powerful contributing factors. The teaching staff of ragged schools could hardly remain insensitive to the relatively far more attractive salaries available in the board schools of the big town boards. The early records of staff taken on by such boards include several from local ragged schools. Again, the superior standards of accommodation, heating, lighting, ventilation, equipment set by the boards could not be ignored by managers who had so long struggled to keep up appearances. When Oldham School Board took over its first ragged school, the newer dispensation must have been very evident.[1]

One exception to a general trend for ragged schools to be absorbed by School Boards may be noted in the Manchester and Salford Sunday Ragged School Union. Its sponsors claimed it fulfilled a very useful function in keeping children off the streets at weekends, when their exposure to temptation was greatest and their occupation least; they added that no board school opened at weekends. It conformed to the general pattern of organisation, as its first 'Articles of Government' in 1858 show, modifying or adding to them thereafter as changing circumstances warranted. Here perhaps is the first tentative formulation of the idea of voluntary youth clubs; and now, as then, a central test for success must be 'how effective is the system of management?'

[1] Board Minutes, 21st Oct. 1871; 1st Jan. 1872; 6th Nov. 1872.

Chapter Nine

BOARD INSPECTORS AND ORGANISERS

IT soon became abundantly clear that, whatever type of general supervision might be preferred by individual boards, they all needed a certain number of specialists to help in pressing this supervision home. Just as Clerks, Solicitors, Surveyors, Architects, Attendance Officers were all being appointed to meet particular needs, so, too, was the organising inspector. He made his debut under devious title and sundry connection in all the bigger school boards, irrespective of the type of school management adopted; and in all cases, his immediate loyalty was to the Clerk and the School Management Committee.

Initially, the greatest single objection to appointments of this kind was that already there existed government inspectors of schools whose work might thus be duplicated. A full-dress debate on the question by the London School Board fittingly epitomised the principles involved. W. S. Grover put the case for a separate School Board inspectorate:

> If the Board undertook to control, manage and regulate their own schools, how was it possible to discharge that duty unless they had their own inspectors, so that they might see with their own eyes, hear with their own ears, and judge with their own judgment, and have their regulations carried out effectively.

This was very much in line with Huxley's view that, at all costs, the evil of all evils should be averted, meddling with education by the State:

> If there was one thing more important than another for the school

97

boards, it was that inspection should be given up by the government and left to the energy of the school boards.

As Chairman of the Scheme of Education Committee he moved, on 26th July, 1871:

> that inspectors be appointed by the Board to examine its schools and pupil teachers in all the subjects taught in each school, and to report to the Board from time to time upon the discipline and general efficiency of the schools provided by the Board.

This motion was twice postponed, but was finally approved 11th October, 1871, in a modified form:

> that officers be appointed by the Board to visit its schools, and to report to the Board from time to time upon the discipline and general efficiency of the schools provided by the Board.

This amendment was a significant one, because it indicated the rate-payers' fear of an unnecessary duplication of, and possible friction, or even collision, between inspectorates owing different allegiance.

The duties prescribed for the first inspectors were set down quite clearly:

> to assist in organising schools provided by the Board; to examine the scholars and pupil teachers in the subjects taught in each school; to ascertain whether the books and apparatus are in good condition and whether the log-books and registers are duly kept; to make a report to the Board upon the efficiency of each school, and to carry out the general instructions of the Board.

The wisdom of choosing Heads of elementary schools as inspectors was emphasised in a motion of 15th May, 1872:

> that an examination of candidates (for pupil-teachers) be held by one of the Board's inspectors, and that the Board agree to pay the advanced salary in the case of each candidate who passes, until such time as he, or she, passes the examination of the government inspector and can duly claim the grant under the scale.

Advisory duties devolved quickly upon the Board inspectors; for example, only a month later, their advice was sought about wall-maps in schools (with comment to be made upon the existing ones in use). Their existence contributed substantially to the Board's pre-disposition to make suggestions to teachers rather than issue directives in such matters as the use of appropriate text-books or copy-books (for hand-writing): only a bare minimum of methodology was prescribed. Their reports, along with those of Her Majesty's inspectors, were laid before the School Management Committee.

Lest it be thought London School Board was the only pioneer in this field, it may serve to quote a big 'provincial' Board like Sheffield. After 20 years' sound teaching experience, B. D. Davis was appointed 'General Superintendent' to this Board in March 1872. His main task was 'thorough and systematic inspection of schools', which he subsequently enlarged upon for the benefit of his Committee as follows:

1. to make personal enquiries in all cases of absence from duty on the part of head teachers, assistants, and pupil-teachers.

2. to make a point of visiting all the Board schools at least once in each month, not later than ten minutes to nine o'clock: in the summer months not later than ten minutes to eight in the mornings. Cases of absence or late attendance to be noted. During the winter months, the schools are to be visited occasionally while instruction is being given to the pupil teachers.

3. to examine the scholars of all schools once a year, individually, on the same plan as that adopted by Her Majesty's Inspectors, and report thereon to the Board.

4. to examine all the scholars in Biblical knowledge according to the syllabus approved by the Board.

5. to fill up for the Committee of Council on Education balance sheets of the income and expenditure of each department of the schools, which at present number thirty, and will gradually increase: to test the accuracy of the returns respecting the attendances of children entered on examination schedules, and to ascertain the correctness of the entries made by teachers on (Government) Form IX.

6. to apprentice pupil teachers, calculate the amount of payment due to candidates and make a list of salaries (monthly) due to pupil teachers.

7. to call at the office at 12.30 each day to meet candidates for appointment as pupil teachers, and see to any matters requiring special attention.

8. to hold quarterly examinations of candidates and pupil

teachers. This is a most important and at the same time laborious part of my employment. At every examination there may be pupil teachers in each quarter of each year of apprenticeship. In order that the work involved in the preparation of the questions and examination of the papers may be more clearly seen, allow me to submit to you a copy of one of the papers. . . . The work of compiling and arranging these questions will require considerable diligence and careful thought, and the subsequent task of reading and valuing each paper, and tabulating and reporting on the whole, will demand for its efficient performance a large amount of time, which can only be secured after my usual day's work is over. . . . Other duties engage me during the morning of Saturday, such as the calls of teachers on matters connected with their work, of candidates and their parents, and of many other persons interested in the operation of the schools of the Board.

As a result of this analysis of all he did, the Board soon felt able to put up his salary from £200 to £250 a year![1]

Perhaps the greatest compliment that could be paid to the work of these early organising inspectors was the relative speed with which other Boards came to appoint them—Nottingham, Newcastle, Norwich and Hull, for example. Even in cases where the idea was discussed but rejected (e.g. in Brighton), the value of the work done by these inspectors elsewhere was not in question. Meantime, as the expansion of activities by the bigger, more progressive boards continued, so the number of their general inspectors grew. Thus, in London, by 1886 there were five inspectors, whose duties were set down as follows:

(*a*) to report week by week to the School Management Committee the results of observations made during their visits to schools, upon the state of the schools, particularly as to the tone, efficiency of staff, and the intelligence of the methods employed in teaching.

(*b*) to give special attention to the Scripture instruction and to object lessons, and also generally to the weaker schools.

(*c*) to report upon matters referred to them by the School Management Committee, and to thoroughly examine and report upon such schools as the Committee shall from time to time direct.

(*d*) to visit the pupil-teachers' schools and to superintend the general examinations held under the authority of the Board for scholarships, for Scripture prizes, and so on.

[1] Sheffield School Board Minute, 28th Oct. 1875.

Board Inspectors and Organisers

The Sub-Committee further recommend that a reference be forwarded to the Stock-taking and Requisition Sub-Committee, asking them if they could devise some means by which the Board inspectors could be relieved from the duty of examining and checking requisitions.

This plea still has relevance today for some local inspectors, though properly interpreted, it can be turned to mutual advantage of school and local authority.

The qualms of the Board inspectors, however, were hardly allayed in view of the steadily increasing number of schools to be visited, and a letter by one of them, R. McWilliam, to the Board touched off the whole question again, for, on 27th October, 1890, a special sub-committee met to consider his letter and its implications. For some six years past, from 1880 to 1886, the inspectors had shared responsibility for inspection of the Board's industrial schools;[1] then, at the end of 1886, G. Ricks had been requested by the Board to be solely responsible. Inevitably, he had to ask his four colleagues for some relief from his ordinary duties, and, though hurt by the lack of consultation beforehand, they had shared out his schools among them. McWilliam now asked if the industrial schools could be shared among the five inspectors again, believing that these (relatively) country schools could be inspected at 'slack times of the year . . . when no Committees are sitting and there are no references to attend to'. The duties of Board inspectors were, therefore, asked for under specific headings, the replies, perhaps, expressing silently the burden carried by them. Quite apart from the long hours worked, the five inspectors had an impossible task to examine effectively an average of 87 schools a year. For purposes of comparison, T. G. Wright, sole inspector to the Bristol School Board, had only 35 schools to inspect; W. Brook, Hull's 'organising teacher and inspector', had the coverage of 25 schools: it is not surprising, therefore, that the London School Board appointed a sixth inspector.

It is important to realise that the Board inspector's function stemmed from the School Management Committee's duty to 'consider and report' upon matters referred to it by the Board.

[1] For a brief comment on the nature of these schools *v.* Cross Commission *Final Report*, p. 104.

101

H

Unlike the London Technical Education Board, which could make its own executive decisions without first reporting back to the L.C.C., this School Board committee could not act of its own accord, emergencies excepted. What it wanted from its inspector(s) was not a treatise upon matters referred but a definite recommendation from which executive decision could flow when confirmed by the Board. In this context, some six phases of work undertaken by the Board inspectors may be discerned, all of which were likely to grow in size and importance.

The prime duty was that of visiting, inspecting or examining, and reporting on every school department under the Board at least once a year. It was largely objective in character at first; and the 'periodical and systematic examination' applied to the children: on their standards of attainment the class teachers were judged. Reports upon teachers individually, or departments and schools as a whole, had to be laid before the School Management Committee, and inspectors often preferred to be present at the Committee meetings when these reports were discussed. In view of twentieth century developments, the early relationship of the Board inspector's report to Her Majesty's Inspector's report is noteworthy. Both reports were made annually, usually with a six-month interval between them. Her Majesty's Inspector's report did not recommend any executive action to the Board: teachers were the servants of the Board which paid their salaries, and, very properly, it was left to the Board to make such decisions. Her Majesty's Inspectors reported to the Education Department which issued their reports as from itself. Its power to influence boards lay in the right it could and did exercise to withhold government grant-in-aid. The value of Board inspectors having been Heads of schools was thus enhanced, for they understood perfectly the intricacies of the Government Code. The Rev. Canon Warburton, a veteran Her Majesty's Inspector, when he gave evidence before the Cross Commission, observed that his colleagues might know little about schools in the first year of their appointment, whereas Board inspectors did: he added:

> teachers do not like examination by ex-teachers, but the latter know where to find weak spots better than inspectors.

This is of importance when one considers the attitude of

inspectors of school boards towards examinations at the turn of the century; but it should also be stressed that, from the first, Board inspectors' work went far beyond preparation for Her Majesty's Inspector's annual examination: 'to visit the schools (of the Board) at different times, and to see that the work is carried on in accordance with the Code and also in accordance with the regulations of the Board' was only a beginning. These inspectors knew that any inspector who visits a school solely for the purpose of making a written report upon it, and irrespective of the wishes of the Head, can never be truly welcome in a school, no matter how much notice he gives beforehand of such intention. Despite their executive connotations therefore, Board inspectors were fortunate that they had many other reasons for visits to schools. A few consecutive examples, culled from the Manchester School Board Minutes between 12th August, 1875 and 22nd June, 1876, are as follows: to see individual teachers at work; to visit particular teachers in day schools with a view to their selection for evening school work; to draw up lists of possible requirements for evening schools; to check attendance and punctuality of teachers and pupils; periodically to call over class-registers; to accept pupils for 'night school' one evening a week (at a charge of 1d. a night); to assess candidates for teaching posts under the Board, sometimes going outside the Board's own area; to draw up promotion lists based upon personal assessment of the class-room ability of teachers being considered for the posts of principal (head) teacher. The versatility of the Board inspector has, perhaps, never been fully appreciated; nor has his continuous need for great flexibility of mind. Every aspect of school life had to be scanned; bricks and mortar, heating, lighting, accommodation, ventilation, equipment, stock and stock-books, apparatus, stationery, books, cloakroom facilities, outside offices. Time-tables had to be scrutinised, as had class-registers, fee-books and teachers' time-books. Matters of health (e.g. defective eye-sight in children) were brought to his attention by heads for appropriate action by him. To be a highly-qualified 'snooper' at the beginning of a visit and then become an adviser upon questions of staffing, temporary or otherwise, help class-teachers, or perhaps investigate one of the endless cornucopia of complaints against teachers, made tremendous demands upon any inspector, not only in time but also in personality. That several of them broke down intermittently was hardly surprising; that they should multiply in number was inevitable.

One particular phase of Board inspectors' work was related to specialist examinations, both in school and 'extra-murally', as it were. Thus, London Board inspectors examined children for the prizes offered by the Religious Society and Mr. Francis Peek, and for prizes in animal physiology offered by the National Health Society. Ricks actually conducted a needlework examination in early days (being allowed to co-opt examiners, however!). He was also made responsible for selecting children's drawings for an Art Exhibition. Liverpool Board inspectors severally conducted an examination in animal physiology for girls, the syllabus being Mrs. C. M. Buckton's 'Health in the Home', Lectures I to XIV; an examination of the boys of the training ship *Indefatigable*; and one of the children of an orphan asylum. Kingston-upon-Hull School Board delegated to its inspector, William Brook, the task of examining for the award of Bailey scholarships at the Sir Henry Cooper School. In Leeds, a list of candidates in order of merit was laid before the Committee, together with a list of those who, in the opinion of the Superintendent, were educationally fitted to take up the scholarships at the Central Higher Grade School.

The concern of Board inspectors with the examination in Religious Instruction varied greatly. Some Boards (Bristol, for example) conducted the examination through their own members who were frequently well qualified for the task. Sometimes a single 'clerical gentleman' was employed and paid, as in the case of Bradford. Nottingham provided a munificent example of no fewer than 27 'examiners' making written reports upon the Scripture Knowledge of the children in the local Board schools: all denominations were included except Roman Catholics. If the Board inspector was at all qualified to inspect in the subject, he was sometimes assigned the duty initially, as in the case of Sheffield's B. D. Davis and W. Jenkins. Leeds provided an example of having its inspector make arrangements for carrying out the examination, thereafter collating and reporting on the results. London School Board inspectors not only conducted the examination and marked the scripts, but inspected the teaching as well, though latterly this became once in every three years only. Smaller boards, of course, more usually relied upon the services of the local expert(s), usually in Holy Orders, as in the case of Fleetwood or Oldham. A handful of boards did not require any examiner, for no religious instruction at all was allowed. It should be emphasised that no Board inspector drew up an 'Agreed Syllabus' for use in board schools; perhaps the closest approximation to it was when Miss Bailey, inspectress under the Liverpool Board, submitted, by request, a 'Proposed Course of Lessons in Religious Knowledge in Infant Schools' in November, 1875. In another case, London Board's School Management Committee, by a Minute of 27th June, 1894, instructed two inspectors, Nickall and McWilliam, to meet heads of Jewish schools with a view to helping draft an appropriately modified scheme of Religious Instruction. One other type of examination may be mentioned: Leeds School Board, fearing, with some justification, that children committed to the denominational industrial schools outside the Board's administrative fiat might have their educational training sub-ordinated to 'turning of their labour to profitable account in the finances of the managers', resolved that an examination of every child towards whose maintenance the Board contributed be held every year by the Board's own Superintendent.

One increasingly important phase of Board inspectors' work was in connection with supervision of pupil-teachers. The link between training and inspecting of teachers was not accidental. In Liverpool, a dual appointment was instituted of Board inspectress and Principal of the (girls) pupil-teacher centre. Aston School Board inspector, H. C. Buckley, was principal of the pupil-teacher centre as well. In Bristol, T. G. Wright was appointed Superintendent of the Pupil-Teachers' Instruction Centre Classes. Board inspectors' administrative experience was useful in other ways, such as drawing up the form of agreement to be used by managers of board schools when engaging stipendiary monitors. Quarterly or half-yearly examinations of pupil-teachers by Board inspectors were accepted practice, though on 25th January, 1884, the Bristol Board resolved that the special half-yearly examination by T. G. Wright should be discontinued: instead, his half-yearly report on pupil-teachers was to be 'founded on the papers worked by them at the periodical examination conducted by the Bristol and Bath Association'. Examples also occur of additional

'occasional' examinations; Edwin Foster of Liverpool conducted such a one in grammar in Liverpool Board Schools in
February, 1880. In Nottingham, pupil-teachers underwent a
General Knowledge Test; if this sounds harsh, the answer
lies in the comment of W. J. Abel in his first report to the School
Management Committee, 1st June, 1882: they were 'lament-
ably deficient in knowledge and teaching ability'. This was not
peculiar to Nottingham. The Minutes of a Sub-Committee of
Leeds School Board, 24th June, 1889, recorded that:

> in considering what steps could be taken to improve the work of
> the pupil-teachers, both Superintendents expressed the opinion
> that it would be desirable to deal more rigorously with pupil-
> teachers who are found to be intellectually deficient, and to
> take a new departure by closing the engagement of several on
> this ground.

Instances of a similar kind can be found in the Minutes of the
School Boards of Birmingham and Liverpool. On the other
hand, examples can be quoted of Board inspectors' genuine
concern over the interests of the pupil-teachers: discovery of
a Head's failure to fill in full particulars in a pupil-teacher's
journal of instruction, or checking of a Head shuffling off
complete responsibility for his own class on to the pupil-
teacher. Bristol School Board instructed its inspector to make a
special investigation into the health of its pupil-teachers. One
of William Breakwell's duties, as Inspector to the Newcastle
Board, was 'to superintend the moral and technical training
of the pupil-teachers, and to personally interest himself in their
welfare'. In short, the Board inspectors had a more continuous
contact with the pupil-teacher than ever Her Majesty's
Inspector could have: they needed every bit of such a contact,
for, as the Instructions to Inspectors of 1878 pointed out:

> My Lords have reason to believe that sufficient care has not been
> bestowed upon (them) in many cases, either by managers or
> teachers.

Other duties devolving upon Board inspectors were those of
advising the appropriate Committee upon questions of in-
service promotion of teachers, and also of writing adverse
reports on individual teachers. Such decisions of a comparative nature called for tact, discretion and a wisdom born of

experience of the job, for boards wanted definiteness from their inspectors. London had an eight point grading scale, and inquiry was called for in the case of teachers in the bottom three grades. A year's service emolument could be withheld by the Board as a result of their inspector's adverse reports; the ultimate executive act of dismissal of a teacher for incompetence would also seem to have been frequently threatened if far less frequently implemented. The usual reason was alleged lack of class-control; perhaps hardly surprising in view of the very large classes of 60 to 80 children, amongst whom at least a proportion had not come willingly to school. Finally, the Board inspector was a sort of liaison officer between the Board and the school managers of individual schools:

> the action of these local bodies is harmonised with that of the School Management Committee of the Board through the aid of the Board's inspector, who attends, as technical adviser, all meetings of the local bodies of Managers at which head or assistant teachers are appointed. He is consequently in frequent intercourse with these bodies and is consulted on other questions, and as he also attends the meetings of the School Management Committee of the Board, he contributes materially to keep the two authorities responsible for a school in touch with one another.

The restless energy of these more progressive Boards showed no sign of flagging towards the close of the century; if anything, the opposite would be true. In the all-round growth of functions by the Boards, their organising inspectors participated, and true to form, the Boards re-defined their duties. Thus, the 1893 Regulations for the Management of Schools under the Norwich Board included (as an Appendix) an impossibly long list for one inspector. Obviously, he would have them all to do at some time or other, but would also have to draw up his own list of priorities. Where additional inspectors were appointed, within a suitable hierarchy of office, the fresh 'Scheme of Work' for them again illustrates that blend of the administrative with activities more truly 'creative of development'. Bristol School Board's scheme for its two inspectors, as re-drafted December, 1898, is such an example. Manchester School Board had three inspectors by 1899, each in charge of a division. Their 'Instructions', as adopted by the Board in May of that year, read thus:

Board Inspectors and Organisers

It shall be the duty of each Inspector in his own Division:

1. To carefully ensure the carrying out of the rules of the Education Department and the regulations of the Board in the schools.

2. Where necessary to direct Principal Teachers in the better organisation of their Schools.

3. To see that the School Staffs are efficiently maintained in accordance with the rules of the Board, and that an adequate supply of Pupil Teachers is kept up in each School. The moving of Assistant Teachers from School to School to be as far as possible avoided. All appointments and changes in the Schools to be first approved by the Managers.

4. To examine once a year in Religious Knowledge, and to inspect periodically, not less than once in three months, each School Department. At these inspections, Organisation, Method, and General Work to be observed, and at the direction of the Inspector, classes examined. Close supervision to be exercised with regard to the Principal Teachers' periodical Examinations and their results. The papers and schedules marked and copy of tests applied to be forwarded to the Inspector of the Division. The Schools in which there is weakness of instruction to be reported to the School Managers in the ninth month, and the inspectors, if so instructed shall hold a special Examination of such Schools before the close of the year. Reports of these Examinations and Inspections, also an Annual Report on each Department, to be submitted to the School Managers. The Clerk of the Board to be supplied with the dates of the Examinations, in advance, in order that the same may appear on the Monthly Remembrancer for the information of the Members of the Board. Should further Examinations be required they will be ordered by the School Managers.

5. To check all Class Registers four times a year, and make the necessary entries in the Log Book.

6. To visit the Schools during the times set apart for the instruction of the children in Religious Knowledge, and to ensure the Pupil Teachers have practice in Teaching.

7. To carefully check requisitions from the Day Schools for Books, Apparatus and Stationery; write off in the Stock and Stores Book all Stock past use; and cause unused Stock to be returned to the Stores.

8. To examine each year the Pupil Teachers of the Board in Religious and Secular Knowledge, and report thereon to the School Managers.

9. To conduct annually an Entrance Examination for Pupil Teachers, and at such other times as may be found necessary.

10. To report the absence from duty of any Teacher in the employ of the Board.

11. To attend the Government Examinations of the Day Schools.

12. To advise the Clerk of any matter requiring attention in the Schools, and to perform any other duty required by the Schools Managers.

Each Inspector shall keep a Staff Book for his Division, showing the Teachers of all grades employed in each School Department, with their respective salaries, dates of appointment, qualifications, and the average number of children in attendance for the preceding year. The Staff Book shall be corrected where necessary, from week to week, and shall be laid before the School Managers at each ordinary Meeting.

Each Inspector shall make a Weekly Return of his work for the information of the School Managers. A similar Return to be made by each Inspector's Assistant.

In order that the Inspectors may spend as much time as possible in the Schools, they shall be relieved from attendance at Committee Meetings, except when required by the Managers, and from office work during School hours.

All Reports and Returns for the School Managers shall be delivered by the Inspectors to the Clerk each Saturday; the instructions of the Managers shall be communicated to them by the Clerk; and the Inspectors shall act under his direction.

On the close of payment by results, by 1895, Board inspectors were actively concerned with the drawing up of schemes of work by heads of schools, and they had to approve such schemes. School administration was already with heads of schools, who were required to keep at least eight separate returns-books, to be available for inspection at any time. In the case of a young head (often internally promoted and even supported by the particular inspector) who better to tender advice of an authoritative kind than an inspector? This inspector's examination of his school was also diagnostic in that it helped staff tighten up the looser joints before the annual inspection from Her Majesty's Inspector. Women heads, too, could derive a deal of inspiration and help from inspectresses and inspectors who, once upon a time, had been heads of large schools themselves and had clearly handled similar problems with success. They knew thoroughly what the changing Board policy entailed in relation to a changing government 'Code': they could interpret it and explain how it operated in schools.

The link with advice was already being forged because inspectors were running courses for teachers on such things as 'school organisation'; Bradford's Board inspectors set a good example here. Particular features of school work, such as object lessons, had no terrors for the inspector who had himself taught them. The danger, in fact, was that he lost contact with a changing educational climate: when one has made a success of something in school, there is ever-present the failure to realise that it might date; and the conditions of work of the Board inspector sometimes made for 'immobilisme' because he was constantly giving out and never taking in—at any rate, not taking in proportionately. It had yet to be realised that a primary function of any inspection system is to adjust the old to the new all the time.

Besides using the inspectors to issue instructions of a general type to teachers, various Boards also appointed organisers for special subjects; the duties of the latter frequently appeared to overlap those of the inspectors, but the big difference was that the organiser was expected to teach his special subject or group of subjects. Neither school board nor government inspector was expected to do this: their role was that of the catechist: teachers, pupil-teachers and children were their catechumens. It was no part of Her Majesty's inspector's task to do any demonstration-teaching, not even to the pupil-teachers whom he examined annually in proficiency. This was not necessarily because he was not capable of so doing, as some critics alleged: it was part of a large body of public opinion that asseverated 'it is not expedient or safe for government to act as the teacher'; it grew out of that deep-rooted suspicion of any 'extension of the government patronage and influence'. To have done 'a method', in fact, might even be considered a disqualification for H.M. inspectorate. The expansion of organising teachers under the bigger boards had a three-fold inspiration:

(*a*) to raise the standards of subject teaching in schools, thereby earning larger government grants and proportionately keeping down the size of the rate-precept. With the substitution of a block grant for a percentage grant based on numbers of passes, this particular incentive to appoint organisers became null and void. It was just as well, for the dangerous opportunity presented itself so easily of organisers' work having a cash-nexus value only.

(*b*) more altruistically, to help train the 'general subjects' teacher in a particular subject, showing how by personal example, then watching teachers teach, correcting faults, improving technique, adapting to particular age-ranges, etc. Such work might begin in the form of peripatetic teaching, but it usually ended in supervising the work of other teachers. It extended to both the newly appointed teacher in his first school and to the more established teacher in search (or in need) of refresher training. Conceptions of how certain subjects should be taught changed considerably in the last quarter of the century; and the organising teacher had a very strong part to play as adjuster to the newer ideas and their putting into practice: if he himself could not adjust, his services might be dispensed with.

(*c*) when added together, to help achieve in a subject, or group of subjects, that ideal scheme of work which, mirage-like, floated in and out of successive boards' collective minds.

Board Minutes are frequently illuminated by progressive thinking of a very high order: evening school teaching, for example, or teaching of physically and mentally handicapped children, beautifying of schools, vocational teaching in higher grade schools, and so on. More often than not, the Boards turned to their organisers for help in putting these ideals into practice.

Appointments of this kind naturally varied from Board to Board: the subjects most frequently committed to the care of such organising-inspectors were Needlework, Cookery, Laundry-work, Drawing, Singing, Science and Physical Education. Quite appropriately, a number of these organisers were women. The part played by these early organisers in pioneering educational advance was, then, considerable. In-service education for teachers was in its infancy, though by no means new in conception: other forms were developing, like the refresher courses in Summer run by the Science and Art Department. The organiser, in the main, was not a powerful original thinker—his previous career and the very nature of organising work militated against that—but he had to have the ability to translate current trends into terms acceptable to teachers. Relationships with local inspectors were, perhaps purposely, left undefined. A report on the work of two London instructors of the blind by T. M. Williams in 1879 might indicate that general inspectors supervised the work of specialist organisers on occasion, but there is little evidence fully to substantiate such a statement. From time to time, however, examples of movement from organising work into more patently inspectorial work do occur. Thus, Mrs. Roadknight, of the Nottingham Board, moved from a 'specialist staff' appointment in kindergarten work to become inspectress; in Sheffield, C. T. Gould, a peripatetic Science Demonstrator became Assistant Inspector of Schools also under the School Board in 1899. Such examples might indicate a ladder of promotion from one to the other. The early organiser was essentially an 'A' teacher: had he been less, the Cross Commission certainly would have been less emphatic in its assertion that by their use in voluntary schools, particularly to teach cookery and elementary science, such schools might

> not only strengthen their position financially but also improve the quality of the education given in them.

The Education Department itself was not ignorant of their worth: some Her Majesty's Inspectors had even watched them at work. The Instructions to Inspectors of 1882 specially drew Her Majesty's Inspectors' attention to the fact that:

> You will often find that these subjects are most thoroughly taught when a special teacher is engaged by a group of schools to give instruction in such subjects once or twice a week, his teaching being supplemented in the interval by the teachers of the school.

By 1899 the Education Department's Code of Regulations for Day Schools could include 'Organising Teacher' in its list of definitions, as one 'who either inspects schools and advises managers and teachers in view of the inspector's visit, or instructs and examines teachers in any special subjects or educational methods, or instructs and examines candidates for the office of pupil teacher.'

The bigger school boards have, perhaps, never received credit for their development of the organising principle as part of an advisory service for teachers, sometimes in the teeth of opposition comment about luxury staff and unnecessary expenditure. Provincial Boards like Liverpool, Bradford, Sheffield, Nottingham, Leeds, all did valuable pioneer work in formulating a tradition of education for physically and mentally handicapped children; and all used organising teachers at some stage, as indeed some Authorities do today. Nottingham and Leeds had suitably encouraged swimming instruction in a similar fashion. Boards were quite ready, it seemed, to encourage their organisers to move about and see what other boards were doing in their own 'specialism'. London allowed its Superintendent of Instruction of blind and deaf children to visit other boards and see what was being done: Oldham sent its drill sergeant to Bolton and Manchester to see work there and report upon it, a very good memorandum being subsequently presented by him: Nottingham sent its newly appointed instructress of a class for defective children, Mrs. E. Thornton, to Leicester to see the work already being done there: Boards, like these, in fact, had anticipated almost every improvement under the various Government codes.

Chapter Ten

HER MAJESTY'S INSPECTOR AND OTHER INSPECTORS

IN spite of such worthy efforts on the part of the Boards, when institutions in this country have acquired the dignity of long-standing, younger, would-be rivals rarely escape initially detrimental comparison; at least, it would appear so in the case of these school board inspectorates born in the shadow of an almighty government inspector who seemed to 'bestride the narrow world like a colossus'. Children in schools were trained to tremble at his name; and much evidence before the Cross Commission served to indicate his 'failure to show as much consideration for and sympathy with the managers, teachers and children as might be expected'. Many teachers were fearful of him, muting their own criticism or complaint for fear of reprisals in the annual examination, or, knowing how school boards relied upon him for reporting and for recommending of teachers on more personal lines, accepting from him much that hardly conformed with the spirit of the Instructions to Inspectors of 1878, that 'it is no part of an inspector's duty either to find fault with or to reprove a teacher'. In law, their function fundamentally remained the same as before, 'to assess the amount which the Treasury should pay; and this was done by a rapid examination of every child above seven years of age who had attended 250 times in the school year'. In practice, however, their influence was infinitely wider. Canon W. P. Warburton, a doughty Her Majesty's Inspector, stated openly to the Cross Commission that the inspector's report largely determined the success and reputation of a teacher. The prescribed duties of managers before the advent of Her Majesty's Inspector also helped to build up this 'mystique' surrounding him. A form of annual return, and examination schedules had to be duly completed beforehand and available for his inspection, along with the register, log-book, portfolio and accounts; the summary of his report, as soon as it was communicated to the managers, as well as any remarks made by the Education Department had to be copied verbatim into the log-book and signed by the correspondent of the managers. Yet again, he had to be notified of usual or special holidays, any closure for sickness, local elections and such occasions as the diocesan inspection, under a fine of £1 for failure in these matters by the Managers. He might not inspect religious instruction but he could ask to see the last report of the examination. School boards, likewise, had to keep him carefully informed, copies of Board Minutes and any maps or embryo development plans being forwarded to him regularly. The mercurial Chairman of London School Board in 1887, the Rev. J. R. Diggle, was quite ready to admit that, proud as his Board was of its own inspectors, they were nonetheless inferior both as inspectors and (in their exterior manner and bearing) as persons to the government inspectors. Professor Huxley had foreseen the dangers in just such a position when he appealed from the very first for Board inspectors to be

> of equal rank and authority with the government inspectors. They (the Board) did not want mere agents or reporters, or commercial gentlemen who would have no weight or authority with the public.

Other difficulties stemmed from this position in which Board inspectors found themselves, for, whatever personal dignity or creative thinking might be theirs, their 'genius was rebuked' in the risk of its being considered but pale imitation of what Her Majesty's Inspectors had said, or verging on criticism of an unwelcome kind of the Education Department: into this latter category came their criticism of payment by results. For Board inspectors were the servants of some rate-sensitive councillors whose dream was ever lower costs with better results; so that evidence of local inspectors' work was very useful information for the hustings about trienniel election time (and invaluable to inspectors asking for salary upgrading). One School Board went so far as to dismiss teachers not earning over a certain amount of government grant! Another dismissed a teacher after a poor report from Her Majesty's inspector. Managing elementary education was like farming: if a benevolent government paid for certain crops, then those crops only were grown. Fresh ideas or new ventures meant outlay of money: but only examination results brought it in, in the form of increased government grant. Some local inspectors, then, fell into the trap Her Majesty's inspectors had been driven into, of being merely agents of a restrictive administrative policy.

From evidence given before the Cross Commission it was made abundantly clear that many responsible educationists believed that the Board inspections were frequently of more value than inspections by Her Majesty's Inspectors.

Asked what difference there was between him and Her Majesty's Inspector, T. G. Wright, of the Bristol School Board, pointed out:

> I would give and I do give greater allowance for the difficulties of the school.

From the Leeds Board, Wesley Lee's evidence was similar in tenor:

> *Q.38,116d.* What is the necessity of having board and voluntary school inspectors: why should not Her Majesty's inspector give all the information that is required?—Her Majesty's inspector cannot enter into those relationships with managers of a friendly and suggestive kind that the school superintendent would find it in his power to do.

> *Q.38,116e.* Does not Her Majesty's inspector give all the information as to proficiency and efficiency of a school that could be required both for the use of the board as well as for the Department?—Yes, but I think that a school superintendent attending a school in the interest of improvement in the character of the education and so forth is in a different position quite from that of Her Majesty's inspector who is there as a critic, and who has the means of testing the attainments of the children with a view to the grant.

> *Q.38,116f.* Is it not the fact that Her Majesty's inspector reports of passes in particular examinations while the board inspector gives a more general report as to the conduct and efficiency of the school?—It is so.

They thus had a width of insight into the educational life of a school unhappily denied at the time to Her Majesty's inspector. Again, as both 'the acting manager and organising master' in some areas, their points of common interest with teachers were more numerous and more consecutive than the government inspector's. The need for such an inspector at local level was further enhanced by the seemingly 'base usage' to which government inspectors had descended. A. P. Graves draws a picture of a complete inspectorial slide-rule under payment by results when he estimated (in his evidence before the Cross Commission) that no fewer than 46,000 Manchester school-children had been 'presented' to him in one year. Full dress parades of this kind were the last way anyone could hope to assess a school's educational life. The full impact of Revised Code procedure upon Her Majesty's inspectors has, perhaps, never been fully stated; but it may be read in the Minutes of School Board meetings. It was not merely a case of the long criticised variation of standards: that was inevitable in a rapidly expanding inspectorate, and the wonder is that there was not more. But even as late as 1882, the Instructions to Inspectors left them with no simple task of assessment, as the following excerpt may show:

Examination and Inspection of Schools Generally

Schools not entitled to inherit grant.
30. From bad or unsatisfactory schools it is manifest that the merit grant should be withheld altogether. The cases which you dealt with under Article 32b of the former Code, and in which a deduction of one or more tenths was made for 'faults of instruction or discipline', or in which you have not recommended the grant for 'discipline and organisation' would, of course, fall under this head. Other cases will occur which are not serious enough to justify actual deduction; but in which you observe that there is a preponderance of indifferent passes, preventible disorder, dullness, or irregularity; or that the teacher is satisfied with a low standard of duty. To schools of this class no merit grant should be awarded. But a school of

Fair schools.
humble aims, which passes only a moderately successful examination, may properly be designated 'Fair', if its work is conscientiously done, and is sound as far as it goes; and if the school is free from any conspicuous faults.

117

Good schools. 31. Generally, a school may be expected to receive the mark 'Good', when both the number and the quality of the passes are satisfactory; when the scholars pass well in such class subjects as are taken up; and when the organisation, discipline, tone and general intelligence are such as to deserve commendation.

Excellent schools. 32. It is the intention of their Lordships that the mark 'Excellent' should be reserved for cases of distinguished merit. A thoroughly good school in favourable conditions is characterised by cheerful and yet exact discipline, maintained without harshness and without noisy demonstration of authority. Its premises are cleanly and well-ordered; its time-table provides a proper variety of mental employment and of physical exercise; its organisation is such as to distribute the teaching power judiciously, and to secure for every scholar—whether he is likely to bring credit to the school by examination or not—a fair share of instruction and of attention. The teaching is animated and interesting, and yet thorough and accurate. The reading is fluent, careful and expressive, and the children are helped by questioning and explanation to follow the meaning of what they read. Arithmetic is so taught as to enable the scholars not only to obtain correct answers to sums, but also to understand the reason of the processes employed. If higher subjects are attempted, the lessons are not confined to memory work and to the learning of technical terms, but are designed to give a clear knowledge of facts, and to train the learner in the practice of thinking and observing. Besides fulfilling these conditions, which are all expressed or implied in the Code, such a school seeks by other means to be of service to the children who attend it. It provides for the upper classes a regular system of home-exercises, and arrangements for correcting them expeditiously and thoroughly. Where circumstances permit, it has also its lending library, its savings bank, and an orderly collection of simple objects and apparatus adapted to illustrate the school lessons, and formed in part by the co-operation of the scholars themselves. Above all, its teaching and discipline are such as to exert a right influence on the manners, the conduct, and the character of the children, to awaken in them a love of reading, and such an interest in their own mental improvement as may reasonably be expected to last beyond the period of school life. Your attention may be usefully recalled to the following extract from the Code of 1881:—

'The Inspector will bear in mind, in reporting on the organisation and discipline, the results of any visits without notice made in the course of the school year; and will not interfere with any method of organisation adopted in a training college under inspection if it is satisfactorily carried out in the school. To meet the requirements respecting discipline, the managers and teachers will be expected to satisfy the Inspector that all reasonable care is taken, in the ordinary management of the school, to bring up the children in habits of punctuality, of good manners and language, of cleanliness and neatness, and also to impress upon the children the importance of cheerful obedience to duty, of consideration and respect for others, and of honour and truthfulness in word and act.'

Excellent as this is, as long as graded payment on it continued, (and even some time after) Her Majesty's Inspectors appeared to arouse the suspicions of teachers and managers alike. It is an odd, but fascinating, inversion that, seemingly lacking so much in so many ways, visits to schools by Board inspectors were for a time more in line with Kay-Shuttleworth's idea of what good school inspection should entail than were those of his own 'brain-children', Her Majesty's inspectors. A. P. Graves' comments would have horrified him:

(Our) occasional visits now are what you may also call spying visits; at least they are visits without notice; they are visits paid in order to make sure that the registers are being properly kept and the schools worked according to the time-table and that the managers have carried out the instructions which they were called upon to carry out in a previous report. But I should like to see visits of a friendly character, of an organising character, made which are now rarely, if ever, made.

It may well be that H.M. Inspector suffered unjust criticism through well-meaning efforts to break through the barriers; trick questions, for instance, could be fun with children who knew an inspector well, but this was pre-requisite, for without it both he and the children could be—and are—made uncomfortable and the teacher discomfited. Freed from this incubus of having to be detective-cum-accountant, turning everything observed into a balance sheet, Board inspectors, by contrast, were able to examine, not every child, but 'a sufficient proportion of each class in each subject to be able to assess the value of the education that is being given'.

Again, they had a headquarters close at hand and visible to teachers; and conditions of service of some Board inspectors included their being available on Saturday mornings 'at the office' for such interviews as were requested. The handicap of having no such local habitation was a very real one to government inspectors. Assistant teachers saw him come and saw him go, but they never established such continuous contact that they could ask advice of him—the very worst basis, therefore, one might suppose, for advice ever being accepted. There was, however, one danger to which Board inspectors alone were exposed. For obvious reasons, their work never brought them into contact with voluntary schools, and the stimulus that comes from comparative study was so denied them. Worse still, the exacting nature of their continuous contact with teachers in their own area militated against cross-visiting with other areas, even assuming the Board agreed to its officials having time off of this kind; development of the broader vision was thus inhibited and the risk of parochial outlook intensified.

In spite of all this, however, it was the Board inspector who was regarded as the teachers' friend (so far as any inspector ever can be), the government inspector as their foe. The National Union of Teachers, in its memorandum submitted to the Bryce Commission in 1894, neatly summed up both the differences between the two groups of inspectors and the value of their work in schools:

> The chief factor in any inspection is the personality of the inspector. An inspector of schools should not only be just, cautious, and accurate in his habit of mind; he should also be sympathetic, genial, courteous, and a lover of children. Above all, he should possess practical knowledge of teaching and should have had

experience of the difficulties alike of teacher and taught. Now experience has shown that whereas the school boards, when appointing advisory inspectors as their eyes and ears in the schools have almost invariably chosen men experienced in the difficulties of the work, and practised in the art of teaching, my Lords of the Education Department on the other hand have almost invariably appointed as Her Majesty's Inspectors of Schools men who lack such experience and practice. And whilst the work of inspectors appointed by school boards has been generally helpful to the schools, the work of many of the inspectors appointed by the Education Department has, to a very serious extent, been harmful to the schools. It follows, therefore, in the opinion of the Union, that the appointment of inspectors of secondary schools would more wisely rest with the local authority than with a Minister and a bureau.

Government and Board inspectors were not, of course, the only ones in the field; some of the voluntary bodies still cherished an active inspectorate, though, between 1870 and 1900, several changes took place. By far the most compactly organised inspectorial system among the voluntary societies, though not the biggest, was that of the British Society, and in 1871 its annual report stated:

> the creation of a body of official inspectors, upon whose report the pecuniary success of the school mainly depends, rendered the regular visitation of schools less necessary. The new arrangement, by which each inspector is to take charge of the schools of a limited district and supervise the education within an area small enough to make him feel personally responsible for its condition will reduce the necessity to a minimum . . .
>
> If the School Boards should appoint for their own distrcts or (by combination) for several districts together, school agents to advise with managers, guide young teachers, explain terse or uncertain regulations, hold public meetings or conduct examinations, this branch of work may decrease. At present, it seems more necessary than ever.

This activity was to be a final flourish. The four agent-inspectors of that year (2 in Wales, 1 in the metropolitan area and 1 in the 'provincial' districts) became but 2 in 1872 (1 for Wales and 1 for the metropolitan area), for the two others due to retire were not replaced; assistance from time to time was to be sought from 'local' men. The report for 1872 indicates the changing functions of their agents: 'occasional services are more in demand than regular and systematic visitation'. The next year's report stressed the 'scope for the sympathy and thoughtful direction and advice of an agent' who could, at the appropriate time, give 'cheering words of encouragement' or of 'caution and warning' concerning the moral tone of the schools.

The report for 1882 mentions six agents, but the summing up is to the point:

> There has not been much activity in the Agency Department. There are no funds wherewith to subsidise local effort, even if it were desirable to stave off the establishment of School Boards; and it would be a waste of power to send agents about for the purpose of stirring up educational zeal when the Committee of Council can secure adequate and suitable school accommodation by means which the Legislature has provided.

In 1883 the aims of the Society were reviewed, one of them being 'the inspection of these schools for the encouragement of managers and teachers and with the view of keeping them up to the mark'. Thus, the principle of 'inspectability' had, in their case, always been liberally interpreted, whereas in the later days of Her Majesty's inspectorate it had not. The end came in 1884. The monies spent in this way, it was suggested, could be better spent in other ways. Replies to the circular containing this suggestion were mixed, but enough 'ayes' were obtained for a resolution to be carried:

> to discontinue the present scheme for the periodical visitation of schools, and make the visitation when desired the object of a special arrangement.

A similar course of events is traceable at first in the Minutes of the Wesleyan Education Committee, near relative of the British Society; indeed, up to 1864 Her Majesty's inspector was appointed jointly to inspect both types of school, though the Wesleyan Education Committee was always careful to observe its rights under the concordat and to record that such appointments were made only with their 'entire concurrence'. But the urgency of separate denominational inspection had disappeared after 1870, and many Wesleyan schools were ultimately taken over by school boards. But, unlike the British

Society, the Wesleyans continued to attach great importance to their own system of inspection. In 1869 the Rev. J. Clulow was required to combine visitation of day-schools with that of Sunday-schools,[1] having the assistance later of Mr. James Bailey, though not for long, as he was called upon for the duties of Secretary. The Report of the Committee for 1874 speaks strongly of the feeling of isolation existing among Wesleyan schools, and this led on directly to the appointment of two lay men as 'Visitors'; one of these died suddenly in 1877, but the other completed twenty-five years of service before retiring in 1901.

The Roman Catholic diocesan inspectorate had a similar varied career. In 1870 the Roman Catholic Church quickly recognised the added importance of the ecclesiastical inspector, and could point with some satisfaction to the patterns of procedure and system of rewards already worked out. It was, however, desirable that a uniform system of inspection should be established after due comparison had been made of existing standards in the various dioceses. As a result of efforts in this direction the cost of inspection rose rapidly, and by 1884 more than half the total income was spent in this way, inspectors being paid a salary of £50 a year as well as travelling expenses.[2] At the same time the Roman Catholic Training Colleges began requiring more money for development, and, under the promptings of Cardinal Manning, much of the income for education was diverted after 1884 from inspection to training colleges, where appropriate systems of inducement were introduced, such as efficiency grants for teachers and books, as rewards, for pupil-teachers.

The National Society was quick off the mark in 1870, and all bishops were circularised for their views upon what forms diocesan inspection should take—local or central, paid or unpaid. Some 50 per cent replied, the majority favouring local inspection based on the diocese. A joint meeting of the General Committee of the Society and Secretaries of the Diocesan Boards was called in 1870 to consider whether diocesan inspectorates should be so constituted as to have a hierarchy

---

[1] Wesleyan Education Committee, *Annual Report*, 1870, p. 24. Wesleyan Sunday schools traditionally paid great attention to reading and were a valuable supplement to the day schools in this way.

[2] Roman Catholic Poor Schools Committee, *Annual Report*, 1884.

headed by a Chief Inspector. Opinion was against the appointment of such higher co-ordinating grades of inspector; but
payment of diocesan inspectors was deemed desirable, most
of the salary to come from grants-in-aid from the parent
National Society.

Another topic for discussion was whether diocesan inspectors
should inspect all subjects in the curriculum, or the non-secular
ones only, a final decision being in favour of the latter. Diocesan
boards were already well equipped to take the strain of
'directing and testing of religious instruction in church-
schools'. Inevitably, some of the increased costs would have to
be passed on to the schools; e.g. the Minutes of the Doncaster
National School Committee recorded on 13th June, 1871:

> it was unanimously agreed to reply to the Archbishop of York's
> inquiries, that the parish church schools be inspected in Religious
> Knowledge by the Diocesan Inspector appointed for that pur-
> pose, and that a sum of £3 0s. 0d. per annum be contributed
> towards the expenses of the inspection, provided that such
> inspection be annual.

Subsequent reports were included in the agenda papers, just
as Her Majesty's inspectors' reports were.

An expansion of the various diocesan inspectorates is
noticeable: Chichester had one inspector at first (a former
pupil-teacher who had gone on to a Church training college,
then taught in a day elementary school, subsequently being
ordained); by 1887 there were three inspectors, all examining
Religious Knowledge on a prescribed syllabus. No financial
gain (or loss) accrued to teachers from such diocesan inspection,
though a few school managing boards refused to have the
examination, usually because the school was small or because
the endowment made the examination difficult under the
trust-deed. The inspection-examination was annual—there
was hardly enough staff for occasional visits besides—fourteen
days' notice beforehand being required, though, in practice,
it was usually a month. Inspectors' reports indicate that the
examination took into consideration the children's knowledge
of the Old and New Testaments, the Catechism and Prayer
Book, and also their Scripture repetition and hymn-singing. In
general, if a large number of children did not pass, the diocesan

inspector must needs remain firm and do his duty by reporting the teacher(s) as inefficient in the subject: in the very bad cases they then reported to the bishop who in turn reported it to the clergyman of the parish concerned. Conversely, a good report upon children passing well was usually followed by a letter of commendation from the bishop. Schools were so keen to get a good report in some cases that it led to cramming, an interesting variant upon the oft-expressed theme that Religious Knowledge tended to be edged out of the curriculum under Payment by Results. The pattern of the examination was different from that of the school boards' own examination of the subject in that it was more closely akin to the class examination. The Rev. J. J. Scott, one of the honorary secretaries of the Manchester Diocesan Board of Education, had the unique experience of also examining for the Manchester School Board, as their officer, not the bishop's, and he was able to compare the two syllabuses: he said that the School Board's scheme, 'has always seemed to me to be a very large scheme, and to be occupied very much with intellectual work; the amount of work to be done under it is much more than we require in the Church school'.

If the bigger school boards offered a challenge to the voluntary schools in their thoroughness of inspection of Religious Knowledge, an even bigger one was to be presented in the other curricular subjects. The boards had many natural advantages. Their school planning was based on wider experience; Birmingham, for instance, could send a deputation up to London to look at that Board's new 'special' schools; G. B. Davis or J. F. Moss, Clerks of the Birmingham and Sheffield Boards respectively, could undertake visits to the Continent and bring back valuable lessons to add to the ever-widening horizons of administrators, inspectors and teachers.[1] By 1884, the Boards were no longer eschewing comparison with the voluntary schools; they were inviting it. The latter might have peculiar strengths—continuity of managers as opposed to possible triennial school board changes; freedom of heads, for instance, in the matter of discipline; or greater choice in curriculum to be adopted. In their favour, too, some managers and others took a real interest in their school(s) and staff, and

[1] *Reports on Schools in Germany and Switzerland,* 1879; *Notes on National Education in Continental Europe,* 1873.

were content to delegate responsibility to teachers in the proper manner.

But in the main there could be no gain-saying the superiority of the rate-aided school of the bigger boards. Nor can it be denied that some voluntary schools clung on to continuity, with many inadequacies, even when school boards put up a case to the Education Department for their closure. A. P. Graves listed these defects in Church schools in Huddersfield:

1. old type buildings, lacking class-room and porch accommodation 'and too often encumbered with Sunday school fittings' (a complaint as old as 1840!).

2. small, ill-ventilated, inadequately heated class-rooms.

3. play-grounds insufficiently drained and badly surfaced.

4. 'objectionable financial arrangements' like the "farming" of schools by teachers.

5. poor staff, compared with that of board schools, more especially in the infants' departments, and further aggravated by shortage of staff.

6. apathy and inability among managers, which led to such abuses as farming or low staffing position.

Graves then went on:

Matters had begun to reach a crisis with regard to these schools. Some of those in Huddersfield were on the point of breaking down before the strenuous competition of the board, when the Church-managers met and wisely determined to take a leaf out of its book by associating their schools under a central executive committee and by appointing an organising master to visit each of them twice a year in order to test their progress, and report it to the school managers and central committee. A very competent inspector, as it proved, was chosen, and four months of his work fully convinced me of the wisdom that dictated this recent action of the Church party.

Thus was born the Church School Association, not a moment too soon:

with regard to the actual efficiency of the church schools, it should be noted that while the total percentage in the ordinary subjects is 79 as against 73 three years ago, the Huddersfield Board schools have just passed 88%. Looking at it from another point of view, the Church schools have suffered 18 deductions in the grant for faults or failures in instruction and discipline, whereas the Board had only just two failures of grant for insufficient teaching of extra subjects, and that in the same school, although the number of their scholars is nearly half that in the Church schools.

The inspector had to prove his worth in a practical way, for grants from the Association to individual bodies of managers were usually out of the question. As it was, his salary of £250 a year was by no means excessive, for he had 62 schools to cover, with 120 departments in all. But he would seem to have justified the confidence placed in him as an ex-teacher: six years after his appointment in 1882, percentage of passes in 'his' schools had gone up by 10; the grant per capita had increased from 15/7¼d. to 18/6d. and merit-grant percentages were high on the national average.

If Huddersfield received a deal of publicity over this, it must not be assumed that the original idea was theirs. The Church Day School Association of Manchester and Salford could claim that distinction in their appointing as organising master, in 1881, James F. Seabrook, formerly Method Master at York Training College; in 1884 he went to be organising master to the Rochester Diocesan Board of Education, and it was in this capacity that he gave evidence before the Cross Commission. Manchester's scheme differed from Huddersfield's in that the former offered Seabrook's services but not all schools accepted the offer; in Huddersfield, the organising master closely resembled Her Majesty's Inspector in his role of assessor— only he called twice a year, as was the case in Bradford also, whereas Her Majesty's Inspector only called once as a general rule. It is interesting to hear Sir (then Mr.) Herbert Birley's opinion why such an advisory officer was not welcomed into some of the Manchester Church schools:

> the reason is that the teachers of voluntary schools practically farm the schools, and they will not have his interference.

Yet another variation on this same theme is heard in Rochester, where a fee of one pound was charged from the schools for the twice yearly visit of the organising master. Salaries, too, varied a great deal: Manchester paid £300 a year for a full-time appointment, whereas Bradford paid £75 a year for a half-time appointment (five half days a week). Sheffield approximated to the average with £200 a year for another full-time appointment. The number of schools to be visited also varied according to area. Bradford Church of England Society had 56 departments: Rochester Diocesan Board of Education (retaining responsibility for inspection of secular subjects in Church schools) had 168—far too many in Seabrook's opinion. Again, Huddersfield's Church Association had no surplus funds for additional grants to managers, whereas Sheffield's School Aid Society carried an annual surplus of £200 for just such a purpose. Liverpool's School Managers' Conference could afford neither organising master nor grants-in-aid, the Diocesan Education Board still being the responsible body for awarding grants to those most needy cases.

But certain common characteristics do begin to emerge among all these organising masters:

1. a ceaseless concern for higher standards in voluntary schools. They may not always have had the success claimed for their schools, though J. F. Seabrook had 100 per cent passes in one or more of the basic three R's in some of the schools he visited in the South London area. But these inspectors had to know just what attainment levels to expect from every class in the school; not surprisingly, therefore, they were all ex-teachers, with training college staff experience as well in some cases.

2. They were more patently in school by permission of the local managers, hence, perhaps, their popular soubriquet of 'pollen carriers'. In turn, teachers felt more at liberty to discuss matters with them, and even challenge their opinions, than was the case with Her Majesty's Inspectors. The reports of the organising master upon individual schools were sent direct to the managers: only a general report went forward to the Association's head-quarters. Their possible role as liaison officers was, therefore, not unrecognised at this time.

3. The attitude of school boards to these organising masters was not likely to find expression in any Minutes, as it was no concern of theirs directly; but the Clerk of Leeds School Board publicly welcomed the idea: 'It cannot but do good'.

4. They were not born in juxtaposition to government inspectors; indeed, the latter seem to have brooded over their birth. Thus, it was a recommendation in 1883 from the district Her Majesty's Inspector, Mr. Legard, that prompted the Leeds voluntary schools to follow Huddersfield's example and appoint their own 'visiting inspector'; they chose a teacher from one of the best voluntary schools in the city.

It may have been such encouragement, coupled with the known readiness of school boards to consult Her Majesty's Inspector about appointments (and at least an equal readiness by the latter to volunteer advice to the former) that prompted the Bryce Commission to make its extraordinary suggestion about the appointing of local inspectors from a list 'approved' by Her Majesty's Inspectors. The over-all success of the idea of an organising master in voluntary schools may, perhaps, be adjudged from his fairly extensive reproduction by the 1880s. Leeds and Nottingham could be added to Manchester, Sheffield, Huddersfield and Bradford, and London had at least two:

> the principle of having an organising master is now followed out in many parts of the country.

In view of this permutation of organiser and inspector, it may be worth noting the use of both by the Science and Art Department. The origin of this Department lay in the 'Council of the Government School of Design' set up in 1837 under the aegis of the Board of Trade, with a School of Design in Somerset House which was to turn out trained teachers. In 1841, the Government 'ear-marked' £10,000 for promoting the establishment of provincial schools of design, and many towns developed these. Inevitably, this government grant implied the right of inspection, though the first inspector was expected to combine this job with that of Director of the Central School, and it was not until 1850 that a full-time inspector of higher education was appointed. After 1853, the duties of 'visiting and reporting on the institutions in connection with the Department' were initially undertaken by the two joint-secretaries, Playfair and Cole. Such schools as these, however, needed less inspection than specialist advice, the more so in their early stages, and the embryo (Science and) Art Department partly met this need by switching masters from one locality to another. These men were therefore peripatetic in a sense; and in a rather different form the system is still in use in some local authority areas today. All this was very similar to the appointments that were being made by some Mechanics' Institutes at the same time.

A tradition of using inspectors to visit and produce increased efficiency in the various schools and institutions was steadily laid down from 1854 onwards; from the first, the inspectors seem to have had a ready welcome from teachers, for at the very least, they represented the 'pecuniary value' of the Department. This could take many forms: prizes, medals, scholarships, liberal grants-in-aid (up to half the purchase price of models, diagrams, samples, apparatus); grants to teachers, pupil-teachers and students; lists of recommended text-books, appropriately illustrated by better-known scientists; and of course increased grants for that most evident of all improvements, namely, better examination results.

Such a system of payment by results had advantages. It was administratively easy to work; the examination papers going out to the candidates at established centres invigilated by paid local secretaries and many more voluntary helpers. The worked papers were gathered up and returned to the Department's headquarters at South Kensington for marking. Schedules of results and grants earned were then circulated, plus the inevitable examiners' comments, e.g. in 1871 'crops of these inefficient teachers spring up from year to year'. Supervision as exercised by the few inspectors in the field cost very little, yet it gave them a reason for existence for they could judge of local equipment and facilities using a national yard-stick. Above all, it was easy to understand: as the Department's report for 1871 stated simply, 'if a teacher produces nothing, he gets no pay . . . The object of the State is to have results; the machinery for producing them is immaterial'. Type of school did not matter a great deal; both the higher grade schools and the endowed secondary schools were drawn naturally into this examination system. But apart from the underlying weakness of any system attempting to regulate education by economic laws, with all its attendant symptoms, there was one weakness in the inspectorate, noted by (then) Captain Donnelly in The Department's Report for 1871:

this inspection is primarily to check and supervise administrative details . . . There is another branch of inspection which this system does not wholly meet—I mean in the way of giving advice and assistance as to teaching.

It would undoubtedly be a very good thing if men of eminence in the various branches of science which are taught could from time to time visit the schools and each in his own special line give assistance and advice to the teachers.

The spate of audit work, checking, cross-checking, collating of results, allocation of grants and visiting the schools of the mounting number of candidates inevitably led to an increase in the number of inspectors: two in 1870 became three in 1871, four in 1882. Other single specialists were called in from time to time; but one ingenious attempt to exercise administrative supervision over the processes of local examination on a temporary basis deserves to be better known. In a memorandum on 'the Corps of Royal Engineers as civil servants of the Crown', Cole had suggested that 'Royal Engineer Officers furnish a ready means of trying experiments in administration. New actions can be tried without creating a new office for life, or entailing the cost of retirement and superannuation on the State . . . In time of peace, the civil service should have perfect freedom in borrowing officers from the War Department, and the Officers should be allowed to retain their rank in their Corps.'[1] The precedent for 'borrowing' had been first established in the case of H. C. Cunliffe-Owen in 1851. Now a further extension was proposed by drawing upon Officers of the Royal Engineers, stationed in different parts of the country, to act as area inspectors; they were to make any preliminary inspection of a school, help the local committee with examination arrangements, and check to see that the rules and regulations were properly obeyed in the interests of national uniformity. These officers proved of great value, as the rise in numbers seconded to such duties might indicate: 73 in 1870, 86 in 1873, 90 in 1879.

After 1893, the inspectorial hierarchy at South Kensington took more definite shape. Acland appointed 13 inspectors bringing up the total number to 17, all with high technical qualifications. So it was that, when the Code of 1894–95 announced that grants would be paid 'partly on the results of

[1] Sir Henry Cole, *Fifty Years of Public Work*, Vol. II, p. 323.

inspection and partly on examination', the field-workers were in position with duties carefully explained to them.[1] The services of the Royal Engineers Officers could now be dispensed with, use being made instead of a permanent body of some 80 first and second class sub-inspectors of the Education Department, already stationed in districts. These men were to inspect elementary classes in science as well as in art, and also to supervise (for purposes of government grant) the literary quantum of the curriculum in organised science schools. With the growth of such a team, movement towards internal hierarchy of office at the top was inevitable: in 1899 there was one Senior Chief Inspector and three (later four) Senior Inspectors in charge of divisions. After the Board of Education Act of that year, however, their independent existence came to an end: an Order-in-Council dated 13th May 1901 appointed all 17 Science and 3 Art inspectors Her Majesty's Inspectors.

With the passing of the Technical Instruction Act of 1889 and the making of more money available to local authorities for this purpose (including the windfall 'whisky money' from 1890 onwards), there was inevitable increase in local inspection of secondary schools receiving grants-in-aid from local sources. As so often, men of scholastic distinction were sought, for example, A. Smithells, who inspected science teaching in certain Yorkshire grammar schools, was Professor of Chemistry at the Yorkshire College. Some evening classes, too, were inspected, and, to create more inspectorial congeries, the Board of Agriculture, created in 1889, offered £5,000 a year for the promotion of agricultural education, and undertook to inspect any school other than elementary (where there were government inspectors in any case) where technical instruction, practical or scientific, in any way connected with agriculture or forestry was given. All this meant an increase in the number of inspectors and led to a restatement of the problem, 'which schools ought to be inspected?' The Schools Inquiry commission had drawn the attention of the Assistant Commissioners to it in 1864:

It is not possible to draw the boundary precisely in a country in which no class of society is separated from that which is above it and that which is below it. But you will understand that you are

[1] Science and Art Department *Report*, 1894, p. LXVI.

required to give your chief attention to the schools attended by the children of such of the gentry, clergy, professional and commercial men as are of limited means, and of farmers and tradesmen.

The schools which you have thus to inspect seem to be divisible into three classes:

1. The grammar schools and those endowed schools which, though not grammar schools, do not appear to have been intended for the children of labourers.

2. Proprietary schools, which, not being endowed, are private property, but are owned by single proprietors, or by proprietary bodies, distinct from the school master.

3. Private schools, which are the property of the school-masters who teach in them.

J. G. Fitch, probably the best known of the Assistant Commissioners, went straight to the heart of the matter:

On the whole, it is clear that in the lower stratum of the middle class there is a great demand for the sort of good primary education which trained teachers can give. At present, that demand is very inadequately met. Except in the case of the Mechanics' Institute and the Congregational Board, no-one initiates schools expressly for this class. The promoters of National and British schools sometimes ... make a provision for the necessity which is forced upon them as a consequence of their own unexpected success. But they never contemplate it at first ... for it is the duty of the Education Department to concern itself wholly with the instruction of the poor. If other children come into the schools, the Government cannot prevent it, but it is bound to consider them as intruders, and to guard the Parliamentary grant from being in any way diverted to their benefit. Even the advantage of inspection and examination is often necessarily withheld from them. For it is the chief business of an inspector to verify the fulfilment of conditions under which a certain sum of public money is to be paid; and ... he is not unnaturally led to disregard those scholars whose failure or success would not affect the substantial part of his report.

Some means are clearly wanting for providing primary schools under trained masters and mistresses for the children just above the rank of those for whom the National Schools were intended. Nothing more would be needed than the provision of a good school-room and some governing authority with powers enough

K

to choose a master, to dismiss him if he prove incompetent, and to enforce annual inspection.

Fitch, as a matter of fact, represents within himself over some forty years, the tug-of-war between the claims of inspection and examination as a means of assessing post-primary schools: Before the Bryce Commission in 1895 he said:

> A collective and class examination may be the best for determining the share which a school should receive from a public fund, but for all other purposes contemplated in the examination of a school—for the encouragement of merit, for the information of parents, for the discovery of defects, for securing thoroughness, for the promotion of the scholar to a higher class, for the award of prizes, scholarships and leaving certificates, the examination of the individual scholar is indispensable. In fact, all examination which is worth anything must always be that of individuals. And although the proportion of scholars who can pass an examination appropriate to their age is not a perfect measure of a school's efficiency, it is on the whole one of the best and fairest measures which has yet been adopted.

Out of its context this may seem contrary to the broad catholicity of Fitch's views on inspection: but he draws both sides together as he goes on:

> There is another very important aspect of the question as it concerns the comparative usefulness of inspection and examination. Inspecting a school implies a critical observation of the methods of its daily work. It also implies that the authority which orders the inspection is more concerned with the processes and organisation in use in a school than with the value of the results achieved. To make such a scrutiny efficient, there should be many visits without notice, and this means considerable expense and some chance of irritation.
>
> An examining body which undertakes to certify not that the work of the school has been successfully done, but that it has been done in the right way, assumes two things:
>
> 1. that there is one—and only one—'right way', and
>
> 2. that the inspector knows it.

But these are large assumptions. We have not yet reached a stage in the development of either the art or the science of education as will justify us in saying that any method of teaching or organisation is the best, or that the opinion on these points of any one person—however skilled or experienced—ought to be conclusive.

Fitch is here feeling his way towards the idea of general inspection of a secondary school by the team of inspectors—an idea which was to come to fruition in the early twentieth century. He sums up:

> ... although inspection and a general estimate of a school as a whole may be valuable for some purposes, and although a skilled inspector may often render great service in calling attention to the methods which are obviously wrong, yet in contemplating any future action whereby secondary schools may be brought under public supervision, examination is of more importance than inspection. It is more likely to be just and impartial. It is more helpful to scholars and more serviceable and satisfactory to their parents. It certainly interferes less with the independence, originality, and personal enthusiasm of the teachers—educational factors which, under any conceivable system, it is of the highest importance to encourage.

A last expression of view-point may be allowed to Fitch: in 1902, speaking of 'possible amendments to the Education Act', he says:

> Examination has been superseded by general inspection ... This change of policy was doubtless designed to leave larger freedom to both teachers and managers, and to encourage in them a stronger sense of responsibility. But it must not be expected to effect this result in all cases. Freedom to improve may easily be interpreted to imply freedom to continue unimproved: and some stimulus is needed ...[1]

He did feel, however, that inspection, done properly, could achieve much. He disapproved of specialist inspectors on the grounds that they were a waste of power, and paid too little attention to the general aims of the schools: instead, he recommended that:

> every district of sufficient size should be provided with one chief inspector, presumably a scholarly man with a large general knowledge of both primary and secondary education, and under him a staff of assistants, all of whom should be competent to take a general share in school inspection, but of whom one should be specially conversant with science, one with art and manual training, one with music and one with modern languages. The chief should assign to each his share of the work of inspecting each

[1] Board of Education, *Miscellanies XXX*, No. 53, p. 960.

school, and should take care that opportunity was afforded for testing by a competent judge any special form of excellence it professed. He should receive from his assistants all their detailed reports, and should be responsible for welding them together and presenting to the local and to the central authority a complete account of all that particular institution professed to do, and of all that it had actually achieved. . . . Additional inspectors destined for work in higher schools, should be men of the same academic and social rank.

He adds significantly that, though some will be found better fitted for inspection in particular types of schools:

all of them would be the better for knowing something of the methods and ideals prevailing in schools either higher or lower than those which they habitually visited.

This little anthology from one of the wisest of all inspectors should be set against the fact that of the three inspectorates amalgamated under the 1899 Act, the least effective by far had been that of the Charity Commission. It was to be regretted that A. J. Mundella's suggestion to the Childers Committee— that endowed schools be subject to inspection—had not been given more publicity. J. Percival, President of Trinity College, Oxford, elaborated on such a proposal (in a letter to Mundella 1st April, 1885) to the effect that Mundella and three co-opted colleagues should report on all the endowed schools, which in return for the privilege of inspection by assistant commissioners, would pay on a sliding scale according to number of pupils on roll. But the idea seemed still-born. The Charity Commission was promised an adequate inspecting staff but never got it, even after 1888 when it began inspections of those endowed schools regulated by schemes it had formulated. With some justification, the Bryce Commission called its mode of inspection 'official and administrative, rather than educational'.

Chapter Eleven

THE EARLY TWENTIETH CENTURY

OF the three main types of inspectorate, the least to be affected at once by administrative re-organisation and change in methodology was the denominational one. Anglican diocesan inspection continued to be popular in the appropriate voluntary schools; the standard report form was the same. In the case of Her Majesty's inspectorate at the turn of the century, the hierarchy of office comprised one Senior Chief Inspector (also in charge of the Metropolitan District); eleven Chief Inspectors, of whom two were specially responsible for training colleges; and some 366 other inspectors in all branches. This total was not unduly large, despite the indictment of Sir George Kekewich later, if viewed against a school population of well over five and a half millions. But when Kekewich was semi-compulsorily retired six months before time in October 1902, to be succeeded as Secretary to the Board of Education by Robert Morant, three urgently needed reforms were put in hand: re-organisation to prevent over-lapping of function, improvement of co-ordination, and some clearer definition of inspectors' roles. Morant approximated most nearly to the Local Authority Chief Education Officer but on a national scale; and inevitably his work in the wider field of public educational administration was to be more publicised (and criticised!). But insofar as His Majesty's inspectorate was concerned, he left as lasting an impress upon it as Kay-Shuttleworth had done, both in an administrative and an inspirational sense. Perhaps the greatest single contribution was his quickness to seize on the lesson of successful use of women as factory inspectors a decade earlier, and his ability to recommend the right initial appointments as His Majesty's Inspector

of Schools. The re-deployment of inspectors was a master-
piece of administrative simplicity: three main groupings only,
Elementary, Secondary, Technological, of which the first was
naturally the largest. They were arranged in nine territorial
divisions in England and one for Wales (a separate Welsh
Department was established in 1907 with its own Chief
Inspector). The three Branches had their own Chief Inspector,
constituting a triumvirate as it were, all responsible to the
Permanent Secretary but without one of them being even
'primus inter pares'. Each division had its Divisional Inspector
who, in addition to co-ordinating the work of his colleagues,
the district inspectors, usually was responsible for a (small)
district himself. Every district inspector had the help of an
assistant, a man of considerable academic and professional
education in his own right. Within each district there were also
to be found secondary inspectors as well as a few specialist
inspectors with high technical qualifications, as for example
the twenty former Science and Art Department Inspectors.
Every inspector thus had an immediate sense of 'belonging', a
constant inducement to look at the all-round development of
the whole child—as enjoined in the current Board of Education
Code. The possibility of pamphlets for the guidance of teachers
became a reality, as did courses run for teachers. Full inspections
of secondary (grammar) schools by a variable team of inspectors with appropriate qualifications were one natural out-
come: the success of these may be judged from the fact that
half a century later they are an integral feature of Her Majesty's
inspectors' work, though not universally approved of by
teachers. It should be added that only sampling inspection was
possible when the growth of Local Authority maintained
grammar schools was so considerable—491 in 1904–5, 802 in
1908–9, 1,161 in 1925. The willingness of some of the bigger
public (independent) schools at the time to invite inspection
was not unassociated with the success, as a method, of 'full'
inspection. In short, the inspectorate had re-developed its
capacity for educational guidance and leadership of the very
finest quality.

The new management at local authority level (as provided
for in the Act of 1902) also brought increased administrative
clarity and order. There had been little equality of opportunity
too between a big school board whose spending ran into

thousands and the smallest board where it came to less than a pound. The bigger school-boards themselves in some cases had found that, excellent as the principle of delegation was, too many sub-committees could delay decision and even blur the outline of delegated responsibility. But the basic four-fold separation of function was sound and was absorbed into the newer Education Committees of County and County Borough Councils: Sites and Buildings; Finance (sometimes with General Purposes); Attendance; and School Management, now of necessity divided into primary and 'higher' education. In theory, at any rate, group-visitation of schools was still possible, but in effect the sheer bulk of administrative decisions to be taken made for increased reliance by committees upon their Chief Officer, whether called Secretary or Director of Education. In turn, this called for expansion of staff and creation of suitable hierarchies under the Education Officer. In the bigger Authorities, this necessitated clarification of function as between the executive and the advisory officer; it also made for appointment of a chief advisory officer, a Chief Inspector, directly responsible to the Chief Education Officer (as for example in London County Council). As the Local Education Authorities assumed certain responsibilities for voluntary schools under the Act of 1902, inspectorial hierarchies also grew, as in Birmingham, Bradford, Hull, Nottingham, Manchester. All these were County Boroughs, all included in those twelve largest towns which, as E. G. A. Holmes said, had 75 local inspectors 'besides a great host of specialists' (i.e. organisers). The growth in County Council inspecting-organising was obviously less immediate; but it did take place with increasing momentum, the moreso as these Councils developed their secondary and further education building programmes.

The Board of Education was fully seized of the need to establish harmonious relationships with the 300 Local Education Authorities; (49 County, 71 County Borough, 134 non-County Borough and 46 Urban District Councils) and the people to do it were His Majesty's inspectors usually at District level.

'The inspector in charge of a district ought to act as the Board's ambassador; it is not merely his duty to report the things he sees and hears, whether for good or evil, and to act as the Board's eyes and ears in connection with individual schools and teachers; he has to settle a great many cases with the local education authority without reference to the Board, and he has also—it is part of his duty—to give the local education authority any advice or assistance he can render; and even when the inspector refers to the Board, there are many things in which it is much better that communications between the Board and the authorities should be made verbally by the inspector rather than by official correspondence. . . . The inspector in fact is, I think, one of the most effective instruments of de-centralisation and in leaving a great deal of discretion to the inspector we feel we are leaving a great deal to the discretion of the local education authority.'

No finer statement could be wished for of the relationship that should exist between Board and Local Authority, than these words of Selby-Bigge before the Royal Commission on the Civil Service in 1912. Ironically enough, the previous twelve years belied it all; never before, or since, were there so many tensions between the Central and the Local Education Authority. In these, inspectors were directly involved and their differing philosophies of education, as well as their administrative loyalties, called into question.

It is sometimes assumed that, with the ending of Payment by Results at the close of the nineteenth century, everybody breathed freely again and teachers got on with experimenting in the newer methods, watched over and encouraged by a benign inspectorate. Nothing could be less true. Her Majesty's Inspector Mr. A. P. Graves had lamented that they were 'become too much examiners'; but freed from the task of writing long reports, they found the conception of their role as 'itinerant ambassadors of technical competence and good will' a difficult one for teachers to endorse at once. Few inspectors, and even fewer elementary school teachers in their middle years, understood the full implications of the new philosophy of infant education: indeed, as E. G. A. Holmes stated in a letter to Sir John Gorst, 4th March, 1902, infant teachers themselves frequently stood in need of far more personal as well as vocational education. A bare handful of progressive teachers were doing excellent experimental work; but many others favoured the older ways. The immediate result was that ideas and methods all too frequently lacked suitable preliminary exegesis; and, in the ensuing confusion of criticism and counter-criticism, local authority inspectors were unhappily caught up.

The Early Twentieth Century

Five specific charges were levelled against the prevailing trend away from individual examination, finding expression in a joint report by the seven London School Board inspectors in 1901 (and representing a complete change of attitude by them from that of the previous few years).

In the first place, the Head's examination was now far less authoritative than that of the inspectors which it had replaced. This should be set in context with the then Education Department's expressed policy of making heads responsible for the state of their own schools, a policy also being followed by some of the bigger school boards. Some extenuation may be made in that the doctrine of the Head's supremacy in his own school not only found little support outside Britain at this time, but had never really extended to elementary school heads in any case; indeed, the words 'secondary' and 'elementary' were veritable dragon's teeth, able to produce in a moment whole fields of warring giants! Nevertheless, the raising of the point at all indicated how far heads and inspectors had to go towards appreciating the true nature of inspection and its vast creative possibilities. In Scotland, it may be worth noting, Her Majesty's Inspectors have still retained a closer connection with school examinations than in England.

Secondly, results were now of far less importance than teaching, the teaching being no longer 'pressed home'. In this, London Board inspectors were settling their eyes, if not their hearts, upon the panacea of an ideal attainment test as the measure of 'efficiency' in a school. It lingered on into this century, and is still with some people when mention is made of 'transfer at 11+'! It was a thousand pities that, at this particular stage in their history, school board inspectors should have put up this barricade to their progress towards a conception of a more child-centred education. As ex-heads themselves, but now translated into the administrative arena and all too frequently exposed to its prevailing cynicisms, they saw very clearly the danger of some teachers 'free wheeling' under the new dispensation; the blurring of those hard and fast lines delimiting efficient from non-efficient. They knew that inspection by sampling, unless conducted with great skill and sagacity, might call into being evils greater than those the new system was meant to eradicate. In some cases, the conservatist attitude of age may also have predisposed them to look back to their own teaching days, when standards certainly proved the teacher.

In the third place, notebooks of children were now mere 'flattery to deceive'; they were showy, and often a great amount of time had been spent in getting up fair copies, etc.; time which could have been more profitably devoted to actual teaching. These notebooks, with their arithmetic sums of fabulous amounts, or with their highly artificial moral precepts so difficult to comprehend and transcribe, were hardly the kind an inspector sometimes meets today, when a 'best book' still has a proper place. But the endless copying from the blackboard could with justice be criticised by the London inspectors. Nevertheless, the imputation upon teachers' integrity (in the suggestion of 'window dressing' for an inspector's approving eye) in itself indicated a wrong teacher-inspector relationship. Indirectly it also reflected upon inspectorial habits, for over-copying out in a 'best' book (to the neglect of any creative work at all) is not usually difficult to detect and discourage.

The fourth charge was that the Board of Education at Whitehall now failed to distinguish in many of its inspectors' reports between genuine efficiency and non-efficiency, and more specifically between efficient and non-efficient teachers. In this, perhaps. lies the fundamental opposition to a more general type of school inspection. Individual examination gives an accurate assessment of what children have learnt, and, if this be the criterion, it therefore assesses directly the teachers' own efficiency. Many teachers preferred to be so assessed, and arguments were brought forward in favour of it.[1] The more general type of inspection by catechetical sample extending to every phase of the life of a school had been over-laid in consequence of Payment by Results; as Huxley said, very pointedly:

> The Revised Code did not compel any school-master to leave off teaching anything; but, by the very simple process of refusing to pay for many kinds of teaching, it has practically put an end to them.[2]

In this climate, school board inspectors had been weaned as

[1] *v.* J. G. Fitch, *The Inspection of Secondary Schools.* National Education, 1901.

[2] T. H. Huxley, *Science and Education: Collected Essays*, vol. III, p. 379.

teachers. What the London School Board inspectors were now saying was that the only accurate measure of efficiency was the number of passes a teacher got for his class on examination day. It would have been better to have criticised the real cause of confusion, namely that, even with such a measure, the hands that use it may vary enormously. This had been one of the teachers' complaints against Her Majesty's inspectors: they eventually changed to other areas, according to prescribed policy, and standards changed with them. Had the regular conferences of Her Majesty's inspectors begun by Landsdowne and Kay-Shuttleworth been so developed as to include teachers as well, accurate over-all assessments by inspectors might have been worked out by 1870. Instead, the scaled degrees, 'Excellent', 'Good' and 'Fair', had tended to change unexpectedly, with consequent protests from school boards and teachers. Edge was given to these complaints because inspectors' opinions could still increase or decrease salaries of teachers. The only answer was a capitation grant to schools, and 'Burnham' salary scales: and some local inspectors, as well as some managers, had been reaching out to the idea. One might have expected School Board inspectors, as ex-heads themselves, to be unanimous in support of this idea, accepting as a calculated risk the fact that some teachers are always less (or more) efficient than others . . . It should be added that the curve of distribution of teaching efficiency spread far more widely at that time than today. E. G. A. Holmes' Memorandum on teacher-training in 1902 gives startling illustration of this.

Fifthly, it was alleged that heads of schools were now diffident about, and shrank from their duty of, writing adverse reports on members of their staff. It might seem complimentary to inspectors that teachers should prefer them to write such reports, but in just this lay the greatest danger that any inspectorate has to negotiate, namely, that of cutting across head-staff relationships. At this particular time, too, it was doubly dangerous, because the teaching profession was beginning to feel its strength in unity: hence the natural reluctance of heads to criticise members of staff in public—for, rough-hew it how one will, that is what a written report amounted to, with all its possible financial implications. It was a manifestation of the growing pains of a profession, and persisted well into the twentieth century. But it may also be candidly stated that nothing was guaranteed to insulate inspectors from the true current of feeling in a school more than a 'pencil and paper' approach, whether it be by choice or necessity.

Support for the stand thus taken came from all over the country: most regrettably, it brought local and central government inspectors into head-on collision, sometimes extending from day school to evening school policy. In that the Board of Education and the new Local Education Authorities were in duty bound to support their respective inspectors, it exacerbated their relations.[1] Yet again, in the case of the London Board which so dwarfed all others, it brought local inspectors into an open quarrel with the teachers whose counsellors they had long been.[2] After contributing so much to the progressive attitude of the Board, it now seemed they had become reactionary, or so the National Union of Teachers thought.[3]

To complete this unhappy picture, inspectorial tensions were thrown into sharper relief, partly as a result of this clash of opinion, but partly too of a deep-seated socio-economic origin. E. G. A. Holmes was expressing a valid (and personal) point of view when he said that 'as compared with the ex-elementary teacher usually engaged in the hopeless task of surveying or trying to survey a wide field of action from a well-worn groove, the inspector of public schools of the 'varsity type has the advantage of being able to look at elementary education from a point of view of complete detachment and therefore of being able to handle its problems with freshness and originality'.

He could have easily substantiated this by reference to the high quality of the contribution being made by Her Majesty's inspectors to various phases of Board planning. But Local Authority inspectors were ex-elementary school heads, presumably among the best of their profession. All resented in varying degrees what the School Guardian called 'amateur' inspection by Her Majesty's Inspector, implying the latter's lack of previous 'shop-floor' experience; yet those who had such experience were de-barred from what seemed to them a

[1] London School Board, Evening Continuation Schools Committee *Minutes*, 16th Nov. 1903.
[2] London School Board School Management Committee *Minutes*, 2nd May 1904.
[3] London School Board *Minutes*, 26th Nov. 1903.

natural promotion to full Her Majesty's Inspector. Selby-Bigge might later dismiss the 'Holmes-Morant' Circular (E. (Elementary Branch) Memorandum No. 21 dated 6th Jan. 1910) as 'a lively controversy over a matter of no importance'; but the 140 resolutions of protest mostly by N.U.T. local associations, and the relentless agitation of the *Schoolmaster* indicated a different opinion among elementary school teachers. G. A. Christian, a London County Council inspector, condemned those parts of the Circular which did find their way into print as 'scurrilous reports'; a colleague, F. H. Hayward, was regrettably even more vehement in public expression of opinion. A similar tension, socio-economic in origin, was reflected at this time within the ranks of His Majesty's inspectorate. Inspectors' assistants, as provided for in the Revised Code, had continued to be appointed up to 1882. In that year, the post of sub-inspector was created, with duties approximating to those of a second inspector. The dissatisfied voice of the old inspector's assistant could be heard in the evidence of J. Finch before the Cross Commission in 1887–8: doing similar work to their masters, they were but 'excellent drudges' on a much lower salary and starved of promotion. From 1893 to 1896 (during Acland's Vice-Presidency) sub-inspectors saw more systematic promotion for themselves, but in the following ten years only four were promoted out of about 40 appointments to H.M.I. Meanwhile a Junior Inspector's post was created as a specific recruiting ground for full inspectorships: they were placed above the sub-inspectors in the hierarchy—notwithstanding the former were appointed to learn the job previously done by sub-inspectors—nor could sub-inspectors apply for junior inspectorships. The Board assured sub-inspectors that they were under a misapprehension if they regarded themselves as inferior to junior inspectors: but salary differential and rate of promotion still served to make them dissatisfied. Perhaps the root-cause of the trouble was the principle of selection by nomination to His Majesty's inspectorate and its operation in favour of 'Oxbridge' antecedents in three cases out of every four. Selby-Bigge ably defended it in evidence before the Royal Commission on the Civil Service 1912–14; but the National Union of Teachers detested it, submitting to the same Commission that

the manner in which inspectors of schools are selected and

appointed by the Board of Education is very unsatisfactory, and that, owing to serious defect in the method of selection, much injury has been inflicted upon teachers and scholars.

It should be added that the N.U.T. had also previously expressed alarm at the prospect of local authorities appointing one or two young university graduates to their advisory staffs:[1] some of these appointments of course, were made with a view to meeting increasing responsibilities for 'higher' education. Perhaps the most powerful vindication of the kind of man the Board of Education had 'nominated' was the increasing readiness of the proprietary schools to accept the principle and practice of inspection. A memorandum from the Public Schools in 1901 hinted such a readiness: 25 years later, only 14 out of 127 schools on the Headmaster's Conference List were still not visited by Her Majesty's inspectors.

The Board of Education, however, could not remain insensitive to criticism from the National Union of Teachers and began to strengthen its 'Elementary Branch' in the inspectorate by drawing into its service more experienced teachers. From 1913, it ceased to recruit to its junior inspectorate, recruiting instead to a new assistant-inspector class. A minimum of eight years' teaching experience was required, preferably to include some experience as Head-teacher as well. The upper age-limit of appointment was raised to 45, later to 50. The result of these complementary tendencies was to bring together the motivating philosophies of both sets of inspectors. Indeed, there were occasional signs, early in the century, that professional and personal relationships could be very cordial, within the framework of differing executive loyalties.

It might be thought that, with the rising standards of teaching, the need for inspectors would grow less. This tendency was certainly observable in the case of some specialist subjects, in the second decade of this century, though with changing emphases in methodology, organisers again were to prove their value. But inspectors' inspirational value found expression in ways other than in school. Teachers' courses became popular; for example, Marion Richardson's art classes for teachers in London in the early 1930s attracted 1,500 applications for

[1] London Teachers Association Letter to the London School Board, 20th Nov. 1909.

150 places. The Board of Education, too, was finding a ready response from teachers to the ever-widening range of short courses it offered: the tutors and lecturers were all Her Majesty's inspectors or people by precept and practice similar to them. Such courses proved of value to inspectorial thinking not less than to teachers' thinking. In some cases, the more so since the last War, local follow-up discussion groups have been started at the prompting of teachers.

Chapter Twelve

SINCE 1944

THE full implications of the 1944 Education Act are still being worked out, but certain 'hints for a prothesis' may be made if only to show how time present has grown out of time past. The Act states

> It shall be the duty of the local education authority for every area, so far as their powers extend, to contribute towards the spiritual, moral, mental and physical development of the community by securing that efficient education throughout those stages shall be available to meet the needs of the population of their area.

These are great responsibilities and are linked with changes in the pattern of local administration in the interests of increased efficiency. The main 'all purpose' education authority becomes the 62 county and 83 county borough councils, with suitable provision made in the former case for delegation of certain powers to the divisional executive and the excepted area. Furthermore, as a result of this Act (and subsequent Acts) much needed systemisation has been achieved: the functions to be exercised in relation to maintained schools by the head, bodies of managers and of governors, and the local authority are clearly set down in the various Instrument and Articles of Management or Government.[1]

No local education committee today can consider itself as simply a specialised employment agency for teaching and non-teaching staff. The Authority is a consortium of teachers, administrators, members of the lay-committee (on which there

[1] v. W. P. Alexander and F. Barraclough, *County and Voluntary Schools*, 2nd edition, 1953.

will be co-opted teacher-representatives); to fulfil its duties under the Act it must be able to offer educational guidance to all those who, under the Head, are engaged in the 'management' of schools. In the process of selecting and training its future leaders, an Authority will offer some of the following, which are examples only:

(1) running courses and/or conferences for different groups of teaching and non-teaching staffs in the area often in response to specific requests;

(2) encouraging teachers to see as much good teaching as they can both in the area and outside it;

(3) assisting financially all teachers who wish to attend courses of their own choice at regional or national level; such courses may be not only the familiar short course, but also longer ones involving a period of secondment;

(4) stimulating and encouraging all forms of experimental teaching in schools;

(5) offering grants-in-aid to the various teacher-associations in the area to run their own study-groups or courses, and helping them publish their reports where research has been undertaken;

(6) developing all forms of joint-participation between teachers, professional officers and lay committee in planning phases of educational policies, in relation to local needs and priorities.

Though Authorities vary in their 'creativity quotient', the result of such activities can only be to develop 'education for responsibility'. In some areas, a combination of activities of this kind has enabled the Authority to plan imaginatively for future spiritual, moral, physical, emotional and mental needs, in terms, for example, of education for work, for leisure, for citizenship, for home-making and parenthood. It has also enabled specific attention to be paid to particular problems in the school community, such as detection, diagnosis and treatment of brightness, or dullness, or backwardness.

In all this, the role of the local authority inspector is variable; in his case, as in the case of managers and governors, present duties have grown out of past ones. Through them passes the two-way flow of ideas and recommendations between teacher and administrator. This indeed underlies one of the most recent definitions of inspection as

> a service to interpret to teachers and the public the educational policies of the authorities and also to interpret to the competent authorities, the experiences, needs and aspirations of teachers and local committees.[1]

This of course applies equally to Local Authority and Ministry inspectors. It should be added that not all local authorities employ their own inspectors, though there is a permissive clause (Section 77 Sub-section 3) in the 1944 Act. On the other hand, some local authorities make full use of teams of inspectors with their own structure of office headed (in ten cases) by a Chief Inspector. A tradition is still preserved in that the majority of them have been heads of schools and/or have teacher-training experience. The over-all increase in numbers is somewhat difficult to determine, because nomenclature, conditions of service and allocation of duties vary so greatly. With the development of fresh emphases in teaching, particularly in relation to the all-sided growth of the child, some Authorities, certainly until quite recently, have appointed specialist subject-organisers, as in Physical Education, or in Rural Science, Domestic Subjects, Art, Music, Handicrafts. Their work is more patently advisory, though there are elements in it of a more executive nature, such as writing individual reports, sharing in full inspections of schools, advising governors or managers who (subject to the usual confirmations) appoint staff. The present use of organisers in the form of peripatetic teachers in such shortage subjects as Science is particularly relevant in this context and this may be a pattern for the future. Over-all, there seems to have been a 60 per cent increase in number of organisers and inspectors over the period 1939–1951: their size varies but in London County, a figure of 0·3 per cent of the whole education service may be quoted and 5 per cent of administrative costs.[2]

At the top of the national pyramid of responsibility is the Minister of Education, with mandatory powers now 'to secure

---

[1] International Bureau of Education Bulletin 1956, No. 120, p. 100.
[2] A. G. Hughes, *The Functions and Status of Local Inspectors*, p. 4, p. 10; *cf. Education in Kent 1933–38*, p. 193; and A. C. Ford, *Education in London in 1931*, p. 14.

the effective execution by local authorities under his control and direction of the national policy for providing a varied and comprehensive service in every area'. As was the case a century earlier, fears have been expressed of possible centralising ambitions on the part of government: others have pointed out that freedom to improve can also mean 'freedom to continue unimproved: and some stimulus is needed'. Perhaps the compromise in practice has best been suggested in the Second Report of the Local Government Manpower Committee for 1951:

> The Minister should in general rely on regulations only where the accepted key-points of control, including financial control, demand them . . . There are wide fields of educational administration where variation of practice is permissible within broad lines of policy which should be indicated in manuals of guidance, circulars, etc., rather than by regulations.

Any Minister of Education has and must have his battery of financial controls. If the state of the national economy demands that only so much money be allocated to the education service, then even the most progressive local authority recognises the need for rationing in terms of major (and minor) building programmes, or of teacher-pupil ratios.[1] But within such limits local educational programmes both in type of school and kind of work done in them have flourished with astonishing and laudable diversity.[2] This could hardly have happened where a Ministry of Education dealt out 'uncircumscribed imperatives' to local authorities. Selby-Bigge said some fifty years ago that the then Board of Education did regard itself as being in partnership with local authorities; and this is still true today. Indeed, in several cases, co-operation has extended to joint planning of schools, as the Ministry's Building Bulletin No. 3 (1961) shows. In such projects, Her Majesty's inspectors and local authority inspectors have played a part (in one latter case in the form of teachers seconded for advisory work).

In a period of rapid educational expansion inspectors often

---

[1] *cf.* for example Ministry of Education Administrative Memorandum No. 12/61 dated 8th June 1961. *Educational Building—Progress of Work*, and Circular 17/60, dated 29th Dec. 1960, *Employment and Distribution of Teachers*.

[2] *cf.* Ministry of Education List 69 (1960), *Secondary Education in each Local Education Authority Area*.

best fulfil their truest function, to be creative of development. It is in this context that the increase in the size of both central and local authority inspectorates should be judged. In the two decades prior to the last War, some of the changes in the administrative structure of Her Majesty's inspectorate might be glanced at; for example, the Medical Branch, headed by a Chief Inspector, was discontinued, and from 1923 until the re-organisation of the inspectorate in 1944, the post of Chief Inspector of (Teacher) Training was abolished, the duties being performed by a staff-inspector. In 1926, Sir Henry Richards, Chief Inspector of Elementary Schools was also made responsible for the whole inspectorate, and so chief adviser to the Permanent Secretary. But from 1944, built-in discriminations between 'elementary' and 'secondary' branches were finally discarded. After being more or less stationary for half-a-century, in the quinquennial period 1945–49 the number of Her Majesty's inspectors grew rapidly from 337 to 549. A new hierarchy of office emerged comprising one Senior Chief Inspector, six Chief Inspectors, various divisional and staff inspectors, and the inspectors in districts. Today, the over-all number of inspectors for England and Wales is 520.[1] In the highest traditions of the service, they have been associated with every phase of major educational planning at national level: two examples would be in the fields of 'further' education (including technological development and the youth service) and of Area Training Organisations. An even more arduous role is envisaged for them if the recommendations of the Beloe Report are implemented in their present form. Extension of inspectorial work has also taken place. In the process of bringing into operation Part III of the 1944 Education Act, all private schools have had to be reported on from the point of view of being recognised by the Ministry as 'efficient'. Perhaps the most welcome of changes under that Act has been the full realisation that religious education is

> a motion and a spirit that impels
> All thinking things, all objects of all thought.

The former dichotomy in inspection of 'religious' and 'secular' is ended: Her Majesty's inspectors now inspect as of right Religious Instruction given in accordance with any Agreed

[1] 475 for England, 45 for Wales (Ministry Establishment List, June 1961).

Syllabus (though only by invitation that given on denominational lines). The period since 1944 has also seen a succession
of pamphlets compiled for the Ministry by Her Majesty's
inspectors. Modestly described in one case as 'a new anthology
of the ideas and practices which teachers are successfully
developing in the schools', and further elaborated in courses for
teachers, they reflect all that is best in good democratic human
relationships. It may be noted that Her Majesty's inspectors
have their own Association or 'trade union'; so have L.E.A.
inspectors and organisers, which in addition organises its own
educational discussions. Conferences of inspectors, no less than
of heads, can be of great inspirational and practical value, in
solving some of the problems of

> improvement of instruction, education in service, supervision,
> and the development of curriculum materials.[1]

A parallel will be observed with Church-government in this
respect; at the close of the nineteenth century the bishop came
to rely less on visitational procedure and more on regular
synod meetings to explain and carry through to the field
workers in the parishes what official policy and opinion were at
any given time and on any particular issue. Her Majesty's
inspectors of course have always had many of the advantages
which come from discussion, in their area meetings, at national
courses, at panel meetings when pamphlets are being prepared,
or in a variety of overseas assignments. Lacking such powerful
stimulus to their thinking, Local Authority inspectors have
found their National Association of proportionately greater
value to them: it is interesting to see the many recent developments in the work of this Association which have helped give
members a more wide-spread sense of belonging—as well as
providing an opportunity to develop the wider view, to formulate at national level a body of thinking on educational matters
of moment and give it the publicity it may merit. Two other
tendencies might be noted in the history of local organising
inspectors over the last ninety years: more than occasional
breakdown; and a high 'turn-over' in members. This latter
point has relevance when the question of training for inspectors
is raised.

[1] R. C. Hammock and R. S. Owings, *Supervising Instruction in Secondary Schools*, p. 19.

Chapter Thirteen

WOMEN AS INSPECTORS AND ORGANISERS

THROUGHOUT the nineteenth century the general attitude to the work of women in the inspectorial field was curiously reticent, the Bryce Report merely commenting that:

> duly qualified women should be chosen where there is likely to be sufficient work for them.

Over and over again one hears of the stratagems to which Her Majesty's Inspectors were reduced when inspecting needlework in the schools,[1] and yet it was not until the coming of the School Boards that the full incongruity of the situation was fully revealed and remedied. Such a situation is all the more remarkable when one recalls the energies of pioneer Ladies' Committees in founding, supervising, and even financing, schools in the later eighteenth century: inspection by local committees of women was flourishing in some areas. Such a group of 'co-adjutors' led by Mrs. Cappe and Mrs. Gray nursed a spinning school into being in York between 1782 and 1785, adding a knitting school in 1786 'for the reception of children too young to spin worsted. From this, the spinners are taken as vacancies happen in the spinning school and as they become eligible by knitting a stocking in the course of a week, which is previously required.'[2] The school conformed to

[1] *cf.* A. P. Graves, *To Return to All That*, p. 175; *cf.* p. 171 and also E. M. Sneyd-Kynnersley, H.M.I. *Some Passages in the Life of one of Her Majesty's Inspectors of Schools*, p. 250-260.

[2] C. Cappe, *An Account of Two Charity Schools for the Education of Girls: And of a Female Friendly Society in York: Interspersed with Reflections on Charity Schools and Friendly Societies in General*, 1800.

a fairly general pattern in such things as the close link with Sunday worship, when the ladies conducted the girls to church. Moreover, its administration was characterised by thoroughness, vision and humanity. By 1798, its stability was so assured that the 15 ladies of the committee were able: 'to divide the business of general superintendence into particular departments. . . . First division, to keep the Books; receive Subscriptions; pay the wages of the Mistresses and Children (which requires attendance in person or by deputy, at least every Saturday morning); to draw up and state the annual accounts; and to be responsible for the whole of the expenditure. Second, to provide materials for clothing; to cut out the clothes; to appropriate the sewing work; and to keep an account of the several articles given to each individual. Thirdly, to superintend the wool spinning; to see it weighed both before and after it is spun; to correspond with the manufacturers; and to assist the Mistress in keeping the accounts, and in any other necessary calculation to which she may not be equal. Fourthly, daily superintendence. This to be divided among eight ladies, each to attend in rotation for the term of six weeks. They are to take cognizance from time to time of every thing that passes; to make minutes of whatever may deserve attention; and to state the results of these observations on Saturday, to those ladies who attend on that day to pay the rewards, and to distribute clothes. These propositions being brought forward at the annual general meeting of the patronesses of the institution in January last, were unanimously approved, and the several departments occupied as follows:

The Books and Expenditure—Miss Hasell.
The Clothes, etc.—Miss Salmond, Miss Marsh, Mrs. Perrot,
           Miss Clough and Miss Grimston.
The Wool—Mrs. Withers and Miss Barton.
Six weeks visitors—Mrs. Withers, Mrs. Dalton, Mrs. Dring,
           Mrs. Gray, Miss Royds, Miss Gray, Mrs.
           Cappe and Miss Salmond.'

The linking of visitation with executive decision is very apparent here.

Whilst they were organising the spinning school so efficiently they were appealed to for help by the Gentlemen's Committee which was failing so signally to run the Grey Coat School.

At once these ladies began a series of daily visits, made without flinching a series of unpopular decisions (including dismissal of the master) to create efficiency, and, in fact, achieved their aim so satisfactorily that the governors of the school delegated all power to the ladies. The latter, thereupon, clarified the external and internal government of the school with a set of carefully worded regulations:

1. That four meetings should be held in the course of the year, at which all who had already, or might hereafter choose to take upon themselves the superintendence of the school, should be desired to attend. That at these meetings, all affairs relating to the Charity should be discussed; new regulations, if at any time such appeared necessary, proposed; abuses redressed; and particular instances of merit, whether in the Mistresses or Scholars, rewarded.

2. That at these quarterly meetings, some one Lady should act as President, another as Secretary; to minute whatever particular transaction might deserve notice, in a book appropriated to that purpose.

3. That at every quarterly meeting, two ladies should be appointed particular Superintendents for the next three months, to attend in succession, six weeks at a time.

When such arrangements for general inspection proved insufficient, four other ladies undertook more detailed supervision of the administration of the school; while

the business of the ladies who take upon themselves the office of general inspectors, and who succeed each other every six weeks, is as follows:

To hear every girl read and spell, at least twice; once, when she enters on her superintendence, and again, before she resigns it. To minute down whatever may merit attention, whether as a matter of praise or of blame, in the conduct of the Mistresses, or girls, in a book to be produced at the ensuing general Committee Meeting. To inspect from time to time, the clothes presses, beds, sheets, etc. To see that all things are in proper order, and, in short, to take notice of everything, whether furniture, repairs, or whatever else may be wanted for the benefit of the Institution. Moreover, to call an extraordinary Committee Meeting, if any exigency should arise to make such a proceeding necessary.

This idea of an inspecting women's committee with the same status as any equivalent men's committee was duly taken over by the National Society, and as early as December, 1812, the

General Committee referred to the School Committee for consideration the formation of a Ladies' Committee to superintend the Girls' School at Trowbridge. On 5th March, 1813, the School Committee:

> resolved that the following regulations be submitted for the approbation of the General Committee:

> 1st   That a Committee of Ladies be formed for the purpose of inspecting the Girls' School.

> 2nd   That such Committee consist of those Ladies of the Members of the General Committee of the National Society who are disposed to undertake the duty, assisted by Ladies to be appointed by the School Committee.

> 3rd   That such Ladies be appointed annually at the Meeting of the School Committee next preceding the 25th March, and all vacancies be filled up from time to time as they arise.

> 4th   That three Ladies be appointed 'Monthly Visitors' in rotation for each month; and in order to render the arrangement convenient, every Lady shall be requested to set down those months in the year during which she can undertake to attend.

> 5th   That the general duty of the Committee of Ladies be to repair to the School on uncertain days and hours, and to note in a Journal to be kept for that purpose, whatever they observe worthy of censure or of particular praise, or of wants to be supplied: which Journal shall be laid before the School Committee at each of its meetings.

> 6th   That it be the special duty of the 'Monthly Visitors' to attend the weekly Examination of the Girls in order to watch over their progress in learning and Religious Instruction, to inspect their work and to see their rewards duly distributed—such weekly Examination to take place every Friday, or such other day in the week as shall hereafter seem most desirable.

Two basic conceptions thus emerge, namely, the voluntary nature of such inspection, shared out on a rota system; and the close link between examination and inspection, the two processes being regarded as complementary rather than dichotomous. The absence of any suggestion that the women as inspectors were inferior to the men may also be worth noting.

The six ladies comprising the Committee set to work with

an energy that earned the thanks of the General Committee in 1814 'for their attention and zeal in superintending the girls' school'. The immediate Committee to which they reported, however, was the School Committee, nor was its supervision nominal, for to it they regularly presented bills for payment; they detailed times of examinations; they suggested alterations in time-table arrangements, and 'asked permission' to purchase materials for rewards preparatory to the next examination.

The Annual Report of the Society in 1816 made mention of the ladies' 'assiduous superintendence' of 'the female department' of the Central School; and certainly they took their responsibilities very seriously. In 1817, they suggested to the School Committee that the upper age limit for girls be 14; but about this time the 'Female School' would seem to have run into trouble, for early the following year, a lack of 'due subordination and obedience' was noted. Three recommendation were made:

1. that it would be desirable to retain six girls over the leaving-age of 14;

2. that an extra mistress be appointed;

3. that 'the regular business of the school' be not altered on account of the attendance of visitors.

The whole matter was properly referred back by the School Committee to the Ladies' Committee, who replied that it would receive their full consideration, and asked that one girl be dismissed from the school for obstinacy. The assurance of the Ladies' Committee may be judged from a recommendation of theirs which came before the School Committee in January, 1818, that the girls' school be open to inspection by women visitors only. Perhaps the School Committee took fright at this, for at its meeting in March it rescinded the motion and, eleven months later, carefully emphasised that the Rev. W. Johnson's powers of superintendence extended to the girls' no less than to the boys' departments.

The Ladies' Committee was also closely concerned with staff appointments to the girls' school, and was quite equal to making arrangements for effective functioning of the school during an interregnum of mistresses; their recommendations usually carried great weight. They it was who decided how best to distribute among the teachers in the girls' schools the familiar weekly rewards: the 'approbation of the ladies' had long been a determining factor here. Traditions thus laid down were to be perpetuated; in 1840 the Ladies' Committee prompted the School Committee to give permission to the school mistress at Battersea to authorise her to purchase and distribute clothing to the amount of the money earned by the first class girls during the last six months, viz. £9 5*s*. 6½*d*. Again, in 1842, they suggested to the same Committee an arrangement for hanging up the girls' bonnets and cloaks. Their interest in girls' hygiene generally as a part of their education was of great importance for further developments: not surprisingly, John Flint dedicated his little *Manual of Health* to the ladies, in 1856.

Similar patterns of supervision by ladies' committees might be traced in the British and Foreign School Society. Article X of the 'Rules and Regulations for the government of the Institution' adopted in November, 1817, stated that:

A Committee of 24 ladies shall be appointed by the General Committee, to superintend the concerns of the female department of the School and Training Establishment; they will be expected to make a written report of their proceedings to the General Committee once every month.

The importance of having women visitors for local girls' schools was quickly realised. Thus, among the earliest Minutes of the National Free School in Westminster, a motion was passed:

That the School be visited once a week at the least, and the Scholars examined as to their progress by a Committee who shall enter their observations thereupon in the Secretary's Register, and sign the same; and that the Dean and Chapter of Westminster (or such of their Body as they shall from time to time appoint for that purpose) all the Vice-Presidents, and all the officiating Ministers of the Parish Churches of Saint Margaret and Saint John respectively shall be perpetual members of the visiting Committee, in conjunction with those Members of the Committee of Management, or such other persons as shall be elected annually for that purpose by a general Meeting of the Subscribers. That the visiting Committee do meet at the School upon the first Tuesday in every month at 11 o'clock punctually; and do provide

amongst themselves by rotation or otherwise for the regular
attendance of one or more members of the Committee on the
days of visitation for the rest of the month, and as much oftener
as may suit their convenience.
That the Ladies of the neighbourhood be earnestly requested to
lend their aid in visiting the Girls' School; as the good management and success of this Branch of the Institution must principally
depend upon their patronage and frequent inspection.

Within nine months, by which time fifteen ladies 'had kindly
undertaken to honour this institution by their personal attendance as visitors', the Management Committee ordered
that 'the Secretary do write letters to those ladies respectively
requesting to be informed which are the months it will most
suit their convenience to attend'. A rotation for superintendence was subsequently drawn up on a monthly basis, two
ladies for each month; their names were hung up in the girls'
school-room in a proper frame. It must be added that a similar
scheme operated for the men-visitors of the boys' school;
judging by the frequency of the same names, several husbands
and wives were engaged on the same duties. This rota system
was mapped out well ahead, subsequently on a March to
March basis. The ladies were by no means reluctant to criticise
where they felt criticism was needful; the Minutes of the
Committee of Management for 13th July, 1813, record their
complaints about the 'offensive effluvia' pervading the girls'
school from a nearby cow-yard—it was left to the gentlemen
to deal with the matter! These ladies also detailed the various
rewards to the girls, items such as petticoats, stockings, shifts
and frocks being recorded, almost invariably with the addition
of one shilling in cash.

Ladies' Committees were also in evidence in the provinces;
for example, the report of Sheldwick (in the diocese of Canterbury) for 1818, after noting the establishing in 1815 of two
National Schools, one for the boys and one for the girls, draws
attention to a committee of ladies 'who appoint two visitors
every month' in order to inspect 'the works of industry',
needlework usually. A more informal, but none the less pains-
taking system of inspection operated in Birmingham, where
there were no visitors as such: yet—

the girls' school is sufficiently superintended by two or three

Women as Inspectors and Organisers

ladies; who without any regular appointment as visitors, which they decline, bestow much time and attention on it.[1]

It would seem that all the various National District Societies, with their healthy regard for the segregation of sexes, inclined greatly to the idea of a committee of ladies being made responsible for the girls' department, with powers and functions almost identical to those of the men's committee; and the protocol of patronage demanded regular public recognition of the fact. The Report of the Lincoln School (in union with the National Society) for the year ended 25th March, 1821, states graciously:

> The Committee return thanks to the ladies and gentlemen who have acted as monthly visitors: the permanent success of the system will be greatly owing to the attention of those who execute this office. It is trusted that the lady visitors have found it a more agreeable duty since the separation of the children, as each division has now sufficient space, and there is considerably less interruption from noise.

The Gloucester Diocesan Society Report for 1820 proudly records:

> the Committee of Ladies have never failed to give their valuable attention to the conduct of the girls' school; and a Committee of Gentlemen have lately been formed to visit weekly that of the boys. Under this constant superintendence, which in fact is the animating spirit of every institution, your Committee trust that no relaxation will be suffered to take place in the adherence to system, and no failure in the attention to duty, either on the part of the instructors or scholars.

The Minutes of the Sheffield National District Society show the operation of the administrative-cum-supervisory machinery in some detail. At the first meeting of subscribers and friends on 12th May, 1813, certain broad principles and regulations were formulated, one being that the general management of the girls' school should be in the hands of a committee of 24 ladies, whilst a gentlemen's committee, also of 24 members, should be responsible for the welfare of the boys' school. Both committees were to meet once a month, exigency apart, and both were empowered to approve their own sub-committees

[1] National Society *Annual Report*, 1818, p. 194.

meeting together where necessary. The Ladies' Sub-Committee of three members had, as its first task, that of 'enquiring into the merits of the candidates for mistress'. They showed a remarkable spirit of independence, recommending none of the first list of candidates and suggesting further advertisement: then, an appointment of a candidate being recommended and duly confirmed by the General Committee, the girls' school opened 30th August, 1813. A next step was the appointment of visitors for the school on a weekly basis; on the subsequent rota drawn up, two a week were to act as visitors, the whole committee of 24 taking a turn in this way every twelve weeks. These two visitors, along with the three members of the Ladies' Sub-Committee, met weekly at the school, dealing with any unexpected difficulties and soon coming to assume the role of 'School Attendance Committee' in their zeal for investigating girls' absences from school. The connection with the larger Ladies' Committee, which at first met monthly, was clearly a strong one: the 24 Ladies, whose enthusiasm was such that they fined themselves 1/- for failure to attend meetings (subject, of course, to illness and to a ten-mile travelling radius)[1] took many administrative decisions which might properly come within the purview of a modern board of school managers. They drew up dates of term and holiday times; they decided rewards should be given to the three most deserving girls in each class, and were expected to provide those rewards. In the earliest days they ruled that the girls should make slips as far as they were able, four ladies working in rotation then being required to finish them off. They recommended to the full Committee for appointment the sewing mistress who was subsequently appointed at £20 a year. They decided that all girls should go to church on Sundays in holiday time, the visitors replacing for that day the mistress of the school, whose attendance was not made compulsory on these occasions. They standardised the rate of selling articles made by the girls in school (usually sold to the poor at prime cost). To the Treasurer and Secretary of the District Society they addressed a request that water should be supplied to the school. They 'examined and approved' the work in sewing of all girls before being 'permitted to work for hire';

[1] For four consecutively recorded three-monthly meetings, 1st July 1814, to 4th May 1815, only 7/- was recorded as paid in fines.

girls received thimble and scissors free but, if they lost them, the ladies decreed that the girls must pay for replacements. Within seven years, this Ladies' Committee, without, it seemed, a wrong word to anyone anywhere, was so established as to be able to formulate 'rules of management':

1. that the management of the mechanical part of the school be vested in Anne Somerset;

2. that the management of the sewing department be vested in Anne Watson;

3. that both mistresses should strictly conform to the discretions of Mrs. Holmes as Superintendent, and that no deviation from the instructions be allowed without permission of the Ladies' Sub-Committee.

Seen in this light, the 'best thanks' amicably extended to the Ladies' Committee at the General Meeting each year were no polite formality but a well-earned tribute.

The development of a similar supervisory role may be traced at Doncaster National School, where, on 25th November, 1816, the Committee gave the names of 40 ladies who should act as visitors to the girls' school, on the basis of four a month; within a fortnight the rota was drawn up and in action. The honour was no sinecure: in February, 1817, the Minutes record 'that it being thought necessary that the girls in this school should be furnished with slips and pockets, those ladies who are visitors for the present month be requested to provide same'. Other activities of this Ladies' Committee included the giving of rewards for good conduct and the presenting of complaints to the Corporation about 'the extreme badness of the footpath in front of the National School'. One particular sphere of inspection the ladies could expect to make their own: that was the girls' needlework and the teaching of it. The Minutes duly reflected this:

> It having been recommended by the ladies visiting the girls' school that in future Wednesday in every week should (after reading is gone through) be wholly devoted to instruction in needlework, Resolved—That the course suggested by the ladies be immediately adopted.

Elsewhere the ladies had recommended with some sagacity that a moiety of the money from the needlework should go to the teacher and to the 'seamstresses'; this was confirmed as general policy at the time by the Committee, though later all such profits were to be applied to the general fund. The ladies' watching brief was occasionally extended to more general aspects of pupils' social training: thus, the children having bought with the money out of the school clothing fund clothes 'scarcely to be denominated useful and warm', the Committee invited some of the more respectable local tradesmen to bring samples of clothing to the school for exhibition, adding that:

> the lady visitors be requested to superintend the purchase of the articles and see that the wishes of the Committee are strictly carried into effect.

That such assiduity was matched elsewhere may be gathered from other societies and schools in union with the National Society. In Louth, for instance, the girls' needlework and knitting were, in 1820:

> under the still uninterrupted and able directions and assistance of the worthy wife of the Vicar, and several truly benevolent ladies, who have for so many years given daily attendance at the school.

Another unsolicited testimonial of this kind came from the pen of J. J. H. Harris, after his organising visit to new schools in Swansea in 1848:

> During my stay at Swansea I have once or twice visited an interesting girls' school, and also an infants' school, situated in York Place. Mr. Tearle recently, and Mr. Fowler some time ago, organised the former of these; and a Committee of Ladies are so active and unceasing in their kind and voluntary self-imposed task of superintending them, that the plans proposed have been pursued most satisfactorily.

One must, however, mention that there were exceptions to this paean of praise: Mrs. Searle, on resigning from teaching at Merton National School, 7th February, 1837, said:

> When the school was founded (in 1831) seven ladies were named to form a Committee of Management. They have never held a single meeting; there has been no examination of the children, and several of the Committee have never been once in the school.[1]

[1] Central Society of Education, *Schools for the Industrious Classes, or the Present State of Education Among the Working People of England*, 1838.

The National Society gave the lead to the district committees in one other way: it considered the idea of peripatetic training mistresses held in the pay of the Society and available for temporary service in exactly the same way as the training masters were. Perhaps early social pressures were very great, for the principle seemed in danger of rejection at first: yet the idea subsequently blossomed with great effect. Again, to the lady members of the Society's Central School Committee in London must go the credit for encouraging the organised teaching of needlework and the raising of standards of performance. It should also be noted that the ladies always took part in the big two-day examination of the school held annually in public: the Ladies' Committees in the provinces carried out similar duties.

It may be interesting to note the later continuance of this feminine visitatorial tradition in the National Society's 'adopted daughter' societies. The diocesan inspector to the Northamptonshire Society (as reconstituted 1854) was the Rev. J. H. Brookes: in 1856, he recommended as desirable 'the further encouragement of sewing in our schools', going on to say:

> As one step in this direction I would suggest the establishing of a committee of ladies who should meet at stated times at Northampton or elsewhere, and to whom the managers of schools should be invited to send in specimens of really good work in knitting, sewing and cutting out, executed by their children. A few prizes of 10s. or 5s. each might be awarded to those whose work was of superior character, while every girl who acquitted herself sufficiently well might have presented to her a formal testimonial that she was a creditable needlewoman. Of course, it should be an understood thing that no girl should be allowed to send in her work whose character was not irreproachable.

The following year's report makes mention of £5 for sewing prizes and includes a report of the Ladies' Committee for Sewing Prizes: 21 schools from the western division of the county sent in specimens of work, prizes and cards of merit being awarded to 34 girls representative of 16 schools. In 1858, only 13 schools out of 64 in the eastern division of the county competed, two schools getting no award, the other eleven showing four first-class and eleven second-class prizes, and twelve cards of merit. The general inspectors' report for 1859 ends with a comment upon girls' 'industrial work' couched in

M

all the elegant, urbane phraseology that an era of patronage could produce:

> Our returns show that while with scarce an exception the girls in our schools are taught sewing and knitting, "darning" is taught in only 40 schools and "cutting out" in no more than 17. In other words, we have met with 78 schools in which it does not appear that the girls learn to make their own clothes, and with 55 in which they are not even instructed in the art of mending their own stockings. We should hope that something might be done to remedy this sad defect. But here we feel at once that we are treading on dangerous ground. We dare not expose ourselves in such a matter to the criticisms of the Ladies' Committee. We will do no more than simply mention the two facts, leaving it to their superior skill to devise and to carry out some plan for an improvement.

The Ladies' Committee duly took note of this comment, and for some time replaced their former method by an examination at one centre, invigilated by one or more Committee members.

Ladies of the Manor often evinced great interest in their local schools and acted as visitors-cum-supervisors, visiting the schools regularly and being both forthright in criticism and generous in praise and help. Early entries in school log-books often bear evidence of this. In other areas, groups of equally enthusiastic ladies did similar work, notably in Poor Law Schools and Ragged Schools. The Hull Ragged School and Industrial Schools Committee, in the first annual report of 1848, expressed their 'most earnest and heartfelt thanks . . . to the Ladies Committee who have, during the existence of this Institution, most zealously and ably carried out our views'. In this, their 'distinguished President' Miss Hill, had had 'the cheering and co-operative influence' of 24 other ladies—a not unfamiliar number on such committees. The Report also included a general comment that:

> It is almost impossible to over-rate the value of the assistance constantly and cheerfully rendered by the ladies. They have, in turn, daily attended the schools, aided the mistress in her duties, and by their kind sympathy, judicious counsel and cheering presence, have done much to elevate and improve the character and condition of the destitute and too long nighted recipients of the benefits of the institution.

Women as Inspectors and Organisers

They were, of course, not the only visitors:

> The Committee have pleasure in stating that the schools have
> been visited by numerous donors and subscribers.

Nevertheless, the ladies were, all so frequently, paragons of
visitatorial virtue in so far as voluntary service was required.
At Vines Court Day Ragged School, Spitalfield:

> about 40 girls are taught needlework by several ladies, who each
> devote one day in the week to this very useful purpose. The ladies
> provide the materials for work, which, when made up, is given
> to the most needy and deserving of scholars.[1]

Inspection of needlework, in fact, would seem to have been the
undisputed province of women examiners at local level: this
might, perhaps, be quoted as another example of how the
locality, in matters inspectorial, had useful lessons to offer to
the central government long before the latter was ready to take
them.

In the case of the Board Schools, too, Ladies' Committees
were called upon to inspect needlecraft on occasion; such
Committees frequently comprising the wives of existing
elected members of the School Boards. The School Management
Committee of the London Board, for example, resolved as early
as 10th January, 1873:

> that the Board inspectors be held responsible for this (needlework)
> inspection, and that they be empowered to ask the assistance of
> ladies on the management of the various schools and where this
> is impracticable to call in other efficient assistance.

Even this was but a temporary measure, and appointment of
specialist women organisers followed quickly. In another field,
that of hygiene in girls' schools, the group principle also acted
with marked cathartic effect. By the end of the century,
Domestic Economy, generally 'at first treated with scant respect
by parents, had become popular with them and is now generally
regarded as a necessity in girls' schools of all grades'; with
which development may be coupled J. C. Buckmaster's advice
to County Councils that District or Local Committees:

> need not exclude ladies, who are often very useful in educational

[1] London Ragged School Union, *Fourth Annual Report*, 1848, p. 15.

167

work, especially when Hygiene, Cookery and Domestic Subjects are taught.[1]

Woman's role, in fact, by the end of the century, had been shown to be an indispensable one in supervision of schools, both in a voluntary, unpaid, group capacity, and in a professional, paid, individual capacity. In the former context may be quoted the 'mass meeting of citizens of London' on 23rd May, 1902, which 'Emphatically condemn(ed) the Education Bill now before Parliament because it . . . excludes women from election to the education authority'. Whether as individuals, as in the case of Miss E. Bayley, Chairman of the Domestic Economy Committee of the L.C.C.'s Technical Education Board, or as groups, as in the case of the Ladies' Technical Instruction Sub-Committee of Nottingham City, women had staked a claim in the supervisory field. The link between unpaid service of this kind and the paid service of the professional servant can clearly be seen in a Special Sub-Committee of the London School Board's School Management Committee, 21st February, 1895–22nd February, 1900. This Sub-Committee, convened in order to investigate problems of accommodation in the Board's Girls' Industrial Schools, duly called upon the expert advice of first Mrs. Millar, then Mrs. Briscoe, both being employed by the Board in a paid capacity.

That the extension of the employment of women in such a capacity could hardly have been envisaged may be judged from an early comment of the Manchester School Board that:

it is inadvisable to employ women as inspectors for this Board.

Most of the bigger School Boards soon had an inspectress of needlework and some had an inspectress of infant schools, too. Leeds School Board combined the two appointments in Miss Louisa Banner, formerly Governess of Derby Training College, nor was this an 'ad hoc' expedient of the Board: though appointed 2nd December, 1884, at a salary of £150 a year, her duties had been carefully prescribed in April of the same year:

1. To supervise generally the needlework in the girls' and infants' departments of the Leeds Board Schools and to see that the necessary garments are prepared for examination by Her Majesty's inspector.

[1] J. C. Buckmaster, *County Councils and Technical Education*, 1891.

2. To direct the class instruction in needlework and to report on a special lesson given each half-year by each female pupil teacher . . .

3. To supervise the instruction of female pupil teachers in needlework, and to examine the needlework exercises at the quarterly examinations.

4. To examine the requirement forms for sewing material: and to report generally on the consumption.

5. To supervise the instruction of girls in domestic economy.

6. To supervise generally the instruction in infants' schools with special attention to correct methods.

7. To advise with the teachers and report as to the various occupations in infants' school . . .

8. To carry out such other incidental duties as may arise under the direction of the Committee through the Clerk to the Board.

Even before her appointment the Leeds School Board had seen the value of women as subject organisers: the Minutes of the Education and Management of Schools Committee for 29th January, 1874, record the proposition:

> In order to test practically whether instruction in physiology and the laws of health can be adapted to the capacities of children in the upper classes of elementary schools, a course of such lessons should be given, and that Mrs. Buckton herself offered to give such course of lessons.

She was one of the Board's liveliest members, and a good example of 'lay' expertise.

Her pilot-scheme of lectures was carefully worked out in conjunction with a prize-scheme: the enthusiastic response led to a repeat performance to over-subscribed courses. In 1876, the lectures were duly published in book form under the title *Health in the House*. Perhaps the sincerest form of compliment to them was the adoption of the first fourteen as the examination syllabus of lessons in Animal Physiology under the Liverpool Board. Mrs. Buckton's lectures touched upon the importance of food preparation and the principles of heat involved, etc.: they led on to a course of lessons being given at the Leeds School of Cookery, and a tremendous expansion of organising, peripatetic teachers of the subject stemmed from them: 4 by 1888, there were 23 by 1902, under Superintendent of Cookery, Miss F. Nicholson. Most other boards of any size had also shown a lively interest in the organisation of cookery instruction; in many there was a blending of specialist teaching-cum-organising of cookery with a group-form of supervision:

> The management of the cookery classes is frequently delegated by school boards to committees of ladies who from time to time devise schemes by which the interest of the girls is kept up in the school cookery classes. These schemes include exhibitions of dishes prepared and cooked entirely by the girls themselves, cookery competitions to which the parents and the public are admitted to watch the girls cooking, prizes being given for the best dishes and for smartness and neatness in working. The sympathy of the public and the interest of the parents are thus enlisted, and the popularity of the subject is increased.[1]

The stimulus given by Mrs. Buckton to the teaching of hygiene in girls' schools in Leeds was such that on 7th August, 1879, the Board appointed Mrs. E. Spencer Instructress in the Laws of Health: who

> goes the round of the girls' schools with great advantage to the pupils, accompanied by the necessary models, apparatus for experiments and diagrams.

Similarly, in 1891–2, after certain requirements had been laid down in the Code with relation to 'object lessons, and suitable occupations for Standard I, II and III', Salford Board appointed Miss E. Lea, formerly a headmistress under the Manchester School Board, to be an 'organising mistress',

> whose duty it will be to supervise and examine the Board's infant schools and also to superintend the juniors' departments and the lower standards of other departments, so far as object lessons and suitable occupations are concerned. The duties of the organising mistress also include the holding of classes for head and assistant teachers, in the kindergarten system, and the visitation from time to time as may be thought desirable, of schools in other districts with a view to obtaining information as to the best methods of instruction.

These classes were also open to teachers in voluntary schools;

[1] *Special Reports on Educational Subjects*, 1896–7, Vol. I, p. 161.

and if infants' departments in these schools (through their Managers) wanted her services, they were to be had 'under an approved scheme and on payment of a guinea per annum'.

Many other Boards and some Technical Education Committees had appointed organising mistresses on similar terms, but in Miss Banner the inspectorial and organising functions were more closely blended. This is even more obvious in the case of Miss Bailey, 'Female Inspector of schools' to the Liverpool Board, for she made five signal contributions to educational planning in Liverpool: 'School needlework and cutting out for the New Code Home Lesson Book for needlework and cutting out for junior teachers and older girls'; 'Hints on introducing the kindergarten into English infant schools'; 'A Syllabus of lessons in animal physiology'; 'A Course of lessons in Religious Knowledge in infant schools'; and 'A plan for the instruction of pupil teachers in sewing and also the mode of teaching that subject'.

The contrast between the attitude of the School Boards and the Education Department is, therefore, all the more striking. It is extraordinary that Her Majesty's inspector, Mr. D. R. Fearon, should publicly recognise that:

> very few men examine infants really well. Women are naturally much better qualified for such a task,[1]

and yet the appointment of women inspectors by the Education Department be so long delayed. By contrast, the School Boards showed themselves much more venturesome; and the expansion in the local field of women-organisers over a whole range of subjects (some of them new) did much to enhance their claim to more general recognition by the lay-public, the more so when their supervisory work was set against a background of a greatly increased number of women-teachers, proportionately far exceeding any corresponding increase in men-teachers. The new Local Education Authorities under the Act of 1902 thus inherited from the School Boards a tradition of inspecting and organising by women, as well as (where relevant) the women themselves. Chosen as they were from the ranks of the most successful women teachers, they found a ready place in inspection, organising and in administration by the bigger Authorities. Robert Blair, in his evidence before the Royal

[1] D. R. Fearon, *School Inspection*, 1876, sect.13.

Commission on the Civil Service in 1912, made reference to this.

Some comparable adjustment in Her Majesty's inspectorate was inevitable: in 1883 a start was made with the appointment of a Directress of Needlework, and an Inspectress of Cookery and Laundry was added in 1890, both appointments being initially on a temporary basis only. After the advent of Robert Morant in 1902, more women inspectors were to work with Her Majesty's inspectors, totalling seven by 1904.

Thereafter, their numbers increased steadily, and though they had certain rights of reference or access to the Chief Woman Inspector, for all intents and purposes they were meant to work as part of the ordinary staff in a district, on exact equality with the other inspectors except that they were not put in charge of a district. (Then they would have had concomitant responsibilities for supervising other inspectors and being the chief administrative link with local authorities in the area.) They participated (according to qualification and experience) in full inspections, the girls' side obviously being one of their main concerns. Equality of pay with men-inspectors was as yet some way off, the ordinary woman inspector earning £200 by £15 to £400. An age-limit on appointment (by nomination) was not set.[1] By 1912, there were 48 women Her Majesty's inspectors, 17 being appointed that year, 11 to the Elementary Branch, 5 as Domestic Science Specialists, one as Physical Training specialist. By 1923, they totalled 78, still constituting a separate corps, with a Woman Staff Inspector in each division filling the post of 'First Lady': all had the advantage of being automatically H.M.I.s, perhaps a source of some disquiet for men assistant-inspectors? But by 1935 final 'aggregation' or full integration of the sexes within the service was being achieved; and some women were appointed district inspectors in both the Elementary and the Secondary Branch (not in the Technological Branch however). In 1936 a woman divisional inspector was appointed. One last change—in nomenclature—may be noted: in 1938 the title of Senior Woman Inspector replaced that of Chief Woman Inspector; and this is the title now commonly used by Local Authorities.

[1] Royal Commission on Civil Service 1912–14, *Second Report*, Appendix Q.8869–Q.8887.

Chapter Fourteen

SOME PROBLEMS OF INSPECTORS

INSPECTION of schools has been a process of growth in this country. With the exception of a single phase associated with payment by results, it has relied on public persuasion rather than executive authority to achieve educational improvement. Its success has been attributable to first-rate scholarship, rich experience and great personal qualities in those who inspect; all are essential. Over the last century and a half, the difficulties of inspectors have centred on two things; recruitment and training, and the degree of relationship with their employing agency. These two problems—which still exist—arise from the very nature of inspectors' functions, which briefly are fourfold, though no hard and fast line can be drawn between them. Firstly, they must find out the facts of any given situation, assemble them, and pass them on to Ministry or Local Authority with appropriate recommendations where called for. This duty extends into many fields; it may take the form of school inspection, it may be study of building, accommodation plans. It might also include investigation of complaints by members of the public, whose right to complain, incidentally, should never be called into question; it is an essential ingredient in any democratic community.

Another function of inspectors is the dispersal of sound practice, based on currently valid principles, over as wide a field as possible. Classroom demonstration is the most obvious form of this, but in general, inspectors fight shy of it, not because they cannot do it but because, quite apart from derogation of a teacher's own status, they realise 'there are already in use many very efficient yet different modes of controlling and instructing a school, and many still better modes have yet to be discovered'.[1]

Of course, if a teacher asks for guidance through being shown how, then the inspector must be able and quite ready to do so. Such demonstration not only sets a standard for the teacher but establishes that very precious bond of confidence between him and the inspector. This may be achieved in other ways, outside the classroom. Influence can be spread through an agreed rubric, drawn up by Ministry or Local Authority in consultation with teachers. Suggestions (no more than that) for improvements in teaching are then widely publicised in the familiar pamphlet-form and pressed home through advertised conferences and courses for those who are inspected. It will be noted that teachers are perfectly free to stay away from such courses; this is entirely consonant with the idea that 'inspectors' advice is really advice and advice that need not be followed'.[2] There is, however, an inherent assumption that the advice is good in that all inspectors, who are drawn from the ranks of the best teachers, have seen what is best in current practice, and thought long and carefully about it. Indeed, inspectors' own best thinking is often an amalgam of what the best teachers and the best administrators are thinking. Mention is made of the latter, because it should not be assumed that original thinking is confined to teachers. Most professional administrative officers have been teachers in any case, but more important, educational advance may often rely ultimately on suitable executive exegesis. A current example is school library development. Here, an additional financial incentive from the Ministry in respect of libraries in newly built secondary schools gives added weight to the recommendations of Her Majesty's Inspectors.

It would be idle to deny that vestiges still remain of the Orwellian function of 'big brother is watching you', so continuing to give rise to the cynical truism that an inspector's greatest value is that he is known to exist, even if those he inspects never see him. This deterrent, inquisitional role is not surprisingly the one inspectors react most against, preferring the much more positive conception of themselves outlined in the Board of Education Report 1922–23: that of 'disseminating in

[1] J. G. Fitch, *Evidence*, Bryce Commission Report, vol. V, p. 435.
[2] Ministry of Education Report, *Education in* 1949, p. 94.

convenient fashion, results and suggestions derived from continuous recorded observations'. This extends to independent and direct grant schools no less than to maintained schools. It might be said in extenuation that a regulative role for Central and Local Education Authority was written into the 1944 Act, which in turn must carry over on to inspectors. An example would be ensuring that the corporate Act of Worship takes place every school day. Nevertheless, teachers do not easily forget what Revised Code days stood for, and watch carefully against any signs of inspectors succumbing to the genetic tendency of all authority to develop its own mystique or cult of power. It is in this connection that the fourth function of inspectors has relevance, namely energising the employing agency as well as assisting teachers in 'the completion of their own design'. Inspectors should know that 'all systems, once established, tend to cease thinking, except intermittently, and operate by their own momentum; and here educational systems are no better than Churches or States or Social Orders. The machine, once started, functions as an end in itself; and self-content forgets the purpose for which it was created'.[1] Autonomous motivation is the greatest danger any inspector has to combat, for he himself can so easily be drawn into it. Perhaps the chronic attempt by inspectors to offset this by the cultivation of a lively inquiring mind causes some inspectors to seem to become eccentrics or faddists.

Much of the controversy over recruitment and training of inspectors has stemmed from the two-fold nature of their allegiance, on the one hand to schools, on the other to those who appoint them inspectors. To be creative of development and yet to interpret and assess current trends requires of an inspector both extensive and intensive educational background of a personal and professional kind. Without some motivating philosophy of education, he can never judge wisely of differing types of school and the quality of teaching in them. This is all the more important when less than 2 per cent of the teaching profession remain unqualified. In the not too distant past, it was by no means axiomatic that 'in the appointment of inspectors, special consideration should be given to scholastic attainments and diplomas, knowledge of psychology and

---

[1] R. W. LIVINGSTONE, *The Rainbow Bridge*, p. 119.

pedagogy, and educational experience, a certain minimum number of years of teaching service being deemed essential'.[1] When the authoritarian role of H.M. Inspectors was most pronounced, so were teachers' criticisms bitterest; T. Runciman even went so far as to term them in print 'unlicked cubs'. Inspectors themselves were likewise embarrassed by seeming to be, in the words of J. G. Fitch 'pedants and detectives'. Their difficulties as grading officers, if such they had to be, were increased by considerable personal variation in assessment, lending further weight to this demand that they have previous training at the level at which they inspect. Yet again, the rapid increase in numbers of H.M. Inspectors (73 in 1870 to 120 in 1877), without the previous common denominators that clergy had had, made introduction of some forms of training a necessity.

Hence the concern in the Instructions to Inspectors, 1878 to ensure 'uniformity of standard (which) will also be further secured by the proposed special training of all inspectors who may hereafter be appointed'. It is not accidental that the demise of Payment by Results should coincide with the Revised Instructions to Inspectors of 1892, where personal discussion was emphasised as the main means of ensuring

> substantial uniformity of judgment and of practice throughout the divisions, without unduly interfering with the methods and with the personal responsibility of individual inspectors.

Yet admirable as this might sound, it was still not enough to meet the wishes, even the demands, of the N.U.T. that training must include having done the job for oneself first.[2]

Four concurrent aspects of training for Her Majesty's inspectors may be discerned which did much to maintain the high traditions of the service;

> (a) Continuous training in the ways of doing things by means of courses after appointment. A familiar feature of 'in-service' training today, it was less so in 1840. The National Education

---

[1] *International Bureau of Education Bulletin*, 1956, No. 120, p. 104.

[2] Royal Commission on the Civil Service 1912–14, *First Appendix to Fourth Report* (Cmd. 7339), Appendix 8.

Some Problems of Inspectors

Board in Ireland effectively applied the idea in 1856;[1] but the real credit for the idea must lie initially with certain Anglican diocesan inspectors.[2]

(b) Institution of certain grades of appointment not carrying full status at once. The best example of this was the inspector's assistant after 1863. His elementary school background, combined with the 'Oxbridge' background of H.M.I. proper, made for a better type of inspection without committing the inspectorate to seeming dilution: in theory at least it also provided for promotion of the assistant to full rank. An ex-pupil teacher like Abel Jones might lend relish to the point.

(c) 'Observation—practice', by being attached to more experienced colleagues for a time. This was current practice over a hundred years ago, but still finds its place in advice circulated to H.M.I.s: 'new inspectors begin by learning from their older colleagues, partly by precept, chiefly by example, often by listening. Each inspector then slowly evolves his own way of doing things, a way that is constantly modified by experience and by new or unfamiliar demands. What to look at on any one occasion, how to look at it, what help to expect from colleagues, what aids to appraisal to use, how much advice to give, how strongly to express criticism, whether and how to report—these are all matters in which tradition and individual experience must instruct. An inspector, if he is wise, will depart from the former only after anxious meditation but he will be expected to learn from and act upon experience and not to await direction from above. In a word, he has the privileges and the responsibilities of independence.'

(d) A final safeguard was the so-called probationary period. The length was a matter of much debate. Her Majesty's Chief Inspector, Mr. H. E. B. Harrison, suggested one as long as three years, but his colleague Mr. J. G. Fitch expressed utmost concern at the whole idea. A two year probation for examiners was mentioned by Sir L. A. Selby-Bigge in his evidence before the Royal Commission on the Civil Service in 1912: that it was infrequently invoked may perhaps be adjudged from his figures

---

[1] P. W. Joyce, (one organiser) summarised the scope of the course in his *Handbook of School Management and Methods of Teaching sanctioned by the Committee of National Education, Ireland.* It ran to a third edition 1867 and an eleventh, 1887.

[2] v. R. Hey *Evidence*, Select Committee on Education, 1865, Q.5045 and F. Close, *National Education*, 1852, p. 28–29.

of two inspectors and two examiners who left before completing such a period: 'I think you may say they resigned,' he added.[1]

It should be added that initial recruitment by nomination also helped reduce any margin of error. Only in the case of the Irish inspectorate were candidates required to take a written examination: this could be a very searching test of suitability. In all these ways, Her Majesty's inspectors were gradually able to overcome the expressed criticism that they were 'crotcheteers', whose greatest weakness was lack of professional training, in turn the cause of so much inefficiency.

A similar problem of training faced Her Majesty's inspectorate in its rapid expansion after 1945. The grade of 'assistant' inspector was abolished (the higher age of recruitment merited no less); but a combination of the other three methods was used most effectively, including a stated probationary period of two years.

Another approach to the problem has been to recruit teachers with the right kind of immediately relevant experience: School Board inspectors and organisers were examples. Specialist inspectors in Ministry and Local Authority today are still appointed on this basis. But if a whole army of inspectors is not to be created, so tending to bureaucracy of a most insidious kind, some inspectors may from time to time have to work in fields additional to those for which they have been specifically trained and of which they have immediate previous experience. It is assumed that after a period of observation and in-service training, such inspectors can extend their effective range in this way; men inspectors of infant or lower junior classes might be a case in point. It was the extreme form of this that once contributed much to those socio-economic tensions in inspectorates of both an external and internal kind.

In view of the inspector's advisory role, some 16 attempts to find a more appropriate title for him have been noted, including Visitor, Agent, Superintendent, Organising Master,

---

[1] *Loc. cit.* Q. 8899, 9049. Two inspectors and one examiner were 'pensioned off' before retirement (*ibid.* Q.9164). Examiners were not officially regarded as educational experts, the Board relying for advice about technical questions or educational policy upon the inspectors and various standing committees which were largely composed of inspectors (*ibid.* Fourth Report, First Appendix, p. 25, footnote).

Secretary, Commissioner, Organiser, Demonstrator, Supervisor, Examiner, Adviser. The generic term 'officer' has been used in such titles as Education Officer, Advisory Officer; and overseas, 'consultant' has found favour. The difficulty with all of these is that each may illustrate only one facet of an inspector's work, and thus be incomplete. Perhaps this is why the suggestion (in the Scottish Education Department's Report on Secondary Education 1947) that the title 'His Majesty's Education Officer' be substituted for 'His Majesty's Inspector' was politely ignored. 'Inspector' has other advantages too, in that it has some prestige value, and permits of hierarchy in such gradations as assistant-inspector, inspector, senior in-inspector, chief inspector; it also can draw on inspectress to indicate a sex difference (though the term is very rarely used in practice); in a sense it is etymologically correct, if an inspector's main function is to 'look into', so militating against endless fragmentation of terminology; above all, it is a distinctive word understood and used generally by teachers, administrators and the lay public.

The question may be asked 'why not second teachers to inspectorial duties for a certain time?' This indeed would eliminate many of the difficulties associated with training. It was first tried out in this country before 1912 when seven women teachers were seconded to the Board of Education; the experiment was not a great success, it seems, though social and administrative pressures may then have been against it. Other countries have had better results with secondment. Austria appoints specialist inspectors for fixed periods (five years usually) from among outstanding teachers. Portugal has a similar scheme in secondary and tertiary education, renewable every three years. Denmark has a half-time appointment, rotating two days teaching and three days inspection. At primary level, Turkey has peripatetic headmasters: in Sweden local inspectors serve for six years. These permutations might give a deal of flexibility to the English system though they might restrict the field of long-term usefulness of an inspector; they would all seem to ignore too that particular relationship existing in this country between the inspector and his master.

To be fully effective, an inspector must be free to give an honest appraisal, without fear or favour, of all he sees and hears. As the Vice-President of the Law Society said 2nd March, 1959, 'a large and not irresponsible section of the public feel that the report of an inspector cannot be relied upon to express an independent view so long as he has to report to the Ministry which controls him'. This reference to a particular type of inspector (in relation to the Administrative Tribunals and Enquiries Report) may serve to illustrate a dilemma for all school inspectors and those who appoint them. The Minister of Education pointed out (in the Jubilee Edition of *The Times* Educational Supplement, 2nd December 1960) that Her Majesty's Inspectors were not 'his' inspectors, though he it is who answers any questions that might be raised in Parliament about their work. The system of appointment by Order-in-Council contributes to public confidence in their independence even if criticism has also been made of it, as for example, before the Royal Commission on the Civil Service in 1929.

Yet they are civil servants, and the restraints and controls placed upon them in the nineteenth century grew out of the need, created by the growth of government responsibilities for national education, for a small body of men performing similar duties and services. The corresponding need for some kind of organisation and code of rules to ensure all were treated alike in such matters as behaviour, remuneration, attention to duties, produced those many tensions of a socio-economic kind. A greater problem still was how much curtailment of complete independence of thought and action by inspectors was desirable. Seymour Tremenheere and one or two colleagues reacted strongly against Executive 'sallies of red tapism' with some success. The Education Department tried again in the later 1850s as recapitulated later by the Select Committee (Inspectors' Reports) 1864.

'The revision (of Her Majesty's Inspector's reports) which before 1858 was principally for the purpose of condensation, was from that time carried into effect in the following manner. The Secretary, considering that the Committee of Council were responsible for the exclusion of irrelevant and objectionable matter from the reports, directed the officer whose duty it was to read for the press, to examine the reports with increased care.

This officer used to call the Secretary's attention to passages which he considered objectionable either by marking them or mentioning them orally. If the Secretary thought the objection invalid or unimportant, he over-ruled it, but if he thought it important, he sent the report to the Vice-President, with the reader's marks, and with observations of his own if he thought necessary.

Mr. Adderley, while he was Vice-President, used to read the manuscript report himself, and to strike out with his own hand those passages which he thought inadmissible.

The inspectors, on receiving back their manuscripts with the proof, had an opportunity of seeing what had been objected to and of correcting the proof accordingly.'

Before Lowe assumed office as Vice-President then in 1859, the principle had been tacitly established within his Department that inspectors' reports, before being printed, were subject to scrutiny and possible amendment by what may euphemistically be termed administrative colleagues. Lowe himself discontinued the practice of striking out passages: the perturbing thing is that the Secretary should continue to mark passages without Lowe's knowledge. The Minute of Committee of Council dated 31st January 1861 was prompted by a case of a Catholic inspector exceeding his brief (his printed report compared Roman Catholic and Protestant morality in a biased way). This Minute stressed that previous Instructions to Her Majesty's Inspectors amounted to the fact that inspectors 'must confine themselves to the state of schools under their inspection, and to practical suggestions for their improvement; if any report, in the judgment of their Lordships, does not conform to this standard, it is to be returned to the inspector for revision; and if on its being again received from him it appears to be open to the same objection, it is to be put aside as a document not proper to be printed at the public expense.'

The sequence of events thereafter is a fascinating example of administrative 'creep'. Accidentally, Lowe became aware in 1862 that reports were being marked and ordered this should cease (by a note of his private secretary, dated 14th February, 1862). This was not a change in policy, however, as reports objected to were not altered then and there, but returned to the inspector(s) with a covering letter drawing attention to the Minute of 1861 and leaving the necessary inference to be drawn: by most inspectors it was. In August the following year the usual circular letter of instruction to inspectors to compile their annual report, on Form No. 17A, 1861, included an additional gloss: 'by the term "state of schools under your inspection" you will understand facts observed within the circle of your official experience; and by the term "practical suggestions for their improvement" you will understand "suggestions consistent with the principles of Minutes sanctioned by Parliament".'

It was the marking in pencil by the Secretary, R. R. W. Lingen, of the Rev. H. Longueville Jones' report 1862–63 which precipitated the Resolution of the House of Commons on 12th April, 1864 that 'the mutilation of the reports of Her Majesty's inspectors of schools and the exclusion from them of statements and opinions adverse to the educational views entertained by the Committee of Council, while matter favourable to them is admitted, are violations of the understanding under which the appointment of inspectors was originally sanctioned by Parliament and tend entirely to destroy the value of their reports.'

Lowe resigned, believing his personal honour to have been impugned; but the Select Committee on Education appointed 12th May, 1864, to inquire into the practice of the Committee of Council with regard to the reports of the inspectors did in fact support his policy: 'the supervision exercised in objecting to the insertion of irrelevant matter, of more dissertation, and of controversial argument, is consistent with the powers of the Committee of Council, and has, on the whole, been exercised fairly and without excessive strictness'.

The Report also added a very illuminating rider:

'The knowledge, or even a reasonable suspicion, that the inspectors' reports are subject to alteration, either directly or indirectly, at the instance of the Department, has, without a doubt, a tendency to lower their value, if they are to be regarded as independent sources of testimony in matters of opinion or controversy touching the educational views of policy of the Committee of Council.'

But the due effect of this is minimised by the next sentence in the Report: 'It appears, however, to your Committee, that whatever may have been the understanding under which the appointment of inspectors was originally sanctioned, Parliament cannot be presumed to be ignorant (since the year 1858 at latest) that the heads of office may have exercised a censorship over the inspectors' reports as to the insertion of argumentative or irrelevant matter; and your Committee are of opinion that some such power is essential to the effectual working of the Department so long as it retains its present constitution and functions.'

The idea of inspectors answering specific questions rather than making general reports was considered but rejected; and possibly as a future safeguard for inspectors, all instructions to inspectors, it was recommended, should be laid before Parliament with the annual report of the Committee of Council. Thereafter, inspectors were more clearly identified as Civil Servants with appropriate allegiance; the Board of Education, for example, perturbed by an incipient tendency of inspectors to take sides (W. P. Turnbull was one) decreed that they must not use their title if publishing any work—a decision recently happily reversed by the Minister of Education. But inspectors were (and still are) allowed a considerable measure of independent discretion in educational matters, provided criticism of official policy is not made in public. Lord Runciman claimed as much in a House of Commons debate, 27th March, 1911: 'the fact that officers of the Board do not hold identical views on all educational matters should not, and I believe does not, prevent them from loyally promoting whatever may be, for the time being, the policy of the Board.' (Selby Bigge made delicate allusion to the same point in his evidence before the Royal Commission on the Civil Service some two years later; so does the Ministry of Education Report 'Education in 1949'.)

In the case of local authority inspectors of schools, the answer to the question 'Quis custodiet ipsos custodes' has never been in doubt. From the first, they have been closely associated with an executive allegiance. Nevertheless, they have shown those qualities of originality and independence which A. J. Balfour thought desirable for such servants of local authorities to have. They are of course as much anonyms as Her Majesty's inspectors; they can contribute to policy-making and even initiate it, but they cannot insist on it. J. Willm caught this aspect of their work when he said that inspectors must

> confine themselves to observing carefully and to reporting what they have observed to the authorities from whom they hold their appointment . . . In their reports, they should, at the same time, state their observations and their views as to what should be done;

183

and the various authorities, from whom they derive their mission, should appreciate and make such use of them as they may judge proper.[1]

It may be worth adding that a comment of Lord Runciman's when President of the Board of Education, that he could not interfere between local authorities and their own inspectors is indicative of those very correct relations which have always subsisted between central and local authority. The point has particular relevance today when, since 1944, the Minister is empowered to intervene in cases where local authorities are proposing to make 'unreasonable exercise of their functions'. A rare point is raised here for if discretionary power is delegated to local authorities, presumably it cannot be half-delegated. If, for example, clearance from first year probation of a teacher is recommended by the local authority, there is every reason to assume that such recommendation should be accepted by the Ministry. The latter's Circular 284 (Revised), 6th February, 1958, has now made this position abundantly clear. In practice, as always, personalising of administrative memoranda through inspectors makes for most effective liaison.

In the ultimate resort then, inspectors resemble nothing so much as the chameleon—except that they can create their own best working environment. Her Majesty's inspectors help safeguard the ever-increasing parliamentary grants, though they are by no means the only safeguard. They represent the Ministry in their dealings with local education authorities. Local inspectors exercise similar responsibilities in relation to their own Authority. Yet it is the advisory side of inspectors' work which today is most in evidence. In New Zealand, for instance,

> The central function of an inspector of schools . . . is simply that of guiding, as well as he can, the efforts of the teachers to serve the children in the schools; in other words that of helping school staffs and individual teachers to do a better professional job. This is a function inspectors can exercise in many different ways; by assisting individual teachers with their personal and professional problems; by consulting with schools over their policies and programmes; by fostering good staff team work; by organising study groups, encouraging professional reading, and actively supporting other forms of in-service training; by judicious

[1] *The Education of the People*, 1847, pp. 181–2.

Some Problems of Inspectors

stimulation and guidance of experimental work in the schools; by working with teachers on such specific projects as a district plan for school library development; by spreading among teachers fresh and useful ideas from whatever source.[1]

Most inspectors in this country might claim a similar function; some would like it to be their sole function. University Institutes of Education might also claim to be doing just this. Other fresh emphases in inspectors' work may be observed overseas. In the United States of America, for instance, joint projects of a community kind have been undertaken in which teachers and supervisors participate. The very extent of the advisory service might also seem to endanger ultimately what that service sets out to achieve.[2] In this country, the simple fact is that *at present* inspectors of schools do inspect schools; they use a sampling technique because they are few; they are few because over-inspection is the greatest deterrent known against growth of self-responsibility. They inspect as representatives of the Ministry or Local Authority, not of the teachers themselves. Teachers share in these inspections in that many are by request of heads, and inspectors have been drawn from the best teachers; in some cases, experienced serving heads have participated in inspections, by all-round agreement. Perhaps the real future lies in the leadership which inspectors must offer: for

> Men (and women) with this ability create a group power rather than express a personal power. . . . The best leader does not persuade men to follow his will—he shows them what it is necessary for them to do in order to meet their responsibility, a responsibility which has been explicitly defined to them. Such a leader is not one who wishes to do people's thinking for them, but one who trains them to think for themselves.[3]

[1] D. G. Ball and N. E. Campbell, 'Changing role of the Inspectorate: a New Zealand view' (*New Era*, Nov. 1955, p. 191); *cf.* also R. C. Hammock and R. S. Owings, 'Supervising instruction in secondary schools', p. 12, p. 292 ff.

[2] *Cf.* G. Corder, 'An evaluation of supervisory services for newly appointed teachers' (*Elementary School Journal*, May 1954); and J. C. Morrison *et al., Current problems of Supervisors*, Columbia University 1930, p. 204.

[3] M. P. Follett, *Freedom and Co-ordination. Lectures in Business Organisation*, p. 52, p. 56.

SELECT BIBLIOGRAPHY

I (a). Works by Denominational Inspectors

BAGSHAWE, F. L., *A catechism of the sacraments of the Catholic Church.* Longhurst, 1871.
FLINT, J., *Plain hints for organising and teaching a church school and conducting its routine for an entire day.* Simpkin, Marshall, 1856.
HARRIS, J. J. H. and TEARLE, F., *The School Room.* Robinson, 1849.
HOPWOOD, H., *Principles of National Education.* Robinson, 1840.
ROSS, J., *The inquirer directed.* London, 1861.
A New Testament Plan of Christian Finance. (3rd Edition) London, 1874.
THOMSON, W., *Work and prospects. A Charge delivered to the clergy of the diocese of York.* Murray, 1865.

I (b). Works by Her Majesty's Inspectors

ARNOLD, M., *The twice revised Code.* Fraser's Magazine, May 1862.
ARNOLD, M., *Schools and universities on the continent.* Macmillan, 1868.
ARNOLD, M., *Culture and anarchy.* (2nd edition) Cambridge, 1948.
ARNOLD, M., *Reports on elementary schools 1852–1882* (F. S. Marvin ed.). H.M.S.O., 1908.
CHARLES, R. H., *Inspection and advice, central and local.* Education Handbook No. 3. Jarrold, 1948.
FEARON, D. R., *School inspection.* Clay, 1876.
FITCH, J. G., *Lectures on teaching.* C.U.P., 1884.
FITCH, J. G., *Thomas and Matthew Arnold.* Heinemann, 1897.
FITCH, J. G., *Educational aims and methods.* C.U.P., 1900.
GRAVES, A. P., *To return to all that.* Cape, 1930.
HOLMES, E. G. A., *What is and what might be.* Constable, 1911.
HOLMES, E. G. A., *The tragedy of education.* Constable, 1913.
HOLMES, E. G. A., *In defence of what might be.* Constable, 1914.
JONES, A. B., *I was privileged.* Abbrevia, 1943.
JONES, A. B., *From an inspector's bag.* Abbrevia, 1944.
SNEYD-KYNNERSLEY, E. M., *HMI. Some passages in the life of one of Her Majesty's Inspectors of Schools.* Macmillan, 1908.

Bibliography

SWINBURNE, A. J., *Memories of a school inspector. Thirty-five years in Lancashire and Suffolk.* (Author c. 1912.)

TREMENHEERE, H. S., *Notes on public subjects made during a tour in the United States and in Canada.* Murray, 1852.

TREMENHEERE, H. S., *A manual of the principles of government.* Kegan Paul, Trench (3rd edition) 1883.

WATKINS, F. W. *Letter to His Grace the Archbishop of York.* Bell, Daldy, 1860.

WILSON, P. *Views and prospects from Curzon Street.* Blackwell, 1961.

1 (c). WORKS BY LOCAL AUTHORITY INSPECTORS

BALLARD, P. B. *Things I cannot forget.* U.L.P., 1937.

*BIRCHENOUGH, C. A. *Inspectors and organisers in the educational system.* National Assoc. of Inspectors and Educational Organisers, 1946.

BRAY, S. E. *School Organisation.* (2nd Edition) U.T.P. 1911.

CHRISTIAN, G. A. *English education from within.* Gandy, 1922.

HAYWARD, F. H. *The psychology of educational administration and criticism.* Ralph, Holland, 1912.

*HUGHES, A. G. *The functions and status of local inspectors.* National Assoc. of Inspectors and Educational Organisers, 1951.

HUGHES, A. G., *Education and the democratic ideal.* Longman, 1951.

HUGHES, A. G., (and E. H. HUGHES), *Learning and teaching.* Longman (3rd edition), 1959.

HUGHES, A. G. (and E. H. HUGHES). *Education, some fundamental problems.* Longman, 1960.

KIMMINS, C. W., *Children's dreams.* Longman, 1920.

SPENCER, F. H. *An inspector's testament.* E.U.P., 1938.

RICHARDSON, M., *Art and the child.* U.L.P., 1948.

2 (a). WORKS ABOUT INSPECTORS OR INSPECTION OF SCHOOLS IN ENGLAND

BOARD OF EDUCATION. *Annual Reports 1913–14, 1922–23, 1949.* H.M.S.O.

BOOTHROYD, H. E., *A history of the inspectorate.* Board of Educ. Inspectors' Assoc., 1923.

*EDMONDS, E. L., *School Inspection. The contribution of the religious denominations.* B.J.E.S., Nov. 1958.

HARRIS, J. S., *British government inspection as a dynamic process.* Stevens, 1955.

* Indicates pamphlet

187

Bibliography

LEESE, J., *Personalities and power in English education.* Arnold, 1950.
LILLEY, A. L., *Sir Joshua Fitch.* Arnold, 1906.
TURNBULL, H. W., *Some memories of W. P. Turnbull.* Bell, 1919.

2 (b). WORKS ABOUT INSPECTION OF SCHOOLS
IN OTHER COUNTRIES

ANDERSON, C. J., BARR, A. S. and BUSH, M. G., *Visiting the teacher at work.* Appleton, New York, 1925.

AYER, F. C., *Fundamentals of instructional supervision.* Harper, 1954.

BALL, D. G., CUNNINGHAM, K. S. and RADFORD, W. C., *Supervision and inspection of primary schools.* Australian Council for Educational Research, 1961.

BARR, A. S., *An introduction to the scientific study of classroom supervision. Appleton, New York,* 1931.

BENNETT, M. E., *Guidance in groups.* McGraw Hill, 1955.

EVERETT, M. (ed.)., *The rural supervisor at work.* National Educ. Assn. of U.S.A., 1949.

*FRANSETH, J., *Supervision in rural schools: a report on belief and practices.* National Educ. Assn. of U.S.A., 1955.

GEST, A. R., *The administration of supervision.* Scribner, New York, 1934.

HAMMOCK, R. C. and OWINGS, R. S., *Supervising instruction in secondary schools.* McGraw Hill, 1955.

HECKEL, M., *Übersicht uber das Schulwesen im Bundesbegiet.* Weidman, Greven-Verlag, 1952.

INTERNAT. BUREAU OF EDUCATION. *School Inspection (XIXth International Conference on Public Education).* I.B.E., 1956.

JOHNSON, F. W., *The administration of supervision of the High Schools.* Ginn, New York, 1925.

MACKENSIE, G. N. and CORBY, S. M., *Instructional leadership.* Horace Mann Lincoln Institution, 1954.

SPEARS, H., *Improving the supervision of instruction.* Prentice Hall, New York, 1953.

SUDAN (MIN. OF ED.). *Province Education Officer's Handbook.* Sudan Ministry of Education.

TALBOT, D. A. (ed.). *Imperial Ethiopian Ministry of Education Yearbook, 1949–51.* Berhanena Selam, 1952.

THAILAND (MIN. OF ED.). *A manual for supervisors.* Ministry of Educ. Thailand, 1953.

UNESCO. *Education Abstracts; inspection and supervision of schools. (May 1956, Vol. VIII, No. 5).* UNESCO, 1956.

* Indicates pamphlet.

Bibliography

WEBER, C. A. and WEBER, M. E., *Fundamentals of educational leadership.* McGraw Hill, 1955.

WILES, K., *Supervision for better schools.* Prentice Hall, New York, 1950.

3 (a). HISTORY OF EDUCATION WITH SOME REFERENCE TO INSPECTION IN ENGLAND

ALLEN, W. O. B. and MCCLURE, E., *Two hundred years: the history of the S.P.C.K.* S.P.C.K., 1898

BANKS, O., *Parity and prestige in English secondary education.* Routledge, 1955

BINNS, H. B., *A century of education 1808–1908 (Brit. and Foreign School Soc.).* Dent, 1908.

BROWN, C. K. FRANCIS. *The Church's part in education, 1833–1941* National Society, 1942.

BURGESS, H. J., *Enterprise in education.* S.P.C.K., 1958.

CHENEY, C. R., *Episcopal visitation of monasteries in the 13th century.* Manchester University Press, 1931.

CLARKE, LOWTHER, W. K., *A history of the S.P.C.K.* S.P.C.K., 1959.

COLE, M. *Servant of the County.* Dobson, 1956.

DENT, H. C., *The educational system of England and Wales.* U.L.P. 1961.

EAGLESHAM, E. *From school board to local authority.* Routledge, 1956.

FINER, H., *English local government.* Methuen, 1950.

GAUTREY, T. (with additions by BALLARD, P. B.) *"Lux Mihi Laus":* School Board memories. Link House, c. 1912.

HELLER, F. A. (ed.). *New developments in industrial leadership.* Polytechnic Management Assoc., 1955.

JONES, M. G., *The Charity School movement: a study of eighteenth century Puritanism in action.* C.U.P., 1938.

JUDGES, A. V. (ed.). *Pioneers of English education.* Faber, 1952.

JUDGES, A. V. (ed.). *Looking forward in education.* Faber, 1955.

KAY-SHUTTLEWORTH, J., *Public education as affected by the Minutes of the Committee of the Privy Council 1846–52 with suggestions as to future policy.* Longman, 1853.

KAY-SHUTTLEWORTH, J., *Four periods of public education as reviewed in 1832–39–46–62, in papers by Sir James Kay-Shuttleworth.* Longman, 1862.

KEKEWICH, G. W., *The Education Department and after.* Constable, 1920.

KNOWLES, D., *The monastic order in England.* C.U.P., 1940.

KNOWLES, D., *The religious orders in England Vol. 1.* C.U.P., 1948.

KNOWLES, D., *The religious orders in England Vol. 2.* C.U.P., 1955.

KNOWLES, D., *The religious orders in England Vol. 3. The Tudor Age.* C.U.P. 1959.

189

Bibliography

KNOX, H. M., *Two hundred and fifty years of Scottish education*. Oliver and Boyd, 1953.

LEACH, A. F., *The schools of medieval England*. Methuen, 1915.

LEACH, A. F., *Educational charters and documents 598 to 1909*. C.U.P. 1911.

LEWIS, R. and MAUDE, A., *Professional people*. Phoenix House, 1952.

LONDON COUNTY COUNCIL, *The London education service*. Staples, 1954, 12th edition 1961.

LOWNDES, G. N., *The English education system*. Hutchinson, 1960.

LOWNDES, G. N., *The silent social revolution*. C.U.P., 1937.

POLLARD, H. M., *Pioneers of popular education*. Murray, 1956.

PURVIS, J. S., *An introduction to ecclesiastical records*. St. Anthony's Press, 1953.

RICHARDS, P. G., *Delegation in local government*. Allen & Unwin, 1956.

ROBSON, A. H., *The education of children engaged in industry 1833–1876*. Devonshire Press, 1931.

SELBY BIGGE, L. A., *The Board of Education*. Putnam, 1934.

SMITH, F., *The life and work of Sir James Kay-Shuttleworth*. Murray, 1923.

SMITH, F., *A History of English elementary education 1760–1902*. U.L.P. 1931.

THOMAS, M. W., *The early factory legislation*. Thames Bank, 1948.

3 (b). HISTORY OF EDUCATION WITH SOME REFERENCE TO INSPECTION IN OTHER COUNTRIES

BYRAM, H. M. and WENRICH, R. C., *Vocational education and practical arts in the community school*. Macmillan (N.Y.), 1956.

HYLLA, E. J. and KEGEL, F. C., *Education in Germany*. Hochschule fur Internationale Pedagogische-Forschung Frankfurt am Main. 2nd edition, 1958.

MORT, P. R. and ROSS, D. H., *Principles of school administration*. 2nd ed. McGraw Hill, 1957.

PARKYN, G. W. (ed.). *The administration of education in New Zealand*. New Zealand Institute of Public Administration, 1954.

UNESCO. *Compulsory education in Australia*. UNESCO—Imprimerie Chantenay, 1951.

INDEX

Abel, W. J., 106
Accounts, 93, 95, 115, 155
Acland, A. H. D., 131, 145
Acts of Parliament:
  Board of Education, 1899, 132
  Education, 1870, 86, 88, 91, 93
    1902, 135, 168, 171
    1944, 148, 150
  Factory, 1802, 25
    1833, 26
    1844, 27
  Mines, 1850, 28
  Technical Instruction, 1889, 132
Act of Worship, 175
Adderley, Sir C. B., 67, 72, 181
Administrative Tribunals and Enquiries Report, 180
Advisory Officer, 179
Age, school-leaving, 52, 158
Age-limit, inspectors', 146, 172
Agent, 121, 178 (see also British Society, S.P.C.K.)
Agreed Syllabus, 152-153
Agriculture, 132
Alexander, Sir W., vii, 148 f
Allen, Rev. John, 36, 41, 42, 43, 50
Allowance, capitation, 52, 143
Althans, Henry, 23-4, 38
Annulment of teacher's certificate, 27
Apparatus, 39, 91, 93, 98, 103, 108, 130
Appointment of teachers, 7, 17, 18, 19, 77, 88, 91, 93, 95, 99, 102, 150, 158 (see under Teachers)
Apprentices, 7, 25, 99
Area Training Organisation, 152

Arithmetic, 41, 44, 74, 80, 82, 118, 142
Armstrong, H., 60
Arnold, Matthew, 66, 67, 79-80
Art, 104, 132, 150
Articles, of Management, 117
Ashley, Lord, 63
Assistant Commissioner, 132
Assistant (Poor Law), 37
Assistant Inspector (see under Inspector)
Association, of Her Majesty's Inspectors, 153
  of L.E.A. Inspectors and Organisers, 153, 182
  of Secretaries of Diocesan and District Boards, 54
  of Teachers, 41 (see also National Union of Teachers)
Attendance at School, 25, 26, 40, 45, 52, 79, 88, 90, 95, 99, 103, 109
Austria, 179

Backwardness in children, 149
Bagshawe, Rev. F. L., 69
Bailey, Miss M. E., 105, 171
Ball, D. G., 185 f
Balfour, A. J., 183
Banner, Miss Louisa, 168, 171
Barraclough, F., 148 f
Barton, Miss, 155
Bath, Archdeaconry of, 21
Bath, Local Committee of National Society, 22
Bayley, Miss E., 168
Beal, J., 28
Bede (The Venerable), 1 f

Bell, Dr. Andrew, 16, 17, 18
Bell, H. C., 2 f
Bellairs, Rev. W. H., 76
"Best Book", 142
Bible, 40, 124
Bills, 13, 17, 93, 158
Birley, Sir Herbert, 127
Blackburn, Church of England Sunday Schools, 13
Blair, Robert, 171
Blind, Instructors of, 112, 113
Board of Agriculture, 132
Board of Education, 137, 138, 139, 140, 142, 144, 146, 174, 179, 183, 184
Board of Education Act (1899), 132
Board of Trade, 129
Bonny, Rev. J., 43
Breakwell, William, 106
Bridges, Mrs., 17
Briscoe, Mrs., 168
British and Foreign Schools Society, ix, 9, 10–11, 15, 22, 23, 24, 30, 37–38, 39, 46, 61, 121, 122
Agents, 23–24, 38, 121–122
Inspectors, 70
Ladies' Committees, 159
Reports of, 23, 38, 61
Brodie, Rev. J. H., 76
Brook, W., 101, 104
Brookfield, Rev. W. H., 76
Brougham, Lord H., 47
Bryce Commission (*see under* Commission)
Buckley, H. C., 105
Buckmaster, J. C., 167
Buckton, Mrs. C. M., 104, 169–170
Building of Schools, 7, 23, 88, 89, 151 f
Building Standards, 67, 103, 126, 173
Bullard, J. V., 2 f
Buncher, Mrs. C., 95
Burn, R., 2 f
Burnham, 143

Campbell, N. E., 185 f
"Cancellarius", 4

Canterbury, Archbishop of, 54
Cappe, Mrs. C., 154, 155
Caretaker, 91
Catechism, 11, 40, 45, 124
Cathedral, 4
Catholic Education Council, ix
Central School,
of National Society, 18, 19, 20, 22, 158, 165
of York Diocesan Board, 34
of Design, 129
Certificate of Attendance, 27
Certificate of Merit, 52, 57
Chadwick, John, 13
Chaffers, Rev. Robert, 35
Chamberlain, Joseph, 94–95
Charity Commission, 136
Chester, Board of Education, 33, 53
Chief Education Officer (Local Authority), 137, 139
Chief Inspector (*see under* Inspector)
Childers Committee, 136
Christian, G. A., 145
Church, Collegiate, 4
Church Day School Association of Manchester and Salford, 127
Church of England, 40, 41, 78
Church, Roman Catholic, 4
Church of Scotland, 40–41
Church School Association, 126, 127
Church, visitatorial tradition of, 1
Churchwardens, 10
Classes, size of, 107, 151
Clerical Superintendant, 16, 21
Clerk, 89, 169
Clothing, 18, 155, 159, 164, 166
Clothing Club, 63, 193
Clothing Fund, 164
Close, Rev. Francis, 57
Clough, Miss, 155
Clulow, Rev. J., 123
Cole, Sir Henry, 129, 131
Collegiate Church, 4
Coghan, the Rev. —., 6
Commissions:
Bryce, 120, 129, 134, 136
Charity, 136
Civil Service (1912–14), 140, 145, 171–172, 177–178, 183

Commissions: *cont.*
Civil Service (1929), 180
Cross, 102, 112, 114, 116, 117, 127, 145
Employment of Children, 35
Middle Class School, 70
Newcastle, 72, 76, 83
School Inquiry, 132
Committees:
Bath, Local C. of, 22
Burnham, 143
Catholic Poor Schools, 38, 46, 59–60
Childers, 136
of Council on Education, 31, 36–37, 39, 40, 43, 46, 47, 49, 50, 51, 83, 122, 180, 181, 182, 183
Doncaster National School, 124
Education, 139, 148
Finance (and General Purposes), L.E.A., 88
Gentlemen's, 155, 161
House of Commons Select C. of, 1835, 28
1864, 180, 182
1865, 83, 177 f
Ladies', 154–168
Local Government Manpower, 151
Methodist Education, ix
National Society (*see under* National Society)
School Board (*see under* School Board)
Soulbury, vii
Wesleyan Education, 11, 38, 46, 60, 122, 123
York Incorporated (C. of E.) Sunday School, 12
Conferences, 13, 143, 149, 153
Congregational Board of Education, 24, 133
Congregational Union, ix
Continent, visitor of, 24
visits to, 125
Cook, Rev. F. C., 33, 56, 76
Cookery, 111, 112, 168, 169
Copy-books, 77, 99

Corder, G., 185 f
Correspondent (National Society), 16
(S.P.C.K.), 9
Corresponding Members (S.P.C.K.), 9
Cost of Education, 79, 150, 151
Council, Fourth Lateran, 4
Council of the Government School of Design, 129
County Borough, 139, 148
County Council, 139, 148
Courses, for Inspectors, 41, 66, 176
for Teachers, 138, 146, 149, 153, 171, 174
Coventry, Archdeaconry of, 21
Cross Commission (*see under* Commissions)
Crosskey, Rev. H. W., 95 f
Cunliffe-Owen, H. C., 131

Dalton, Mrs., 155
Davis, B. D., 99–100, 104
Davis, G. B., 125
Dawes, Rev. Richard, 57
Deaf Children, 113
Defective Children, 113
Demonstration, 173
Denison, Archdeacon, G. A., 50
Denmark, 179
Dictation, 82
Diggle, Rev. J. R., 115
Dioceses, 21, 35, 36, 43, 45, 124
Diocesan Boards, 31, 43, 52, 53, 58, 68, 84, 123
Bath and Wells, 33
Bristol, 33
Chester, 33, 53
Chichester, 33, 34
Durham, 36
Ely, 33, 34
Exeter, 33, 34, 36
Gloucester, 33
Lichfield, 36, 43
Lincoln, 33
Liverpool, 128
London, 33, 36
Manchester, 125

Index

Diocesan Boards: *cont.*
  Norwich, 33
  Peterborough, 36, 43
  Ripon, 33, 36
  Rochester, 36, 127
  Salisbury, 33
  Winchester, 36
  Worcester, 33, 36
  York, 34, 36
Diocesan and District Societies, 15
Diocesan Board Fund, 43
Director, 92
Directress, 172
Discipline, 80, 90, 98, 107, 117–119, 158
Discussion Groups, 147
Dismissal of pupils, 158
  of teachers (*see under* Teachers)
Divisional Executive, 148
Dobson, W., 95 f
Domestic Economy, 167
Domestic Subjects, 150, 168
Doncaster National School Committee, 124, 163
Donnelly, J. F. D., 130
Drawing, 41, 111
Dring, Mrs., 155
Dual Management, 92
Durham, 21, 36
  Diocesan Society, 22

Education Acts (*see under* Acts)
Education Authority, "all-purpose", 148
Education Committee, 139, 148
Education Department, 76, 78, 83, 87, 88, 102, 112, 115, 121, 141, 180, 181, 182
Education Officer, 179
Elections, local, 115
Ellis, Rev. Dr. John, 9
Ellis, Rev. W., 12
Episcopal Church of Scotland, 51
Evening Classes, 132
Evening Institutes, 71
Everard, John, 2
Examination, Civil Service, 83
  Oxford and Cambridge Local, 70

Examinations, 23, 35, 47, 52, 53, 55, 69, 72, 76, 81, 82, 83, 91, 94, 95, 98, 99–100, 101, 102, 103, 104, 109, 114, 115, 116, 117–119, 124, 130, 134, 141, 142, 157, 164, 165, 166, 169
Examination Schedule, 82, 115, 130
Examiners, 33, 140
Excepted Districts, 148
Excommunication, 4
Exhibitions, 52, 68
Exhibit(ion)s, 104, 170
Eye-sight, 103

Fabian, Lieutenant, 23–24, 38
Factory Acts (*see under* Acts)
Factory Inspectors, 25–29
"Farming", 126, 127
Fearon, D. R., 66, 76, 84, 171
Fees, for inspection, 124, 127
  for organisation, 171
Feild, Rev. Edward, 1, 13, 35, 42
Field, Mrs., 17
Fielden, 28
Finch, J., 145
Fines, 27, 115
Fitch, Sir Joshua G., 48, 133–136, 176, 177
Fletcher, Joseph, 38, 41
Follett, M. P., 185 f
Forestry, 132
Friendly Society, 154 f
Further Education, 71, 139, 152
Foster, Edwin, 106
Fowler, Mr., 164
Frazer, S. J. G., 84

Gibson, John, 41
Gentlemen's Committees, 155, 161
Geography, 44, 67, 80
Gloucester Diocesan Society, 161
Gordon, John, 40
Gorst, Sir John, 140
Gould, C. T., 112
Government Inspection, 30–31, 36–38, 78, 79 (*see also* Inspectors, Her Majesty's)
Graham, Sir James, 37
Grammar, 44, 67, 80

Grants-in-aid, to schools, 30, 39, 42, 43, 71, 73–75, 76, 77, 78, 79, 81, 82, 84, 86, 91, 102, 110–111, 114, 116, 117, 126–127, 130, 131–132, 184
to teacher associations, 41, 149
Granville, Lord, 82
Graves, A. P., 119, 126, 154
Gray, Miss, 155
Gray, Rev. H. F., 33
Greg, R. H., 28
Grey, Sir George, 28
Grimston, Miss, 155
Grindal, Edmund, Archbishop (York), 5
Grosseteste, Robert, Bishop of Lincoln, 3
Grover, W. S., 97
Guthrie, T., 64 f

Half-time System, 27
Hall, Richard, 2
Hamilton, Lord George, 78
Handicapped Children, 111, 113
Handicrafts, 150
Hand-writing, 41, 44, 74, 80
Harris, J. J. H., 164
Harrison, H. E. B., 177
Hasell, Miss, 155
Hayward, F. H., 145
Headmasters' Conference, 146
Heads as Inspectors, 98, 102, 128, 141, 143, 144, 146, 150, 185
Heads, responsibilities of, 141
"Hedge Schools", 6
Hey, R., 177 f
Higher Education, Inspector of, 129
Hill, Miss, 166
History, 44, 67, 80
Holidays, 115, 162
Holmes, E. G. A., 139, 140, 143, 144
Holmes, Mrs., 163
Holmes-Morant Circular, 145
Home Office, 26, 28, 35
Hopwood, Rev. Henry, 43
Horner, L., 29
House of Commons, 182, 183
Select Committees of (*see under* Committees)

Huxley, T. H., 87, 97, 115, 142
Hygiene, 159, 167, 170

Industrial School, 91,
Industrial School Officers, 91
Industry, schools of, 61–62
Infant education, 73, 126, 140, 164, 169, 171
Inspection, function of, 1, 16, 30–31, 43, 48, 173–175, 181, 185
general, 135, 138, 150, 172
method of, 67, 80, 107–109, 141–144, 185
right of, 30, 31, 43, 69, 129, 152
Inspector, alternative titles for, 178–179
Assistant, 51, 52, 82, 135, 138, 146, 178, 179
Assistant of, 83–84, 145, 177
British and Foreign Schools Society, 11, 23–24, 38, 61, 70, 122–123
Charity Commission, 136
Charity Schools, 6–7, 9, 10, 154–156
Chief, 135, 137, 152, 172, 179
Chief Woman, 179
Diocesan, 52, 53–54, 55, 56, 57, 68, 84–85, 115, 123–125, 137, 177
District, 135, 136, 138, 152, 172
Divisional, 135, 152
Elementary, 68, 135, 152
Her Majesty's, of Factories, ix, 25–29
Her Majesty's, of Mines, 28, 37
Her Majesty's, of Schools, 38, 39–54, 56, 57, 59, 66–67, 72–85, 109, 110, 112, 113–121, 126–127, 129, 133–136, 137–138, 139–140, 143, 144–147, 151–153, 154, 171–172, 176–179, 180–183, 184–185
Junior, 145
Local Education Authority, 139, 140, 144, 149–150, 171–172, 183–184, 185
National Society, 15–17, 19–22, 35, 41–43, 53, 156–157

Inspector: *cont.*
  of Domestic Subjects, 150
  of Higher Education, 129, 132, 136
  of infants, 169, 170, 171
  of Music, 95
  of Physical Training, 150
  of teacher training, 152
  Organising, 97, 98, 107, 171
  Roman Catholic Schools, 60, 70, 123
  School Board, 91–92, 93, 94–95, 97–112, 114–117, 119–121, 141–144, 167–169, 171, 178
  Science and Art Department, 129–132
  Secondary, 135, 138, 152, 172, 179
  Senior Chief, 132, 137, 152
  specialist, 129, 135, 138, 139, 146, 150, 178, 179
  Staff, 152, 172
  Sub-, of Factories, 26, 28–29
    of Schools, 145
  Sunday Schools, 11–14, 43
  Technological, 152, 172
Inspectorate, Irish, 177, 178
Inspectors, Reports of, 9, 13, 26, 33, 37, 38, 41–45, 51–53, 56, 61, 66, 67, 70, 72, 73–75, 78–80, 82, 94, 98, 100, 103, 104, 109, 116, 124, 136, 140, 141–144, 164, 165, 180–182
  Selection of, 16–17, 24, 28, 32, 35, 36, 37, 38, 50, 98, 126, 144–146, 173, 175, 178, 179
  training of, 27–28, 66–67, 153, 173, 175–178
Inspectress, Cookery and Laundry 172
  Needlework, 95, 168
Instructions to Her Majesty's Inspectors of Schools, 39, 41–43, 75–76, 82, 106, 112, 114, 117–119, 176, 181, 183
  to National Society Inspectors, 35, 41–43
  to School Board Inspectors, 107–109

  to School Managers, 93
  to Schoolmasters, 18
Instrument and Articles of Management, 148
Interviews, 120

Jenkins, W., 104
Johnson, Rev. W., 17, 158
Jones, Abel, 177
Joyce, P. W., 177 f

Kay-Shuttleworth, Sir James, 41, 46–50, 59, 73, 82, 83, 119, 137, 143
Kekewich, Sir George W., 81, 137
Kemp, Dr., 6
Kilgour, A., 71
Kindergarten, 112, 170, 171
Knitting, School of, 154

Ladies' Committees, 154–168
Lady of the Manor, 166
Landsdowne, Lord, 143
Laundry-work, 111
Law Society, 179
Lea, Miss E., 170
Leach, A. F., 2 f
Leaving Certificate, 134
Lecturers, 71, 147
Lee, Wesley, 116
Legard, Mr., 129
Leisure, education for, 149
Library, 118, 174
Licensing of Teachers, 3, 5
Lichfield, 43, 85
Lingen, R. R. W., 182
Liverpool School Managers' Conference, 128
Livingstone, R. W., 175 f
Lloyd, G. C., 95 f
Local Education Authority, 139, 140, 144, 150, 171, 175, 184
Local Government Manpower Committee, 151
Log-book, School, 98, 108, 115
London, 6, 8, 9
  County, 150
  Ragged School Union, 38, 63
  Society, 10

Longueville-Jones, Rev. H., 182
Lonsdale, Rev. J. G., 83, 84
Lowe, Robert, 72, 76, 78, 181–182
Lynch, H. J., 77

Madras system, 16, 17, 18, 22
"magister scholarum", 4
Mair, R. H., 86 f
Managers, 12, 20, 22, 42, 43, 48,
    77, 81, 88, 89, 91, 92, 93, 95,
    96, 107, 109, 114, 115, 119,
    125, 148, 149
Managers' Reports, 93, 94
Manning, Cardinal, 123
"Manual of Health", 159
Manual of Primary Instruction, 37
Maps, 56, 74, 93, 115
Marsh, Miss, 155
Marshall, T. W. M., 59
Mathinson, G. F., 15
McWilliam, R., 101, 105
Mechanics' Institutes, 70, 133
Medical Branch, 152
Meeting, 23, 24, 67, 72, 86, 94
Mere, Thomas de la, 3
Methodist Education Committee, ix
Methodology, 67, 99, 110, 136, 146,
    173–174
Middle Class, 68
Millar, Mrs., 168
Mines Act, 28
Mines Inspector (*see under* Inspector)
Minister of Education, 150, 180,
    183, 184
Monitors, 47, 90
Monitorial system, 37
Monthly Paper, 53, 54, 69
Morant, Robert, 137, 172
Morning Chronicle, 66
Morrison, J. C., 185 f
Moss, J. F., 125
Mundella, A. J., 136
Musgrave, Thomas, Archbishop of
    York, 1
Music, 41, 95, 150

National Association of Inspectors
    and Educational Organisers, ix,
    153

National Education Board (Ireland),
    176–177
National Society, ix, 11, 13, 15–22,
    27, 30–31, 33–36, 41–43, 44,
    52, 55, 57, 58, 59, 123
    Committee of Correspondence,
        34–35, 68
    Committee of Enquiry, 31, 32
    General Committee, 17–18, 58,
        68, 157, 158
    Inspectorate (*see under* Inspector)
    Ladies' Committee, 18, 157–159
    Organising Secretaries, 35
    Reports of, 16, 18, 19, 21–22, 52,
        57–58
    Schools Committee, 17–19, 157, 158
National Union of Teachers, ix, 120,
    144, 145, 146, 176
Needlework, 104, 111, 154, 160, 162,
    163, 165, 167, 169, 171
Newcastle Commission (*see under*
    Commission)
Newcourt, R., 6
Newman, Henry, 10
New Zealand, 184
Nicholson, Miss F., 170
Nickall, J., 105
Night School, 52, 71, 103
Norfolk, County of, 21
Normal School Certificate, 47
Norris, Rev. J. P., 76
Northamptonshire Society, 56, 165
Norwich, St. Stephens, 12

Office, Local Education, 120
Offices, 91, 103
"Official Agent", 11
Order in Council, 30, 132, 180
Organisers   (Local   Education
    Authority), 146, 150
Organising Inspector, 24, 70, 111
    Master, 13, 52, 178
    Mistress, 170
Organising Secretary, 35
    Teachers, 13, 18–19, 20, 22, 52,
        57–59, 110–112, 117, 126, 127,
        128, 165
    Reports of, 128
"Oxbridge", 177

o

Pamphlets, 138, 153, 174
Paris, Matthew, 3 f
Paul, St., 1
Payment by Results, 72, 76, 78, 79, 117, 125, 140, 173, 176
Percival, J., 136
Permanent Secretary, 152
Perrot, Mrs., 155
Philosophy of Education, 175
Physical Education, 111, 113, 118, 150
Physiology, 104, 169
Playfair, Sir Lyon, 129
Playground, 91, 126
"Pollen Carriers", 128
Poor Law Commissioner (assistant), 37
Portugal, 179
Pounds, John, 65
Practice, Educational, 173–174
  Observation, 177
  School, 18
Precentor, 5
Probationary Period, for Inspectors, 177–178
  for Teachers, 184
Psychology, 175
Public (Independent) Schools, 133, 138, 146
Public Works Loans Commissioner, 88
Pupil-Teachers, 47, 49, 52, 60, 75, 78, 90, 98, 99, 100, 105–106, 108, 109, 112, 123, 130, 169, 171, 177
Pupil-Teachers' Centres, 87, 100, 105

Quarter-sessions, 26
Queen's Scholarships, 47, 100

Ragged Schools, 62–66, 95–96
  Inspectors of, 63–64
  Superintendent of, 64
Ragged School Unions, 63, 64, 96
Rate, Education, 86, 88, 89, 115, 126

Reading, 44, 67, 80, 118, 163
Reed, Rev. William, 34
Refresher Courses, 111
Registers, 16, 52, 79, 88, 98, 103, 108, 115, 119
Regulations, 156
Religious Education, 2, 11, 40, 42–43, 45, 56, 60, 75–76, 83–84
  Knowledge, 85, 99, 104–105, 108, 115, 124–125, 152–153, 157, 171
  Approved Syllabus, 99, 105, 124
Repairs, School, 13
"Repertorium", 6
Reports, Inspectors' (Her Majesty's), 41, 51, 94, 102, 114, 181, 182, 183
  (Local), 94, 101, 102, 103, 109, 143, 183
Reports on Teachers, 106–107, 114, 143
Requisitions, 17, 88, 101, 108, 169
Research, 149
Retiring Pensions, 52
Revised Code, 42, 71, 73–79, 82, 84, 86, 91, 117, 142, 145, 175
Rewards, 12, 15, 18, 40, 45, 60, 69, 94, 100, 123, 130, 134, 155, 157, 158, 159, 160, 163
Richards, Sir Henry, 152
Ricks, G., 101, 104
Roadknight, Mrs. J. N., 112
Roman Catholic, Education Council, ix
  Poor School Committee, 38, 46, 59–60
  Reports of, 59–60
  Inspectors, 59–60, 123, 181
Ross, Rev. John, 24
Royal Commissions on the Civil Service (*see under* Commissions)
Royal Engineers, 131–132
Royds, Miss, 155
Rudge, H., 95 f
Runciman, Lord, 183, 184
Runciman, T., 176
Rural Science, 150

Index

Salaries, Inspectors', 6, 20, 26, 29, 33, 35, 36, 37, 43, 55, 63–64, 70, 83, 92, 100, 124, 127–128, 168, 172

Teachers', 7, 9, 27, 47–48, 49–50, 77, 81, 83, 88, 102, 107, 143, 154, 162

Salisbury, 4

Salmond, Miss, 155

Sandford, Rev. H., 79

Sanitation, 79, 80, 103

Savings Bank, 118

Scheme of Education Committee (see under School Boards)

Scholarships, 47, 104, 130, 134

"Scholasticus", 4

School Attendance Committee (see under School Boards)

School Attendance Officer, 10, 88, 97

School Boards, 86–89, 93–95, 97, 100, 106, 110, 112–113, 115, 117, 125, 138–139, 154, 167, 168, 171

Attendance Committee of, 88, 162

Scheme of Education Committee of, 98

Finance (and General Purposes) Committee of, 88, 92

Sites (and Buildings) Committee of, 88

(Educational and) School Management Committee of, 88, 90, 91, 92, 93, 94, 95, 100, 101, 102, 105, 106, 107, 139, 168, 169

School Boards, Named,

Aston, 105

Birmingham, 94–95, 125

Bolton, 113

Bradford, 87–88, 104, 110, 112

Brighton, 100

Bristol, 93–94, 104, 105, 106, 107, 116

Fleetwood, 105

Hull, 100, 104

Leeds, 88–90, 104, 105, 112, 113, 116, 168–170

Leicester, 113

Liverpool, 93, 94, 104, 105, 106, 112, 169

London, 91–93, 94, 95, 97–99, 100–101, 104, 105, 107, 113, 115, 125, 141–144, 168

Manchester, 103, 107–109, 125, 170

Newcastle, 10, 106

Norwich, 90–91, 100, 107

Nottingham, 93, 100, 104, 106, 112, 113

Oldham, 96, 105, 113

Salford, 170

Sheffield, 99–100, 104, 112, 125

"School Guardian", 144

"Schoolmaster", 145

School Pence, 26, 27, 52, 88, 91, 93

School, Types of:

Charity, 5–10, 154 f

Commercial, 33, 43

Direct Grant, 175

Dock Yard and Ships, 48

Elementary, 43, 50, 87

Endowed, 130, 133, 136

Evening, 87, 90, 111, 144

Factory, 48

Grammar, 4, 5, 133, 138

Higher Grade, 87, 104, 111, 130

Hospital, 48

Independent, 133, 138

Industrial, 87, 91, 101, 105, 168

Industry, 61, 62

Knitting, 154

Maintained, 148

Medieval, 1–5

Middle Class, 34, 43, 68–70

Normal, 52

of Design, 129–130

Poor Law, 48, 166

Primary, 133

Prison, 48

Private, 133

"Private Adventure", 87

Post-primary, 133

Proprietary, 133

Ragged, 61–66, 95–96, 166

Roman Catholic, 38, 59–60, 77, 123

School, Types of: *cont.*
  Secondary, 130, 132, 135
  Special, 87, 125
  Spinning, 154
  Sunday, 13–14, 43, 44
  Sunday, Ragged, 96
  Training, 34, 50, 52
  See also British and Foreign
    Schools Society, National
    Society
Schools, Named:
  Adwick-le-Street, 77
  Barton - on - Humber British
    School, 23
  Battersea Girls' National School,
    159
  Beverley C. of E., 79
  Birmingham National, 160
    Industry, 61
  Blackburn C. of E.,
    Sunday, 12
  Bridlington C. of E., 79
  Chelsea, World's End Passage
    Ragged, 63
  Chiswick C. of E., 19
  Clerkenwell Charity, 8
  Croston (Lancs), Industry, 62
  Doncaster National, 163
  Fincham, Industry, 62
  Goathland C. of E., 79
  Halifax C. of E., 79
  Huddersfield C. of E., 126
  Hull, British, 23
    Ragged and Industrial, 62, 166
    Sir Henry Cooper School, 104
    Training Ship "Southampton",
      65
  Humber Industrial Ship, 65
  "Indefatigable", 104
  Leeds, Central Higher Grade, 104
    School of Cookery, 169
    Zion Board, 88–89
  Lincoln National, 161
  Louth National, 164
  Manchester and District Sunday
    Schools Association, C. of E.,
    11, 13
  Merton National, 164
  Middlesbrough C. of E., 79

New Malton, British, 23
Salisbury Cathedral, 4
Scarborough, British, 23
Scarborough C. of E., 79
Sheffield Sunday School Union,
  Wesleyan, 13
Sheldwick National, 160
Sigglesthorpe C. of E., 18
Spitalfields, Vines Court Ragged,
  167
Staines C. of E., 18
Stoke Newington Ragged, 63
Stroud Sunday, 12
Swansea National, 164
Trowbridge, Girls' National, 157
Warwick, Collegiate Church, 4
Westminster, National Free, 159
  "Refuge", Old Pye Street
    (Ragged), 63
Whitby, British, 23
York, British, 23
  Grey Coat, 155–156
  Cathedral, 4
Schools Inquiry Commission
  (Taunton) (*see under* Com-
  missions)
Science, 75, 80, 111, 112, 132
Science and Art Department, 111,
  129, 138
Scott, Rev. J. J., 125
Scottish Education Department, 179
Scottish Society for the Propagation
  of Christian Knowledge, 6
Scripture, 124
Seabrook, James F., 127, 128
Searle, Mrs., 164
Secondment, 149, 151, 179
Secretary, ix, 10, 16, 139, 159, 160,
  162, 178, 180, 181
Selby-Bigge, Sir L. A., 140, 145,
  151, 177, 183
Sharpe, Rev. T. W., 75
Sheffield, National District Society,
  161
  School Aid Society, 128
  Wesleyan Sunday School Union,
    13
Shoe Black Society, 64
Singing, 111, 124

Index

Slates, 77, 82

Smedley, Catherine, 18

Smithells, Professor A., 132

Sneyd-Kynnersley, E. M., 81, 82 f, 154 f

Society for the Establishment and Support of Sunday Schools, 10

Society for the Propagation of Christian Knowledge, ix, 5–10

Society of Secretaries, 20

Somerset, Anne, 163

Spencer, Mrs. E., 170

Sub-inspectors (*see under* Inspector)

Subjects:
  class, 78, 118
  special, 111
  specific, 78

Subscribers, 9, 10, 12, 62

Subscriptions, 7, 9, 155

Sunday School, 10–14, 43, 44
  Inspectors (*see under* Inspector)
  Teachers, 11, 13–14
  Visitors, 11, 12, 13–14

Superintendent, 12, 16, 163, 178

Supervision, 111, 154

Sweden, 179

Swimming, 113

Synod, 153

Tancred, Thomas, 35

Teachers:
  Annulment of Certificate, 27
  Appointment, 7, 17, 18, 19, 77, 88, 91, 93, 95, 99, 102, 150, 158
  Dismissal, 17, 77, 91, 93, 107, 115–116, 156
  Promotion, 103, 106
  Secondment, 149, 151, 179
  Training of, 8, 13–14, 18, 38, 45, 129, 143

Tearle, F., 164

Technical Education Boards, 102, 168

Technical Instruction Act (*see under* Acts)

Technology, 152

Textbooks, 2–3, 7, 17, 18, 22, 23, 27, 39, 41, 56, 91, 93, 98, 99, 103, 108, 130

Theodore, St., 3

Theological College, 4

Thornton, Mrs. E., 113

Times Educational Supplement, 180

Time-table, 90, 103, 119, 158

Training of Teachers (*see under* Teachers)

Training Colleges, 123, 124, 127, 137

Training Colleges, Named:
  Derby, 168
  St. Mary's, Hammersmith (R.C.), 59
  York, 127

Training School, 34, 50, 52

Training Ship, 104

Transfer, at 11 plus, 141

Treasury, 30

Tremenheere, H. S., 13, 36, 37, 38, 39, 41, 42, 72, 83

Trimmer, Mrs. S., 6

Trust Deed, 124

Turkey, 179

Turnbull, W. P., 183

Urban District Council, 139

University Graduates, 146

University Institutes of Education, 184

United States of America, 185

Ventilation, 79, 90, 103, 126

Vicar, 5, 6, 9, 11, 18, 20, 21, 25, 32, 62

Visitation by:
  Archbishop, 5
  Archdeacon, 2, 3
  Bishop, 2, 3, 4, 5, 31–32, 153
  Dean, 3
  Local Order, 1
  Pope's own Legate, 1
  Rural Dean, 2, 34

Visitors:
  Board School, 89, 90–91, 93–94
  Committees, 90, 159, 160, 161, 163, 164, 165, 167
  Subscribers, 9–10, 62, 167

Visitors: *cont.*
  Managers, 89, 90
  Ragged School, 65
  Sunday School, 11–12
Vocational Education, 140
Vocational Teaching, 111
Voluntary Schools, 112, 120, 125, 127, 128, 170

Wales, 138, 152 f
Wall-maps, 98
Walmsley, Rev. Dr. T. T., 16
Warburton, Rev. Canon W. P., 102, 114
Warwick, 4
Watkins, Rev. Frederick, 43–45, 51–53, 76, 81
Watson, Anne, 163
Wesleyan Education Committee, 11, 38, 46, 60, 122
  Inspectors, 60, 70, 123

Westminster, 6, 159
  Dean and Chapter of, 159
  Churches of St. Margaret and St. John, 159
West Sussex, District of, 21,
"Whisky money", 132
Williams, T. M., 112
Willm, J., 183
Withers, Mrs., 155
Women Inspectors, 112, 137, 154, 168, 171, 172, 179
  Organisers, 111–112, 167, 169, 170, 171–172
  Teachers, increase in, 171
Wool, 155
Wright, T. G., 101, 105

York, 4, 154
Yorkshire College, 132
Youth Clubs, 96
Youth Service, 152

For Product Safety Concerns and Information please contact our EU
representative GPSR@taylorandfrancis.com
Taylor & Francis Verlag GmbH, Kaufingerstraße 24, 80331 München, Germany

www.ingramcontent.com/pod-product-compliance
Lightning Source LLC
Chambersburg PA
CBHW070419270326
41926CB00014B/2850